P9-API-333

Perennials

Perennials

CONSULTANT EDITOR
Judy Moore

FOG CITY PRESS

Published by Fog City Press
814 Montgomery Street
San Francisco, CA 94133 USA
Copyright © 2003 Weldon Owen Pty Ltd

FOG CITY PRESS
CHIEF EXECUTIVE OFFICER John Owen
PRESIDENT Terry Newell
PUBLISHER Lynn Humphries
MANAGING EDITOR Janine Flew
ART DIRECTOR Kylie Mulquin
COVER DESIGN John Bull
PICTURE EDITOR Tracey Gibson
EDITORIAL COORDINATORS Kiren Thandi and Paul McNally
PRODUCTION MANAGER Caroline Webber
PRODUCTION COORDINATOR James Blackman
SALES MANAGER Emily Jahn
VICE PRESIDENT INTERNATIONAL SALES Stuart Laurence
EUROPEAN SALES DIRECTOR Vanessa Mori

LIMELIGHT PRESS PTY LTD
PROJECT MANAGEMENT Helen Bateman/Jayne Denshire
PROJECT EDITOR Margaret Whiskin
PROJECT DESIGNER Avril Makula
CONSULTANT EDITOR Judy Moore

ISBN 1 876778 97 0

Color reproduction by Bright Arts Graphics (S) Pte Ltd
Printed by LeeFung-Asco Printers

Printed in China

A Weldon Owen Production

CONTENTS

HOW TO USE THIS BOOK

*T*he *Gardeners Handbooks: Perennials* is divided
into two parts. The first part is the general
section (sample page below) and the second part
is a plant directory (sample page on page 9).
These combine to provide a comprehensive
guide to perennials.

Illustrations show various
perennials. There are many other
helpful illustrations in the book.

Colorful photographs
give you guidance
and inspiration in
planning and planting
your garden.

SOIL SOLUTIONS

Gardening would be easier if soil were
consistent, but it is a complex and
changing mixture of substances—there's
bound to be something (or lack of something) that makes gardening a challenge.

ALKALINE ANEMONE
The delicate Japanese
anemone *Anemone x hybrida*
spreads by creeping underground stems and thrives
in alkaline soil.

ALKALINE SOIL
Most plants can live with a slightly
alkaline soil, but a soil with a pH above
8.0 starts to take its toll. Excessively
alkaline soils have chronic nutrient
deficiencies and resist attempts to acidify
them. In too-alkaline soils, phosphorus
and most micronutrients are insoluble
and unavailable to plants. On the other
hand, minerals such as sodium and
selenium may be abundant enough to be
toxic to plants. You may decide to grow
species that are adapted to high-pH soils.
  The most effective material for
lowering the soil pH is elemental sulfur.
Apply 1 pound (0.5 kg) per 100 square
feet (9.3 sq m) for each whole point you
want to lower the pH. Rake or dig the
sulfur into the soil and keep it moist.

**PLANTS FOR SOIL
pH 7.0 OR HIGHER**
Baby's breath
  *Gypsophila
  paniculata*
Bergenias
  Bergenia spp.
Coral bells
  Heuchera spp.
Japanese anemone
  Anemone x hybrida
Mulleins
  Verbascum spp.
Peonies *Paeonia* spp.
Pinks *Dianthus* spp.

ADAPTABLE PHLOX
Garden phlox can adapt
to alkaline soil, as long as
it has good drainage and
lots of organic matter.

Organic matter can help lower the
pH or keep it low if you've added sulfur.
Avoid fertilizers that raise the soil pH,
including wood ashes, bonemeal, rock
phosphate and guano.

ACID FRIENDLY
Garden mum is a late
summer to autumn be
that is suited to well-dr
soil with a pH under 6.
full sun to light shade.

ACID SOIL
Excess acidity is among the easiest of soil
problems to fix. A slightly acid soil is a
great thing to have because most plants
thrive in it. But in too-acid soil, most
nutrients are bound up in unavailable
forms. A few minerals—aluminum, iron,
manganese—may become too soluble
and reach toxic concentrations. And soil
organisms are inhibited, so organic
matter breaks down more slowly.
  Soil with a pH below 6.2 is too acid
for many plants, but there are some that
will thrive in those conditions. If your
soil is naturally quite acid, you may just
decide to grow adapted species, such as
garden mums *Dendranthema* spp. and
lily-of-the-valley *Convallaria majalis.*
Observe what is growing well in your
neighbor's gardens and in natural areas
around your home.

RAISE THE pH
Add ground limestone
to raise the pH of acid
soil, digging or raking it
into your soil

Gardening tips and ideas,
and suggestions about
problems you may
encounter in your garden.

General information about
planting, propagating,
and caring for your plants
to get the optimum results.

Photograph of each individual plant, showing what it looks like when grown in the right conditions.

Botanical name

Family name

Quick-reference information on climate, height and spread, and flower season. Refer to the Plant Hardiness Zone Maps on page 308.

Common name

Helleborus niger

RANUNCULACEAE

CLIMATE
Zones 3–8.

HEIGHT AND
SPREAD
1–1½ feet
(30–45 cm) tall.
1–2 feet
(30–60 cm) wide.

FLOWERING TIME
Early winter
through spring.

Hemerocallis Hybrids

HEMEROCALLIDACEAE

CLIMATE
Zones 3–9 for
most hybrids.

HEIGHT AND
SPREAD
1–5 feet
(30–150 cm) tall.
2–3 feet
(60–90 cm) wide.
There are miniature
and standard sizes
as well as extremely
tall kinds.

FLOWERING TIME
Late spring through
summer.

CHRISTMAS ROSE

CHRISTMAS ROSE'S LOVELY FOLIAGE IS ATTRACTIVE ALL SEASON. USE THIS PERENNIAL IN SHADE GARDENS OR IN SPRING BORDERS.

Description Has deeply lobed, leathery leaves growing from a stout crown with fleshy roots. The flowers open white and turn pink with age. They have five petal-like sepals surrounded by leafy bracts.

Ideal position Light to partial shade. Established plants tolerate dry soil and deep shade.

Ideal soil conditions Evenly moist, humus-rich soil.

Cultivation In spring, remove any damaged leaves from the plant. Plants take 2–3 years to become established and resent disturbance. Divide only to propagate.

Propagation Lift the clumps after flowering in spring and separate the crowns. Replant the divisions immediately. Sow seed outdoors in spring or early summer.

Pest and disease prevention No serious pests or diseases.

Landscape use Combine with early-spring bulbs, wildflowers and ferns.

Other species *H. argutifolius*, Corsican hellebore, has green flowers. Zones 6–8

H. orientalis, lenten rose, is similar to *H. niger* but has pink, red or white flowers. Zones 4–9.

DAYLILY

STUNNING DAYLILY HYBRIDS ARE AMONG THE MOST POPULAR PERENNIALS—THEY ARE LONG-LIVED, EASY-CARE PLANTS.

Description Each flower only lasts a day but a profusion of new buds keeps the plants in bloom for 1 month or more. Daylily flowers vary in color and form. The majority of the wild species are orange or yellow with wide petals and narrow, petal-like sepals. Modern hybrids come in many colors.

Ideal position Full sun to light shade. Most modern hybrids need at least 8 hours of direct sun to flower well. Some of the older selections and the species will bloom in partial shade.

Ideal soil conditions Evenly moist, average to humus-rich soil.

Cultivation Plant container-grown or bareroot plants in spring or autumn. Place the crowns just below the soil surface. Plants take a year to become established and then spread quickly to form dense clumps. Most hybrids and species can remain in place for many years without disturbance. Some have so many bloom stalks that the flowers crowd together and lose their beauty—divide these every 3 years. Deadhead regularly to keep them looking their best. The foliage of most daylilies remains nice all season. If leaves are yellow, grasp

Detailed information about the plant.

Each section is color-coded for easy reference.

Part One

Know Your Garden

Perpetual Perennials

Gardening with perennials is a joy. Whether your garden is large or small, sunny or shady, wet or dry, a wide variety of perennials will thrive there and provide beauty for years to come.

What Is a Perennial?

Perennial plants live and bloom for more than two growing seasons. Many survive a decade or longer if planted in the right location and hardy perennials come back year after year, so you don't have to buy and replant them each spring. But even the short-lived plants are worth growing. For instance, blanket flower *Gaillardia* x *grandiflora* blooms vigorously for a long

CLOUDS OF COLOR

The delicate Japanese anemone *Anemone* x *hybrida* is one perennial that can be propagated by taking root cuttings or by division.

portion of the summer, although it seldom survives more than 2 years.

Occasionally a biennial plant such as foxglove *Digitalis purpurea*, which grows foliage the first year and flowers the second, will live for a third year. Despite their different life spans, all these plants are called perennials.

Perennials are herbaceous, which means they lack woody stems—trees and shrubs are exempted from this definition because they develop woody stems and limbs.

Usually the foliage of perennials dies down to the underground roots each dormant season. A few, such as rock cress *Arabis* spp., have evergreen foliage.

Unlike annuals, most perennials flower for only a few weeks each season. They don't have to be replanted every year—these beauties come back on their own. They are cheaper than most trees and shrubs and they're relatively simple to move or dig up and replace if you want to change the look and layout of your yard. Perennials are dependable and easy choices for beginners, and they come in enough variety to satisfy even the most experienced gardener.

BEAUTIFUL BRACTS

Perennials come in all shapes and sizes. *Eryngium giganteum* is an unusually shaped, short-lived perennial with fascinating bracts surrounding the flowers.

SHOWY DAYLILY

Daylilies are dependable, hardy plants that produce brightly colored blooms in a range of different climates.

LONG-LASTING COLOR
Centaurea dealbata
'Steenbergii' is a long-
flowering knapweed cultivar,
which is perfect for any
full-sun position.

GRASSY COMPANION
Upright, arching, perennial
grasses such as Japanese
silver grass *Miscanthus
sinensis* are ideal for planting
with other perennials in a
flower border.

NOT JUST FLOWERS
Shade-loving caladiums are
grown for their showy leaves.
Pinch off any of the small
flowers that grow in summer.

A Perennial for Every Position

Now that you know what a perennial is,
you are able to start to explore the many
possibilities for using them in your
garden. With thousands of species and
cultivars to choose from, there's a good
chance that you'll find plenty of plant
forms, leaf textures and flower colors
and shapes to fit the garden you have
in mind. Any yard can be accented with
perennials. A few clusters of perennial
flowers will bring colorful highlights
to drab corners and a garden full of
perennials will become a landscape
feature. You can use perennials as
accents, focal points, masses of color
or scenes of change.

Choose perennials with colors,
textures and forms that enhance your
entire landscape. By combining your
perennials with annuals, biennials, shrubs
and trees in one glorious garden, you
will be able to enjoy the benefits of each
kind of plant. For example, plant early-
blooming perennials such as irises and
peonies with annuals such as cleomes
Cleome spp. and cosmos, which start
blooming in early summer and carry on
until frost. Put smaller clumps of dramatic
perennials in strategic locations to

highlight the entrance to walks, the location of a door or the view from a window. Consider nesting three gold-centered, broad-leaved hostas (such as *Hosta* 'Gold Standard') at each side of the entrance of a woodland path. Or use a clump of common torch lilies *Kniphofia uvaria* to frame the top of a drive.

STANDING IRISES

A stand of irises is an impressive feature for any garden. They look really stunning planted in graduating colors.

Name That Perennial

One of the tricks to growing perennials successfully is to learn their names. Get to know their botanical names so you know exactly which plant you are talking about, planting or ordering.

What's in a Name?

Botanical names are usually given as two words. The first word, the name of the genus, refers to a group of closely related plants. The second word indicates the species, a particular kind of plant in that genus. You may grow several different species from the same genus. *Achillea*

AUTUMNAL FLOWERS

Common sneezeweed *Helenium autumnale* is great for moist soil. As its botanical name indicates, it is an autumn-flowering perennial.

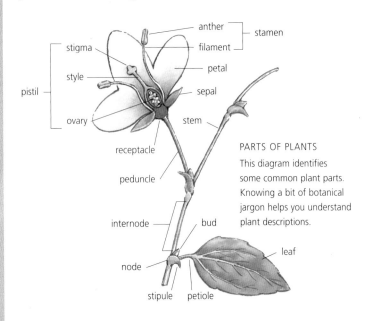

stigma
style
pistil
ovary

anther
filament
stamen

petal
sepal
stem

receptacle
peduncle

internode
bud

node
stipule
petiole
leaf

PARTS OF PLANTS

This diagram identifies some common plant parts. Knowing a bit of botanical jargon helps you understand plant descriptions.

millefolium and *Achillea tomentosa*, for example, both belong to the genus *Achillea*, known as yarrow. But *Achillea millefolium* refers to a species with finely cut leaves, while *Achillea tomentosa* refers to one with fuzzy leaves.

Horticulturists and botanists recognize two other classifications of plants: varieties and cultivars. Plants that develop a natural variation in the wild are called varieties and the varietal name is included as part of the botanical name after the abbreviation "var." Cultivars, whose names are set in single quotes after the botanical name, are plants that have been selected and propagated as part of a breeding program or from a chance mutation in a garden.

You may also come across hybrids, which are blends of two species or, more rarely, two genera. One example is *Anemone* x *hybrida*—the "x" indicates that this plant is a hybrid.

In this book, you will find plants listed by their common name and their botanical name. When we use "spp." we are discussing related species in the same genus. For example, *Iris* spp. includes bearded, Siberian and Japanese irises.

CREEPING AJUGA
"*Reptans*" is Latin for "creeping." *Ajuga reptans* is a creeping perennial.

THE LOGIC OF NAMES

A botanical name tells us something about the plant it identifies, such as its flower color or growth habit. Listed below are some words that appear in botanical names.

Albus: white
Argenteus: silver
Aureus: golden yellow
Caeruleus: blue
Luteus: yellow
Niger: black
Palustris: swampy
Perennis: perennial
Prostratus: trailing
Reptans: creeping
Roseus: rosy
Ruber: red
Spinosus: spiny
Variegatus: variegated
Vulgaris: common

CLIMATE

Climate—the seasonal cycles of rainfall, temperature, humidity and other factors—has a major influence on which perennials will thrive in different parts of your garden landscape.

THINK ABOUT TEMPERATURE

If you want to grow plants that will live for more than 1 year, you have to consider your area's average low and high temperatures. Plants that are naturally adapted to this temperature range will tend to thrive in your garden.

Try to limit your selections to plants that are reliably cold-hardy for your local area. Marginally hardy plants may survive for several years, but it's likely that they won't thrive and an unusually cold spell could even kill them off.

High summer temperatures also limit which perennials you can grow. Even if a plant can tolerate the heat, it may demand frequent watering in return, and it probably won't look great.

WATER WISE

Many delphiniums limp along in hot-climate summers and die out after 1 or 2 years, while the same plants grown in a cooler, moister climate can thrive for several years.

SHADE LOVERS

Moisture-loving plants such as astilbes, primulas and hostas thrive in cool, humid climates that have a high annual rainfall.

RAINFALL

Rainfall, like temperature, has a great impact on determining which plants will grow in an area without supplemental water. If you want to grow just a few moisture-loving plants, site them close to the house where you can give them special attention more easily. But if your goal is to save time, money and natural resources, you'll definitely want to include naturally adapted plants in your landscape. Small, fuzzy or silvery leaves are fairly reliable clues that a particular plant is adapted to low-water conditions.

MICROCLIMATES

Microclimates are small areas where the growing conditions differ from the norm. As an example, an L-shaped corner next to your house might be sheltered enough from the winter wind and hold enough of the heat radiating from the house to allow you to grow a special, marginally hardy plant that would struggle along in an open area. Similar microclimates can also exist for shade and water.

VARIABLE NEEDS
Some daylily cultivars are suited to hot climates, while others can't take the heat at all. Ask your local nursery for advice to match your climate and a particular daylily cultivar.

SILVER-LEAVED YARROW
Plants with silvery leaves are often well adapted to low-water, full-sun conditions.

TOPOGRAPHY

The topography of your yard will influence how you'll design your garden. Each kind of topography has its own advantages and disadvantages for perennial gardening.

GARDENING ON A HILLTOP

A garden on a hilltop will face different conditions than gardens just down the slope. The soil on a hilltop may be thin due to erosion, and is often very well drained. Hilltop sites can be windswept, and strong winds can topple tall plants, so you'll either need to stake your tall perennials or stick with shorter plants. Winds can also dry out plants quickly, so you may have to water more often. If excessive wind is a problem, you can decrease the velocity by setting a fence, hedge or vine-covered trellis between the prevailing wind and your garden.

GARDENING IN A VALLEY

At the base of a slope, perennial gardens are more prone to late-spring and early-autumn frosts. Frost and cold air inevitably concentrate in low-lying areas, known as frost pockets, slowing or damaging spring growth and autumn flowers. The same frost may miss plants growing in warmer areas slightly uphill. Gardeners in low-lying areas may want to wait a little later than those at higher levels to remove protective winter mulches.

Like frost, moisture will collect at the base of the slope. Valleys are rich in rainfall runoff and, often, natural water

OBEDIENT PLANT
Obedient plant is ideal for those spots where water gathers in a valley garden. This moisture-loving plant likes full sun or light shade.

A SUNNY CORNER
A wall can act just like a stand of trees and create a warm, frost-free microclimate ideal for heat-loving plants.

TWO SURE-FIRE FAVORITES
Common bugleweed and hosta are two tough, dependable, moisture-loving perennials that are excellent for easy-care shade gardens.

features, such as ponds and streams. Topsoil eroded from surrounding slopes tends to collect here, but if the soil is clayey, it may not drain well. A common way to deal with this drainage problem is to plant perennials in raised beds. If poor drainage is really a problem, you could install drainage pipes to channel the excess water into another area. In valleys and flat terrain, the best solution to poor drainage is often to use the moisture around creeks, ponds and lakes to your advantage. Let a bubbling brook or the reflective surface of a pond become the focus around which you plant water-loving perennials. Clothe the banks with the flashiest of the moisture-lovers, such as Japanese primroses *Primula japonica*, red-spiked cardinal flowers *Lobelia cardinalis* or rodgersia *Rodgersia pinnata*.

RAISED BEDS
Valley gardens often collect water from surrounding areas. If drainage is poor, try planting in raised beds.

CASCADING COLOR
Slopes tend to be well drained and are natural sites for rock gardens. Choose perennials such as wall rock cress *Arabis caucasica*.

SLOPE STABILIZER
Ajuga reptans takes root and spreads rapidly to form a dense groundcover—perfect for growing on shady slopes.

Gardening on a Slope
With a little imagination and work, you can transform a sloping site from a maintenance headache into a valuable landscape asset. Hillsides are awkward to mow and weed, so the best strategy is to cover them with plants that take care of themselves.

A hilly yard has great potential for interesting settings for your perennials. It also has more microclimates. In general, soils on slopes tend to be well drained but the topsoil may be thin because of erosion. Perennial gardens on slopes are less prone to late-spring and early-autumn frosts, as the cold air tends to settle down in the valley and the warm air rises up over the slope.

Slopes are ideal sites for rock gardens. If the slope isn't naturally rocky, you can add groupings of large boulders or layers of flat rock that resemble natural outcroppings. Leave pockets of soil between the rocks to grow small perennials such as sweet violets *Viola odorata*, primroses *Primula* spp. and candytuft

SLOPING SOLUTIONS

Shallow basins or terraces trap moisture and minimize soil erosion (right). Another alternative is low-growing, spreading perennials such as moss phlox for gently sloping sites (below).

ROBUST COLOR

Clump-forming *Geranium ibericum* forms a glorious groundcover of saucer-shaped, purple-blue flowers in early summer—it needs evenly moist soil to thrive.

Iberis sempervirens, along with small bulbs and dwarf conifers.

If you have a steep slope, think twice before stripping the existing vegetation to plant a perennial garden. The soil might wash away before most of the perennials can root and stabilize the slope. One way to handle slopes is by planting them with perennials that take root and spread aggressively, such as daylilies, common bugleweed *Ajuga reptans* and cranesbills *Geranium* spp. Space the plants closely for more rapid bank stabilization, and use burlap or straw to hold soil in place until the roots do their job.

If you don't want to rely on plants alone to control erosion, you can terrace the hill or install a retaining wall to moderate the slope. A beautiful rock or timber retaining wall will give your landscape interesting structure and let you grow perennials that do not root strongly enough to survive on a slope.

ASPECT

YARROW EXPOSED
Fern-leaved yarrow *Achillea filipendulina* likes full sun and prefers a southern aspect, which provides the maximum amount of light and heat.

Aspect refers to the amount of sun and shade your garden receives. It depends on where each garden is in relation to the house and to other shade-casting features such as trees and fences.

SOUTH–FACING SITES
Southern aspects have maximum light. Heat- and drought-tolerant perennials such as common sundrops *Oenothera fruticosa* subsp. *glauca* thrive here.

EASTERN ASPECT
Eastern sites receive cool morning sun and up to a half day of direct light. They are sheltered from hot afternoon sun. Plants requiring afternoon shade do well here, such as lady's mantle *Alchemilla mollis* and cranesbills *Geranium* spp.

WEST–FACING SITES
West-facing sites are cool and shady in the morning but temperatures rise when strong afternoon sun hits. Try tough, drought-tolerant perennials that can take these conditions, such as daylilies.

NORTHERN ASPECT
North-facing gardens receive less light and remain cool. A bright, evenly cool spot is ideal for perennials that love shade and moist soil, such as hostas, ferns, primroses and some iris species.

SOUTHERN EXPOSURE
South-facing sites in the Northern Hemisphere have exactly the same characteristics (maximum amount of sun and maximum heat in summer) as north-facing sites in the Southern Hemisphere. If you are in the Southern Hemisphere, simply substitute south for north, north for south.

MEETING THE CHALLENGE
Purple coneflowers (right) tolerate west-facing sites, which are a challenge for most plants.

Sun or Shade

How do you tell if a spot has full sun, partial shade or full shade? You'll have to consider not only the exposure, but also the shade cast by trees, shrubs, hedges, fences and other structures.

Understanding Sun and Shade

To understand a garden site, watch it over the course of a day (check on it every hour or so) and note each time whether the spot is sunny or shady. Any site with less than 6 hours of direct sunlight is shady. Perennials that prefer full sun need 6 hours or more of direct sunlight to grow well. A site that receives a few hours of morning or late afternoon sun but no direct midday sun is described as having partial shade. Many perennials that prefer full sun will also tolerate partial shade.

A generally bright site that receives little direct sun but lots of filtered or reflected light is said to have light or dappled shade. Typically, this kind of

SHADY COLOR

Many interesting and colorful perennials, such as astilbes, thrive in the shade.

SECRET TO SUCCESS

The trick to successful perennial gardening is finding and combining plants that thrive in your particular local conditions.

HAPPY HOSTAS

Hostas come in a variety of colors and shapes and are tough, dependable perennials that are excellent for easy-care shade gardens.

PURPLE ROCK CRESS

As its name suggests, purple rock cress is ideal for sunny rock gardens and rock walls.

shade occurs beneath high-branched deciduous trees that don't cast solid shadows. Full, dense or deep shade is darker and fewer plants grow well in it. The area under evergreens is in deep shade all year long. Plants growing under densely branched deciduous trees are in full shade most of the summer.

Shade changes during the year both because the angle of the sun changes and because deciduous trees grow and shed their leaves. A sunny summer site may be shaded by a tree in spring, when the sun is lower in the sky.

The deep shade of a maple tree disappears when it loses its leaves. Many spring wildflowers, including bluebells *Mertensia pulmonarioides*, bloom before overhead trees leaf out. Even if your yard is deeply shaded the rest of the season, you can enjoy masses of color in the spring and beautiful green and patterned foliage the rest of the year.

SOIL COMPOSITION

Learning your soil's characteristics helps you choose the right techniques for dealing with it successfully. When your soil is in good shape your garden will naturally be healthier and more beautiful.

WHAT IS SOIL?

Just as the air you breathe is a mixture of different gases, your garden soil is a mixture of solids, spaces and living organisms. About 97 percent of the solid part is old rock that's been broken down into tiny particles over millions of years. The remaining 3 percent or so is organic matter, made up of decomposed plant and animal tissue. Intermingled with rock and organic matter is an almost equal volume of space, filled with air and water.

This mixture of minerals, organic matter, air and water can support a diverse population of living organisms, from algae and fungi to earthworms and small mammals. Most important to you, as a gardener, is that soil is a habitat for roots, providing the physical support, nutrients and water that your plants need to grow and thrive. Maintaining the right balance of these ingredients is the goal of good soil management.

WELL-DRAINED PEONIES
Peonies grow best in soil that has been enriched with organic matter. They like a nutrient-rich environment and need good drainage to avoid root rot.

SAND, CLAY AND SILT
Sandy soil (left) tends to be dry and low in nutrients; clayey soil (center) can be sticky when wet and hard when dry; and silty soil (right) is fine and powdery and can pack like clay.

THRIVING PLANTS
Once you know the soil conditions of your site, you can choose perennials that will thrive—like these salvia and orange coneflowers.

SOIL MAKEUP

Sand, clay and silt make up your soil and are categorized by size. Sand has the largest mineral particles. These leave loose pockets, called pore spaces, that allow water and nutrients to drain away. Sandy soils tend to be dry and infertile.

Clay particles are ultrafine—about 1,000 times smaller than sand. They can pack together to make a tight, water- and nutrient-rich but poorly oxygenated soil. Between sand and clay are the medium-sized silt particles. Silt tends to have characteristics of both sand and clay.

SOIL pH

Soil pH—the measurement of your soil's acidity or alkalinity—is another factor that can determine which plants will grow well because pH affects the availability of nutrients in your soil. Soils that have pH ratings below 7 are acidic and as the pH drops, the soil becomes increasingly more acidic. Soils with pH ratings above 7 become increasingly more alkaline. An acidic pH (5.5–6.5) is ideal for most flowering plants.

STUDY YOUR SOIL

Soil structure refers to the way in which the sand, silt and clay particles join together to form clumps. A soil with high amounts of sand or clay will usually be too loose or too dense to support good plant growth. A well-balanced soil tends to form soft, crumbly, granular clumps. Soil with this loose, granular structure is also easy to dig.

Organic matter is a critical component of all soils. Healthy soils have 5 percent organic matter or more (humus-rich soil). Soils high in organic matter tend to be dark, loose and crumbly and have a nice, earthy smell. Soil structure can be improved by adding organic matter.

Organic matter improves soil and encourages earthworms and other soil organisms, which in turn contribute nutrients and encourage root growth.

HUMUS-RICH SOIL

Humus, or partially decomposed organic matter, improves the quality of the soil. Ligularias thrive in a moist, humus-rich soil.

CARDINAL FLOWER

The shallow-rooted cardinal flower *Lobelia cardinalis* thrives in rich, evenly moist soil. Mulch if winter is cold.

SIMPLE TEXTURE TESTS

To see how clayey your soil is, rub a moistened ball of soil about the size of a grape between your palms. The goal is to make a "worm" or rope. If you succeed, your soil is more than 15 percent clay. The longer the worm, the higher the percentage of clay.

To check for sand, place a chunk of soil in your palm and wet it enough to form a small puddle. Rub a finger in it: If it's gritty, your soil is sandy; if it's smooth, your soil is silty.

SOIL TUNNELERS

Earthworms tunnel through the soil, consuming and breaking down organic matter and leaving behind nutrient-rich castings.

The depth of your soil has an impact on root growth and this in turn affects what plants—deep- or shallow-rooting—will thrive in your garden. Dig down into the soil with a shovel. If you can go 2 feet (60 cm) without hitting a sheet of rock or a band of dense, tightly compacted soil, you'll be able to grow a wide range of shallow-rooted perennials.

There is also abundant life in healthy soil. Beneficial bacteria can decompose organic and mineral elements, freeing nutrients for plants to use. Soil that is compacted, low in organic matter or excessively wet is low in soil organisms.

Fertility is the availability, not just the presence, of nutrients in the soil. In order to grow, plants draw upon large amounts of nutrients and trace elements. Many of these are released naturally through mineral-rich rocks breaking down. A soil test can tell you if you have the right balance for normal plant growth.

Part Two

Planning Your Garden

PLANNING

NOT JUST PLANTS
Don't restrict yourself to plants when planning your garden. Remember to include features such as birdbaths.

NEVER TOO SMALL
Clouds of Japanese anemone *Anemone* x *hybrida* seem to drift from this window box—they like moist, open shade.

Don't jump into perennial gardening without sufficient planning. By taking the few basic steps below, you'll create a beautiful, healthy garden that suits your landscape and requires the least upkeep.

LOOK AT YOUR LANDSCAPE

Before you start, walk around and look at your garden from all angles. Think about where a perennial garden would enhance your yard. You could have the garden edge your shrub borders, run along the perimeter of the patio or radiate out from the back door or picture window. In short, you want to give the garden a reason for being wherever it is.

PUT YOUR IDEAS ON PAPER

Once you've chosen a site and style for your garden, you can start putting your plans down on paper. Measure the length and width of the area you have targeted for your garden. Determine an appropriate outline and draw it to scale on a piece of graph paper. For example, if you decide to use a perennial border that is 7 feet (2.1 m) wide and 20 feet (6 m) long, you could draw a replica plan with a scale of 1 inch (2.5 cm) on the paper to 2 feet (60 cm) in the garden. The resulting scale drawing would be 3½ inches (9 cm) wide and 10 inches (25 cm) long. To fit a larger

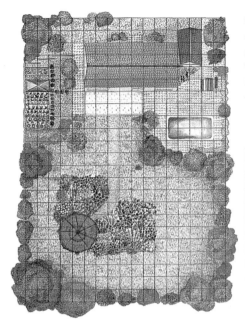

Once you decide on the plants and the effect you want, you're ready to take pencil and paper in hand and turn your list into a landscape design.

SET PRIORITY PROJECTS

How you actually turn your ideas into reality depends on your time and budget. Don't try to convert the whole yard at one time—a better route is to set priority areas based on the sections you feel most strongly about. Deal with the most time-consuming tasks first, which will free up more time to tackle the smaller challenges in the following years.

garden plan onto graph paper, you could adjust the scale, with 1 inch (2.5 cm) on paper equaling up to 5 feet (1.5 m) of garden. If you compress more than about 5 feet (1.5 m) of garden space to 1 inch (2.5 cm) of graph paper your plan may be too small to include details you need.

Draw in the major features that surround your garden, such as buildings, trees, shrubs and existing paths. This is also a good place to jot down notes about the soil conditions in the area (is it frequently wet, often dry or evenly moist?), as well as the amount and type of sunshine available (does it get full sun, just a few hours of morning sun or no direct sun at all?). Now you are ready to choose perennials with colors, textures and forms that enhance your landscape.

A SPOT OF COLOR

Even a small planting such as a patch of pinks *Dianthus* spp. and lamb's ears *Stachys byzantina* adds color.

PLANT FOR ALL SEASONS
Pretty lamb's ears *Stachys byzantina* is a spring bloomer, but its lovely, velvety or fuzzy leaves provide year-long interest.

A MASS OF COLOR
You can depend on asters to produce loads of colorful blooms for your late-summer and autumn garden.

ALL-SEASON INTEREST

A good selection of spring-, summer-, and autumn-blooming perennials, plus a few plants with evergreen leaves for winter interest, will give you a landscape that is truly attractive all year long.

All-season interest starts with flower displays that spread beyond one season. Foliage and plant form are the other features you can use to keep your garden looking beautiful as flowers come and go. From spring through autumn, many perennials have leaves in attractive colors or interesting shapes, such as the starry leaves of blood-red cranesbill *Geranium sanguineum*.

Many wildflowers and shade-loving perennials bloom just as trees leaf out, so spring is a good season to draw attention to areas that will be shady and green later on. Supplement early-blooming perennials with your favorite spring-flowering shrubs and trees.

As spring turns into summer, many old-fashioned perennials, including peonies, irises and columbines *Aquilegia* spp., reach their peak, making it easy to feature flowers.

As summer progresses, daisy-like perennials—including blanket flower *Gaillardia* x *grandiflora* and coreopsis *Coreopsis* spp.—take center stage. Foliage keeps up appearances where early perennials have finished blooming. Silver leaves make dramatic partners for hot- or cool-hued flowers.

Asters, boltonia and Joe-Pye weeds *Eupatorium* spp. keep blooming after autumn frosts nip most annuals. As flowers fade, foliage brightens—leaves of peonies and common sundrops

YEAR-ROUND COLOR

Put in a selection of spring-, summer- and autumn-flowering perennials to ensure all-season interest. Plant spring-flowering wildflowers and old-fashioned peonies and columbines for summer color. For autumn, you can't go past asters and boltonia. For winter choose perennials with showy seedpods, such as astilbes and coneflowers *Rudbeckia* spp.

Oenothera fruticosa subsp. *glauca* turn beautiful shades of red, the leaves of amsonias *Amsonia* spp. turn bright yellow and many ornamental grasses bleach to gold. White baneberry *Actaea alba* and Jack-in-the-pulpit *Arisaema triphyllum* are perennials with dramatic berries that may last through autumn.

After the leaves drop, attention turns to evergreen plants and those with interesting seedpods or fruits. Perennials with showy winter seedpods include blue false indigo *Baptisia australis*, coneflowers *Rudbeckia* and *Echinacea* spp., blackberry lily *Belamcanda chinensis* and astilbes.

DRAMATIC EFFECT
The spiky leaves and flowers of spike gayfeather *Liatris spicata* add summer drama.

CONDITIONS IN COMMON

Phlox (top), amsonia (middle) and bee balm (bergamot) (bottom) do well as companions—they all like moist, well-drained, humus-rich soil and full sun.

EASY SUCCESSES

To get the best growth and flowering for the least work, combine plants that have similar soil and fertility needs.

Match the Plant to the Site

Use the information you have gathered about your site to decide which perennials to grow where. You need to decide whether to match the plant to the site or the site to the plant.

Keep a wish list of all the plants that you really love. Write down the flower color, shape, height, season of bloom, foliage appearance and cultural require-ments so you can compare them all and group together the plants with similar needs. Start matching up the plants with your site conditions. Think about how to organize the garden to get the optimum result—consider factors such as flower and foliage colors, size and bloom season. It makes gardening rewarding and simpler if you can match the plants to the site.

If you have a fairly flat site with moist, well-drained soil, you can plant a wide variety of perennials almost anywhere. But you still need to think about other plant needs, such as sun requirements, or exposure, and frost hardiness. And chances are that you'll have at least one area in the yard with

CONTRASTING STYLE

The color and texture of the foliage of lamb's ears contrasts beautifully with the bold flowers of spike speedwell—and they thrive in the same site conditions.

more challenging conditions, such as slopes or wet spots. If you have a difficult spot, you may decide to ignore it and limit your perennial plantings to the more hospitable areas. Or you may choose to take up the challenge and plan a garden of perennials that are naturally adapted to those tough conditions. You may be pleasantly surprised to see how well-chosen perennial plantings with similar needs can turn a problem site into a pleasing garden.

Quick-reference Guide to Some Favorite Perennials

The secret to having a thriving garden is choosing your plants well. When you have
your list of favorites, check that they will grow in your climate. Group them together
according to the position they like and flower color and season, then start planning.
This table summarizes the vital information for about 60 popular perennials.

BOTANICAL NAME	FLOWER SEASON	COLOR	POSITION	ZONES
Achillea filipendulina	summer	yellow	sun/shade	3–9
Aconitum carmichaelii	late summer/autumn	blue	sun/shade	3–7
Agapanthus africanus	summer/autumn	blue	sun/shade	8–10
Ajuga reptans	late spring/summer	blue	sun/shade	3–9
Alcea rosea	summer/autumn	various	sun/shade	2–8
Alchemilla mollis	summer/autumn	yellow	sun/shade	2–8
Alstroemeria aurea	summer	yellow, orange	sun/shade	7–10
Anemone x hybrida	late summer/autumn	white to rose	sun/shade	5–8
Aquilegia hybrids	spring/summer	various	sun/shade	3–9
Arabis caucasica	late winter/spring	pink, white	sun/shade	3–7
Armeria maritima	late spring/summer	pink	sun	4–8
Aruncus dioicus	late winter/spring	white	sun/shade	3–7
Aster novae-angliae	late summer/autumn	various	sun/shade	3–8
Aster x frikartii	midsummer/autumn	blue-purple	sun/shade	5–8
Aubrieta deltoidea	early spring	white, rose, purple	sun/shade	4–8
Begonia Tuberhybrida Group	summer/autumn	various	partial shade	10
Boltonia asteroides	late summer/autumn	white and yellow	sun/shade	3–9
Brunnera macrophylla	early spring	blue	shade	3–8
Caltha palustris	early to midspring	yellow	sun/shade	2–8
Campanula glomerata	late spring/summer	blue, purple	sun/shade	3–8
Campanula persicifolia	summer	blue	sun/shade	3–8
Centaurea dealbata	late spring/summer	pink	sun	3–7
Cerastium tomentosum	late spring/summer	white	sun	2–7
Ceratostigma plumbaginoides	summer	blue	sun/shade	5–9
Coreopsis verticillata	summer	yellow	sun/shade	3–9
Cyclamen hederifolium	early autumn	pink, white	partial shade	5–9
Delphinium Elatum Group	late spring/summer	white, blue, purple	sun	4–7
Dendranthema x grandiflorum	late summer/autumn	various	sun/shade	3–9

BOTANICAL NAME	FLOWER SEASON	COLOR	POSITION	ZONES
Dianthus plumarius	early to midsummer	white, pink	sun	3–9
Dicentra spectabilis	early spring/summer	pink	partial shade	2–9
Echinacea purpurea	mid- to late summer	red, pink	sun	3–8
Gaillardia x grandiflora	summer	yellow and orange	sun	4–9
Gaura lindheimeri	summer	white	sun	5–9
Geranium endressii	early to midsummer	pink	sun/shade	4–8
Helenium autumnale	late summer/autumn	yellow	sun/shade	3–8
Heliopsis helianthoides	early to midsummer	yellow	sun/shade	3–9
Helleborus niger	early winter/spring	white	light shade	3–8
Hemerocallis Hybrids	late spring/summer	various	sun/shade	3–9
Heuchera sanguinea	late spring/summer	white, pink, red	sun/shade	3–8
Impatiens New Guinea Hybrids	summer	various	sun/shade	5–10
Iris sibirica	early summer	various	sun/shade	3–9
Kniphofia uvaria	late spring/summer	yellow, white, red	sun	5–9
Leucanthemum x superbum	summer	white	sun	3–10
Liatris spicata	midsummer	purple	sun	3–9
Lobelia cardinalis	late summer/autumn	red	sun/shade	2–9
Lupinus polyphyllus	spring/summer	blue, yellow	sun/shade	3–7
Mertensia pulmonarioides	spring	blue	sun/shade	3–9
Monarda didyma	summer	red	sun/shade	4–8
Nepeta x faassenii	spring/midsummer	blue/purple	sun/shade	3–8
Paeonia lactiflora Hybrids	spring/summer	various	sun/shade	2–8
Papaver orientale	early summer	red	sun/shade	2–7
Phlox paniculata	mid- to late summer	various	sun/shade	3–8
Platycodon grandiflorus	summer	blue	sun/shade	3–8
Rudbeckia fulgida	mid- to late summer	yellow/orange	sun/shade	3–9
Salvia x superba	early to midsummer	blue-purple	sun/shade	4–7
Scabiosa caucasica	summer	blue	sun/shade	3–7
Sedum spectabile	mid- to late summer	pink	sun	3–9
Stokesia laevis	summer	blue	sun/shade	5–9
Thalictrum aquilegiifolium	late spring/summer	lavender	sun/shade	5–8
Tiarella cordifolia	sping	white	shade	3–8
Viola odorata	spring	purple	sun/shade	6–9

DESIGNING

Great-looking gardens are basically sequences of many individual plant combinations that consider the quality, color and texture of each plant's foliage as well as its flowers.

COLOR COMBINATIONS

Different colors have different attributes. Warm colors—those related to red, orange or yellow—are bold. They are stimulating and appear closer to the viewer. Cool colors—those related to violet, blue or green—are more tranquil and appear to recede from view. Pure hues—like true yellow or blue—are more vibrant than lighter or darker versions of the same color. Mixing warm and cool colors adds depth and interest.

Combining color in your gardens is just as easy as combining colors in clothes. The green background of the foliage harmonizes with strong colors that you probably wouldn't think to combine in an outfit. While certain types and combinations of colors tend to create specific effects, only you can decide whether you like each particular effect.

Combining similar flower colors in the garden creates a harmonious effect. Try grouping reds with oranges and yellows, yellows with greens and blues, or blues with purples and reds. Colors sharing the same degree of lightness or darkness are also similar, for instance, several different pastels blend more harmoniously than several pure hues.

DRAMATIC EFFECT
It's hard to beat tall, spiky, bold-colored flowers, such as these spike gayfeathers for adding a dramatic touch.

POINT OF INTEREST
A birdbath of complementary color adds interest to this bed of garden mums.

FLOWERS AND FOLIAGE
The lacy leaves of this artemisia combine well with different flower forms and provide season-long interest.

If contrast and excitement are what you're after, choose complementary hues, such as yellow and violet or red and green. Or place a light tint next to a very bright or dark shade of the same hue.

White and gray play an important role in the garden. White can be exciting or soothing. Bright white is surprisingly bold and stands out even in a group of soft pastels. A dash of pure white in a spread of harmonious colors has a dramatic effect. Gray is the great unifier. Silvery or gray foliage works even better than green to soften the transition between two complementary or bold colors. Gray adds drama by contrasting with neighboring green foliage.

COLORFUL SHADE

You can create color and interest in shade gardens by using plants with variegated leaves and colorful flowers, such as this Jacob's ladder.

STRIKING COMBINATIONS

If contrast and excitement are what you're after, choose complementary hues, such as yellow and violet.

SPIDER MUMS

These spidery garden mums illustrate perfectly the use of contrast in color, form and tone to give a great effect.

CONTRASTS AND COMPLEMENTS

Well-planned gardens balance contrast and similarity. Contrasting colors, sizes or other design elements are bold and stimulating. Use contrast to draw attention to a particular location and to add a lively feel. Overusing contrast, too many different textures or too many strong colors can give your garden a jumbled, chaotic look.

Similarity, or the absence of contrasts, increases the sense of harmony. Use variations of closely related colors and gradual height transitions to create soothing garden designs. Too much can be uninteresting, so add a touch of contrast for balance.

Repetition acts as a bridge between similarity and contrast. Repeating similar elements will unify designs. Exact, evenly spaced repetitions of particular plants or combinations create a formal look. Combine different plants with similar features to give an informal garden a cohesive but casual look.

Texture and Form Factors

Two other plant characteristics, texture and form, are as important as color in creating interesting combinations and landscapes with the desired effects. Masses of even-textured foliage can tone down bold colors. Dramatic leaf shapes can add extra zip to a pastel planting. Here are some other tips you can try to plan effective plantings:

- Balance rounded clump formers, such as shasta daisies *Leucanthemum* x *superbum* and coreopsis, with spiky plants, such as mulleins *Verbascum* spp., foxgloves *Digitalis* spp. and spike gayfeather *Liatris spicata*.
- Contrast shiny leaves—like those of bear's breeches *Acanthus mollis* and European ginger *Asarum europaeum*—with velvety or fuzzy leaves, such as those of lamb's ears *Stachys byzantina* or lungworts *Pulmonaria* spp.
- Contrast fine foliage, such as lacy fern fronds, with the smooth, broad leaves of hostas and similar plants.
- Include spiky leaves, like those of irises and blackberry lilies *Belamcanda chinensis*; they'll stand out from matlike or mounded plants long after their flowers fade.
- If you have a small garden that you'll see from a distance, use bold colors, bold textures or bold shapes to make it appear larger and closer to the viewer— the bolder it is, the closer it will appear.

STEELY COLOR

This *Aconitum* sp. cultivar 'Stainless Steel' has beautifully colored flowers. It looks great in borders with flowers of contrasting hues.

CREATING UNITY

Large masses of plants in a single color can add unity to a garden design and avoid a "spotty" look—this adds a sense of serenity to a garden.

STYLES

CASUAL STRUCTURE
This delightful garden blends the casual feeling of a cottage garden with the structure of a double border.

A FLORAL EDGING
The floriferous, semiwoody perennial candytuft *Iberis sempervirens* (above) is perfect for using as an edging in formal plantings (right), walks or walls.

There are traditional and non-traditional styles for flower gardens. These include formal gardens, cottage gardens, herbaceous borders, island beds, cutting gardens and other specialty gardens.

FORMAL GARDENS

Historically, formal gardens were found on large estates. But today, this style is spreading into smaller yards. They are usually laid out in squares or rectangles with low hedges of clipped boxwood, hollies or other evergreens. Plant the beds symmetrically, using the same sequence of perennials and edging plants on either side of a central axis. Make your own patterns with lines, angles and curving rows. Choose carefully—limit your selection to plants that will stay in place and maintain uniform height. Try new cultivars developed for uniformity, such as 'Moonbeam' thread-leaved coreopsis *Coreopsis verticillata* and 'Stella d'Oro' daylily.

Informal Gardens

Informal landscapes use curved lines to create a more natural feeling. These kinds of gardens generally include many different types of plants—trees, shrubs, annuals, herbs and vines as well as perennials. Informal designs are relaxed and lively. Since the plants are free to spread, sprawl and lean on each other, they need less regular maintenance. You won't need to keep sharp edges on the beds and the few weeds that pop up won't immediately be obvious and ruin the look of the garden.

The classic informal garden is the cottage garden, where perennials, annuals, herbs and roses ramble and intertwine. Cottage gardens are at least partially enclosed within walls or fences, making them a natural choice for a small house or a townhouse with an enclosed yard. Unify the scene with a focal point, such as a path through the garden's center to a door, patio or bench.

COLOR AND MOVEMENT
By using trees, paths, beds and borders in an informal way, this garden becomes full of interest and motion.

COTTAGE COLLAGE
Create a pleasing jumble of color and shape by keeping in mind the following "roles" plants can play:

- "Feature" flowers have strong shapes—like spiky lupines and massive peonies—or bright colors.
- "Filler" flowers are less obvious—baby's breath is a filler.
- "Edgers" are low plants used in the fronts of beds or spilling over onto paths. Think of thymes and catmint.

CURVED BEDS

Island beds are suited to casual, or informal, plantings. Just make the beds curved.

BOLD BEDS AND BORDERS

The bold colors of Peruvian lily *Alstroemeria* cultivars are ideal for beds and borders.

PERENNIAL BORDERS

Most perennial borders are designed to be seen from the front, allowing you to set the shorter plants in the foreground and the taller plants in the back.

Borders typically are long, rectangular areas. Generally, the longer a border, the wider it should be—this will help to prevent awkward-looking squares. But there is no reason why you can't make a border any length and width you like. If you want a really wide border, put an access path through it so you can maintain the middle of the garden without walking on it. If you only have room for a small border, place it close to the house and use small groupings of flowers. Look for plants with a long bloom season and attractive foliage.

ISLAND BEDS

Unlike borders, which are usually seen from only one side, island beds are designed for you to walk around and look at from all angles. Because they are located away from structures, they are exposed to maximum sun and air

COOL-CLIMATE BORDER

Aconitum spp. are cool-climate, informal border plants. The hooded flowers form dramatic spikes.

penetration—so the garden tends to be healthier and easier to maintain.

As with a border, tie an island in with existing structures. For the most natural effect, make island beds three times as long as they are wide. If you can view an island bed from all sides, put the tallest plants in the center. If, on the other hand, you can view it primarily from only one angle, make the highest point at the back. Then you can add extra tiers of midborder plants.

FOOD AND WATER

Attract butterflies with a water source and a variety of different plants.

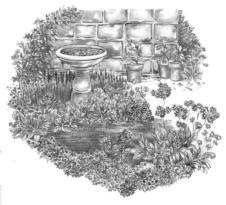

ATTRACTING BUTTERFLIES

If you have an informal landscape, consider planting a meadow garden. If you don't have room, grow some of the many wildflowers that double as garden perennials, such as asters and coneflowers *Echinacea* and *Rudbeckia* spp. Scatter these plants throughout your landscape, or put several together in a butterfly garden. Large splashes of color are easier for butterflies to find than a single plant, so group several plants of the same color together.

You can take a number of steps to encourage butterflies to stay in your yard, including the following: Set flat stones in a sheltered, sunny spot for butterflies to bask on; dig a small, shallow basin and

NOT ONLY COLOR

Besides adding colorful blooms to your garden, orange coneflowers offer nectar for butterflies.

line it with plastic to form a butterfly-luring water source; allow a corner of your yard to go wild—a tangle of brush provides protection from predators; and finally, create a safe, pesticide-free habitat by using safer techniques, such as hand-picking and water sprays, to remove pests.

Perennial Herb Garden

Plan your herb garden as a regular perennial bed or border. A basic garden could consist of raised beds separated by paths. For more formality, lay out the garden beds in geometric shapes, wheel spokes or intricate knots. If you don't have room for a separate herb garden, tuck your favorite herbs into other perennial beds and borders. Most herbs look good in formal designs and make a natural addition to informal gardens.

Sunny sites will suit the widest range of herbs. It is possible to grow some herbs in partial to full shade, but your choices will be limited. (Mints, lemon balm and sweet woodruff are your most likely subjects for success in shade.)

GROUPING OF HERBS
Herbs look wonderful any way you use them—grouped into a special herb garden or mixed with perennials and other plants.

HERB FEATURE
Catmint *Nepeta* x *faassenii* is perfect for spilling over pathways in herb or other types of gardens.

MOISTURE LOVERS

A bog garden is a great site for many kinds of irises. The flowers are beautiful in early summer and the spiky leaves look good all season.

NOT ONLY FRAGRANT

Bee balm (bergamot) *Monarda didyma* leaves have a wonderful citrus aroma. This plant grows well in evenly moist soil.

BOUNTIFUL BOGS

Some perennials have an affinity for wet ground and will thrive at the edge of a pond or in boggy or marshy areas. Perennials suitable for low, moist places are plentiful, including Japanese iris *Iris ensata*, goat's beard *Aruncus dioicus*, turtleheads *Chelone* spp., marsh marigold *Caltha palustris* and cardinal flower *Lobelia cardinalis*.

If you already have a pond or wet spot, a bog garden is the solution. If you don't have a naturally wet area but enjoy bog plants, you can create your own bog. Dig a trench at least 1 foot (30 cm) deep and line it with a heavy plastic pond liner. Put a soaker hose on the top of the plastic and refill the trench with humus-rich soil. The open end of the hose should protrude slightly so that you can attach it to your garden hose and fill the "bog" with water. Repeat as necessary to keep the soil moist.

THE FRAGRANT PERENNIAL GARDEN

When you mention fragrance in the garden, most people automatically think

SHADE AND WATER

Rodgersias grow well in bog and water gardens and along streams. Plant them with hostas, irises, astilbes, ferns and ligularias *Ligularia* spp.

HEADY SCENTS

Lavender is beloved for its beautiful flowers and delightful fragrance.

of flowers. Peonies and lilies are among the most well known, but many others have pleasing scents. Grow scented flowers close to the house for their fragrance, or grow them near outdoor eating areas, patios and porches—any place where people linger.

A number of plants have fragrant foliage, but you need to touch these to smell them. Plant lavender and bee balm (bergamot) *Monarda didyma* where you'll brush against them as you walk by. Grow lemon balm *Melissa officinalis* near a garden seat so you can rub the leaves to release the delicious lemony odor.

The key to having a scented garden that you enjoy is smelling plants before you buy them. As you plan your garden, try to arrange it with just one or two scented plants in bloom at any one time. Then you can enjoy fragrances through the season without being overwhelmed by too many at once.

A COLORFUL CUTTING GARDEN

Few people have enough space to put a cutting garden truly out of sight, but the more removed it is, the less you'll worry about making it look nice. Some gardeners turn over a corner of their vegetable garden to cut flowers; others create separate cutting beds along a garage, in a sunny side yard, or in a sheltered corner of the backyard.

Wherever you put your cutting beds, you want them to be easy to reach and maintain and you want plants that will

STUNNING COLOR

Peruvian lily *Alstroemeria aurea* 'Orange Glory' is a stunning flower to have in your garden or in a vase on your dining room table.

MORNING HARVEST

Using sharp clippers, harvest flowers in the morning before they fully open. Plunge the stems into a bucket of warm water.

NOTHING FANCY

You don't need a complicated design or a particular shape for a cutting garden. Just pick a suitable spot and line up your plants in rows, as you would for vegetables. Cage the stems of floppy perennials, such as delphiniums, or stake them. Add annuals and bulbs to your cutting garden to round out your choice of materials for arrangements.

thrive in your growing conditions—if they don't grow well, they won't produce enough flowers for cutting.

Selecting plants for your cutting garden is much like choosing perennials for any planting. Here are some other things you'll want to consider when you're deciding what to include:

• If space is limited, concentrate on growing perennials in your favorite colors. If, on the other hand, you have lots of room, plant a variety of colors to give yourself lots of arranging options.

• Grow perennials of different shapes. Include spiky flowers and foliage for height, flat or round flowers and leaves for mass, and small, airy flowers and leaves for fillers.

• Look for perennials with long stems. Compact cultivars are great for ornamental plantings but their stems are usually too short for easy arranging.

• Don't forget to include foliage—it adds body and filler to arrangements. Use subtle greens and silvers—variegated leaves make striking accents.

To add extra excitement to your arrangements, include annuals, grasses and hardy bulbs in your cutting garden. Ornamental grasses are great with both flowers and foliage.

LONG LASTING
'Sweet Sultan', *Centaurea moschata* is long-lasting in both dried or fresh flower arrangements.

COLOR THEMES
Gardens based on blue and purple flowers are peaceful and soothing. If you like these colors, grow them in a cutting garden so you can enjoy them indoors as well.

SOLVING PROBLEMS WITH PERENNIALS

Perennials are verstatile plants—you can find the right ones to suit any situation. Use them in foundation plantings, low-maintenance and container gardening and in different soil conditions.

FOUNDATION PLANTING

More and more gardeners are discovering the advantages of using perennials and other colorful, adaptable plants to create a welcoming entrance that is both beautiful and low-care.

Perennials, alone or in combination with hardy bulbs, trees, vines and shrubs, offer attractive and colorful alternatives to a boring row of clipped evergreens.

Well-chosen perennials won't drastically outgrow their location, and they're dormant when snow falls off the roof. Plus, perennials change continually through the season, which is more than can be said for the most commonly planted foundation evergreens.

Planning a perennial garden next to your house is pretty much the same as planning one in any other part of the yard. In some cases, though, foundation sites have extreme growing conditions that you'll need to consider as you choose your plant. Light levels and microclimates can vary dramatically on different sides of your house.

YEAR-LONG INTEREST

Mix perennials with evergreen leaves—such as heart-leaved bergenia *Bergenia cordifolia*—with hardy bulbs to create a planting with year-round appeal.

HAPPY HOSTAS

The ever-dependable hosta comes in a range of sizes and colors. Its tidy growth habit makes it ideal for shady foundation plantings.

HOUSE AND GARDEN

When you choose plants, look for flower colors that will complement the colors of your house.

HIGH FOUNDATIONS

To shield high foundations, include tall perennials that continue to add interest even after they've gone dormant. For instance, the gray seedpods of blue false indigo *Baptisia australis* look attractive all winter. Some tall ornamental grasses also look good after they've dried. Enjoy the stems and leaves all winter, then cut them back in early spring before the new growth sprouts.

INTERESTING SHAPES

Include a mix of rounded and spiky blooms to add interest to your planting. Fragrant flowers are nice, too.

There are no special rules for designing foundation plantings—just choose the plants that can take the conditions and that look good to you.

Including some fragrant flowers, such as peonies and cheddar pinks *Dianthus gratianopolitanus,* adds a welcoming touch. For a formal look, keep the lines straight with a path of bricks or square or rectangular flagstones and straight edges to plantings. For a less formal design, curve the edge of the bed to create a gentle, casual feel and to allow a few of the plants in front to sprawl a bit onto the path.

LOW-CARE COMPACTS
If you love bellflowers, go for
a low-maintenance dwarf
evergreen species, such as
Campanula portenschlagiana.

LOW–MAINTENANCE
SUN LOVERS

The following are all
easy-care and require
full sun to thrive.

Coneflowers
Rudbeckia spp.
Coreopsis
Coreopsis spp.
Daylilies
Hemerocallis spp.
Purple coneflower
Echinacea purpurea
Showy stonecrop
Sedum spectabile
Thrift
Armeria maritima

STUNNINGLY EASY
Salvia superba has long-
blooming showy spikes of
purplish blue flowers, which
are excellent as cut flowers.

LOW–MAINTENANCE PERENNIAL GARDENING

To some people, just the mention
of low maintenance conjures up
images of gravel-covered yards or
expanses of boring, green groundcovers. But there's no reason that
low care has to mean no flowers.
Planning for a low-maintenance
perennial garden requires some
thought. The trick is to choose perennials
that don't need special attention such as
staking, indoor winter storage or frequent
pruning. Look for plants that shrug off
heat, scoff at drought and laugh in the
face of pests. Although going the low-
maintenance route eliminates some
species, you'll still have more to choose
from than you could ever hope to grow.

If you really want to avoid labor,
shun tall or floppy plants—such as
hybrid delphinium *Delphinium* Elatum
Group and baby's breath *Gypsophila
paniculata*—that need staking. Steer
clear of tender perennials, such as canna
Canna x *generalis* and dahlias *Dahlia*
spp., that you have to dig up and store
over the winter. Unless you want to
cover a large area, avoid those that

spread, like lamb's ears *Stachys byzantina* and goutweed *Aegopodium podagraria*. Pass up those that die out after a few years, like many perennial asters *Aster* spp. And ignore those that have a serious pest in your area, unless you can get a resistant strain.

What's left? A lot, starting with dependable spring bulbs such as irises, if iris borer isn't a severe problem in your area; daylilies (there are thousands to choose from); and hostas for shady areas. Try short cultivars of balloon flower *Platycodon grandiflorus* and bellflowers *Campanula* spp. Choose coreopsis *Coreopsis* spp. and other wildflowers, especially in a natural garden. Don't forget old-time favorites such as bleeding heart *Dicentra* spp. Ornamental grasses such as fountain grass *Pennisetum alopecuroides* and blue fescue *Festuca glauca* are great for their foliage and interesting seed heads.

For more ideas, look at gardens that bloom even though you know no one bothers with them. Before you plant any perennial, research its growth needs to be sure it suits your conditions.

ROOM TO MOVE

Spike speedwell *Veronica spicata* is a good choice for a larger, low-maintenance garden—cut them back each year if they get rangy.

EASY IRISES

Irises thrive for years without division and they look great with other easy-care perennials, such as peonies, hostas and astilbes.

CONTAINER SOLUTIONS

OVERFLOWING POT
Geranium cinereum 'Ballerina'
looks great spilling out of a
container and its foliage is
attractive all year round.

CONTAINER LIVING
Many lovely perennials,
including asters and
campanulas, adapt well
to life in containers.

Containers can be the solution to any
troublesome landscape—whether
it be problems with soil, climate or
topography. You can change all these
things simply by using containers.

SOLVING PROBLEMS WITH CONTAINERS

With a little creativity, you'll find many
different ways to use containers to solve
problem spots. If you can't kneel or if
you garden from a wheelchair, you can
grow plants at a convenient height in
raised planters. If your soil is too hard or
rocky to dig, grow flowers in half-barrel
planters instead of in the ground.

If you've got a shady spot that's
crying out for color, try using potted
annuals or perennials to create a rotating
display. As flowers fade, move the shady
pot to a sunnier spot and replace it with
one that's robust from sunshine. Or tuck
a few pots into a dull planting to add
quick color. If space is really limited,
create your own garden paradise
on a rooftop or porch or in a
window box.

Don't limit your container
gardens to just practical uses,
though. Growing perennials
in pots is a great way to
experiment with different
plant combinations before you
commit to putting them in the
ground. If you find that you don't

TOUCH OF INTEREST
Carefully chosen plants in well-placed containers can add another dimension to an otherwise uninteresting area of your garden.

like a particular combination, just separate the pots and group them with other possible perennials.

Containers can also make great garden accents. Choose bold, sculptural perennials such as Adam's needle *Yucca filamentosa* for formal designs—or mix lots of colors and cascading plants for a cottage look. You can achieve any effect you wish with containers.

Choosing a Container

Pot possibilities are endless. You may buy plastic or clay containers or make your own out of old barrels, washtubs or even buckets. Large pots tend to provide the best conditions for growth, since they hold more soil, nutrients and water, but they are also quite heavy if you need to move or hang them.

Pots that are about 8 inches (20 cm) deep are usually able to hold enough soil without getting too heavy. If you don't plan to move the planter, it can be as big as you want. Be creative, almost anything you can put drainage holes in— from clay drainage tiles to old leather work boots—can be pressed into service.

Solid-sided containers, such as plastic pots, hold water longer than porous clay. Plastics are great for hot, dry summers. Plastic pots are lighter and easier to move, but more prone to blowing over than clay pots. Empty your clay pots or bring them indoors before freezing weather because wet soil expands as it freezes and will crack the pot.

COLOR IN A POT
You can combine different plants in one pot to create a particular color combination.

OLD TIMER
The old-time favorite bleeding heart *Dicentra* spp. looks stunning in a container.

FOCAL POINT
A special container can be a focal point in a garden. Clay pots are particularly attractive and natural looking.

OVERFLOWING FLOWERS

A "mass" container planting of baby's breath *Gypsophila muralis* 'Gypsy' not only looks great but gives you an ongoing supply of cut flowers to take indoors.

FOR CONTAINERS

Nearly any perennial will grow well in a pot. Plant several in one pot or group several in individual containers. Good choices include those with a long season of bloom, such as golden orange 'Stella d'Oro' daylily. Others that look great are those with attractive foliage such as lady's mantle *Alchemilla mollis*, spotted lamium *Lamium maculatum*, heart-leaved bergenia *Bergenia cordifolia*, hostas and ornamental grasses. Foliage plants extend the period of interest.

CARING FOR CONTAINERS

Keeping the right water balance is a key part of successful container gardening. To help in this, you need to choose a growing medium that will hold some water but not too much. Improve garden soil by mixing 2 parts soil with 1 part finished compost (or peat moss) and 1 part perlite. Or use sterilized, premixed "soil-less" potting mixes. These mixes are free of soilborne diseases and they weigh much less.

Regular watering is another way you'll balance each container's water supply. Some containers may need watering every day while others will only need water once a week. A good general rule is to wait until the top 1 inch (2.5 cm) of soil is dry; then water until some comes out of the bottom.

Since their rooting space is limited, plants in pots need more fertilizer than plants in the ground. After they've been growing for a month or so, give plants diluted liquid fertilizer every couple of weeks. Use fish emulsion, liquid seaweed or a balanced organic fertilizer. Follow the instructions on the package to find out how often and how much fertilizer you should apply.

Soil Solutions

Gardening would be easier if soil were consistent, but it is a complex and changing mixture of substances—there's bound to be something (or lack of something) that makes gardening a challenge.

Alkaline Soil

Most plants can live with a slightly alkaline soil, but a soil with a pH above 8.0 starts to take its toll. Excessively alkaline soils have chronic nutrient deficiencies and resist attempts to acidify them. In too-alkaline soils, phosphorus and most micronutrients are insoluble and unavailable to plants. On the other hand, minerals such as sodium and selenium may be abundant enough to be toxic to plants. You may decide to grow species that are adapted to high-pH soils.

The most effective material for lowering the soil pH is elemental sulfur. Apply 1 pound (0.5 kg) per 100 square feet (9.3 sq m) for each whole point you want to lower the pH. Rake or dig the sulfur into the soil and keep it moist.

ALKALINE ANEMONE
The delicate Japanese anemone *Anemone* x *hybrida* spreads by creeping underground stems and thrives in alkaline soil.

Plants for Soil pH 7.0 or Higher

Baby's breath
  Gypsophila paniculata
Bergenias
  Bergenia spp.
Coral bells
  Heuchera spp.
Japanese anemone
  Anemone x *hybrida*
Mulleins
  Verbascum spp.
Peonies *Paeonia* spp.
Pinks *Dianthus* spp.

ADAPTABLE PHLOX
Garden phlox can adapt to alkaline soil, as long as it has good drainage and lots of organic matter.

Organic matter can help lower the pH or keep it low if you've added sulfur. Avoid fertilizers that raise the soil pH, including wood ashes, bonemeal, rock phosphate and guano.

ACID SOIL

Excess acidity is among the easiest of soil problems to fix. A slightly acid soil is a great thing to have because most plants thrive in it. But in too-acid soil, most nutrients are bound up in unavailable forms. A few minerals—aluminum, iron, manganese—may become too soluble and reach toxic concentrations. And soil organisms are inhibited, so organic matter breaks down more slowly.

Soil with a pH below 6.2 is too acid for many plants, but there are some that will thrive in those conditions. If your soil is naturally quite acid, you may just decide to grow adapted species, such as garden mums *Dendranthema* spp. and lily-of-the-valley *Convallaria majalis*. Observe what is growing well in your neighbors' gardens and in natural areas around your home.

ACID FRIENDLY
Garden mum is a late-summer to autumn bloomer that is suited to well-drained soil with a pH under 6.5 and full sun to light shade.

RAISE THE pH
Add ground limestone to raise the pH of acid soil, digging or raking it into your soil.

Snow-in-summer is a low-mounding, spring-flowering perennial that can tolerate sandy or loamy soil.

PLANTS FOR SAND

Common torch lily
Kniphofia uvaria
Lance-leaved coreopsis
Coreopsis lanceolata
Lavender cotton
Santolina chamaecyparissus
Sea lavender
Limonium latifolium
Sedums *Sedum* spp.
Snow-in-summer
Cerastium tomentosum
White gaura
Gaura lindheimeri
Yarrows *Achillea* spp.
Yuccas *Yucca* spp.

TOLERANT THRIFT
Thrift *Armeria maritima* will tolerate poor, sandy soil that drains quickly.

MANAGING SANDY SOIL

Sandy soils are light to dig in and don't get sticky when wet. They're well aerated. They warm up quickly in the spring. And it's easy to change their pH because they're not buffered by reserves of acidity or alkalinity. But sands have little clay or humus to hold water and minerals, which wash quickly away. Sand gets hot during the day and cools rapidly at night and there's little or no structure.

Compared to other soil quirks, excessive sandiness is easy to remedy—just dump on organic matter. With enough organic matter, sandy soils can hold water and nutrients while still being well drained and easy to work. Of course, with all that extra moisture to heat up, organically enriched sandy soils won't warm up as fast as they normally do in the spring. But they won't get as hot in the summer, either.

Because sandy soils are well aerated, microorganisms burn through organic matter quickly. In one way, that's good, because humus forms faster; in another way, that's bad, because nutrient-rich organic matter doesn't last long. So add both fast- and slow-digesting organic matter. Manures, grass clippings and

POOR SOIL DELIGHT

Sandy soil is generally infertile, and coreopsis grows best in soil that isn't very fertile—too much nitrogen can cause weak stems.

compost will break down quickly, building humus and improving the soil's ability to hold water and nutrients. Growing green manures over the winter is another good source of organic matter.

Sandy soils are so porous that if the top few inches have dried out, the next few inches below aren't far behind. It doesn't take as much water to soak the soil beyond the root zone, which encourages deep roots. But you will have to water more frequently.

ROCKY BEDS
Use the rocks you find in your landscape as the framework for a raised rock garden. Mound topsoil over the top and plant in crevices and pockets between them.

WORKING WITH ROCKY SOIL

To gardeners facing a thin layer of soil over blocks of rock, the usual advice about deep watering and subsoils and double-digging seems pointless. The obstacles these soils present are many. Plant roots have few places to go. Water and nutrients have little to cling to. Tilling, digging and planting are difficult. The usual remedy for building soil—adding ample amounts of organic matter—helps, but just isn't enough.

The best approach to gardening in rocky soil is to use native plants where possible or to use plants that are suited to rocky conditions—and to import soil for every place else. Plants native to rocky regions have evolved to cope with short supplies of water and nutrients and little room to spread out. They generally

PERENNIALS FOR ROCKY MEADOWS

Basket of gold
Aurinia saxatilis
Butterfly weed
Asclepias tuberosa
Thrift
Armeria maritima
Common wormwood
Artemisia absinthium
Cupid's dart
Catananche caerulea
Dalmation bellflower
Campanula portenschlagiana
Purple rock cress
Aubrieta deltoidea

CASCADING COLOR

Aubrieta deltoidea 'Blue Cascade' is an excellent choice for sunny rock gardens.

WILD ROCK JASMINE

Rock jasmine *Androsace* spp. is a low-growing, unassuming plant with light green or silvery gray foliage.

GRASSES

If you have a moist spot in your rock garden, try ornamental grasses to add depth and interest.

have shallow root systems that reach through whatever soil is available.

It's best to begin with the smallest plant possible. Seeds are ideal, although young potted specimens are more practical for difficult-to-germinate plants. Seeds and young plants can grow roots around obstacles in the soil rather than having to adapt an existing root system to new conditions.

Rocky soils dry out quickly, so water them frequently but for short periods. If you choose plants that are naturally adapted to rocky sites they may not need extra water at all once established.

Meadow gardens normally feature durable, sun-loving flowers. Try turning a rocky outcrop or field into a meadow garden using plants adapted to your rocky area. Look in wildflower gardening books or check with local wildflower societies to find out which plants grow best in your area.

Once you've chosen the plants that will be in your meadow, you'll need to prepare a good seedbed. Keep the soil moist and weed regularly for the first few years. Once the meadow is established, a yearly mowing or slashing in late winter will help control woody plants. Beyond that, once established, you can let these perennials grow and mingle as they will.

Part Three

Planting
Your Garden

Tools and Equipment

Caring for your garden is simpler if you've got good tools. Using the right tool makes any job easier, but when faced with a wall-long display of different tools, it can be hard to decide what you need.

SIMPLE NEEDS

If you garden only with containers or have a very small garden, the tools you need may be just a trowel and hand cultivator.

Basic Collection

Most gardeners can get by with a few basic tools. You'll need a spade to turn the soil and a shovel for digging holes and for moving soil and amendments.

A garden fork is useful for turning the soil, working in amendments and green manures, turning compost and dividing perennials. You'll also need a metal rake to smooth the soil, a hoe for weeding and a trowel for planting and transplanting. Hand pruners may be necessary for pruning perennials.

Caring for Tools

It's easy at the end of a long day in the garden to put tools away dirty. But

EARTH MOVER

If you need to move any significant amount of soil, then a good wheelbarrow is essential to minimize injury and general aches and pains.

You may decide on a whole
collection of garden tools,
or you may buy only a few
of the basics, especially if
you are just starting out.
It depends on your needs
and your budget.

eventually the moist soil clinging to your
tools will make them rust. Use a stick,
wooden spoon or paint stirrer to scrape
off the clinging soil. A good trick is to
keep a tub of sharp sand around and
dip the tool up and down in it until the
soil comes off.

Your spade and hoe will do a
better job for you if you keep them
sharpened. You'll get the best
results if you sharpen them briefly
and often rather than making it a
big job you keep for the end of
the gardening year. For most
gardeners, a metal file is quite
adequate. Use a file that matches
the contour of the tool's surface. The
aim is to keep the angle of the existing
edge but to thin it a bit and remove any
nicks. If you have many tools, a whet-
stone or grindstone will do the job more
quickly. If you don't want to sharpen
them yourself, you can take your tools
to someone who does it professionally.

THE VERSATILE RAKE
A rake is a vital part of any
garden tool collection. Use
rakes for clearing stones,
leaves and sticks from beds
and for making a smooth
planting surface.

Selecting and Buying Plants

A basic step in ensuring a healthy garden is starting with healthy, pest-free plants. They'll become established quickly and you'll avoid importing pests and diseases that could spread to other plants.

INSTANT COLOR
Lenten roses *Helleborus orientalis* are often sold when in flower and have an immediate impact.

Inspect the Root System

Strong, healthy roots are a vital part of plant health. If a plant is growing in a plastic or clay container, gently remove the container and look at the roots. Roots should be uniformly white, moist and without breaks, bumps or brown spots. A few fine, exposed roots don't indicate stress, but avoid plants with lots of matted roots or plants tightly rooted to their neighbors. Separating closely rooted plants can severely damage individual root systems. This shocks the young plants and can set them back by several weeks as they grow new roots.

A HEAD START
Starting with healthy, vigorous perennials, such as these *Lupinus* spp. is a key part of creating a beautiful garden filled with flowers.

SPOT THE DIFFERENCE

Learn to spot the difference
between strong, healthy
plants and weak, sickly ones
that can be cheaper but
won't be worth the money.

CHECK PLANT COLOR

Healthy seedlings are usually deep green,
although you can expect color to vary
among plants and cultivars. An overall
pale, washed-out appearance often
indicates that a nutrient is lacking. If
you're not sure what a particular plant is
supposed to look like, compare it with a
photograph from a book or catalog. This
will help you determine if those stripes,
spots or colors are normal or if they
indicate a problem.

PROBE FOR PROBLEMS

Examine perennials carefully before you
buy them and reject any that have clear
signs of pests or diseases or pest and
disease damage. As you inspect the
foliage of the perennials, make sure you
turn the leaves over and carefully check
their undersides as well as the tops—
remember that the lower leaf surfaces
are favorite pest hideouts.

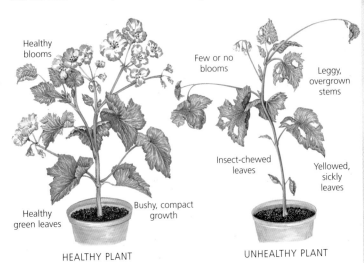

Healthy
blooms

Few or no
blooms

Leggy,
overgrown
stems

Insect-chewed
leaves

Yellowed,
sickly
leaves

Healthy
green leaves

Bushy, compact
growth

HEALTHY PLANT

UNHEALTHY PLANT

Mail Order

Mail-order companies often send plants bareroot to save on space and shipping. Immediately open the box to let some air in. Don't be worried when you find long spidery roots and—at best—a small tuft of foliage. The roots will be wrapped in a protective medium such as shredded newspaper or sphagnum moss— keep this medium moist but not soggy.

CONTAINER-GROWN PERENNIALS

Perennials are most commonly sold in containers. Container-grown perennials are convenient and easy to handle. You can keep the pots in a well-lit location until you are ready to plant. Then you can slide the root ball out and plant it in the garden with minimal disturbance. However, there is a catch. Horticultural researchers are finding that roots tend to stay in the light, fluffy "soil" of synthetic mixes, rather than branching out into the surrounding garden soil. But you can avoid this problem by loosening roots on the outside of the ball and spreading them out into the soil as you plant.

Container-grown perennials come in different sizes, so their prices vary widely. Larger-sized pots, usually 1- and 2-gallon (4.5- and 9-l) containers, are generally more expensive. The cost may be worthwhile if you want immediate garden impact. On the other hand, you can buy younger plants inexpensively in multi-cell packs or small pots. These sizes work fine if you don't mind waiting a season or more for them to fill out and bloom with abandon. In fact, young plants tend to become established in the garden faster than older ones, catching up to the bigger plants in a short time.

CHECK BELOW

Gently slide a plant from iits pot to check the roots before buying. Avoid plants with massed and curling roots, below.

HEALTHY ROOT GROWTH

Good-quality perennials have healthy white roots that you can see are still growing through the soil ball, right.

Bareroot Perennials

You will come across many species of dormant bareroot plants for sale early in the growing season. In late summer or early autumn, you can also find bareroot items such as common bleeding heart *Dicentra spectabilis* and peonies. You may choose to buy bareroot plants to save money—they usually are less expensive than large container-grown plants. These plants look more dead than alive, but fortunately, in this case, looks are deceiving. If you keep the roots moist and cool and plant them quickly and properly, plants will recover.

Your plants' roots should be wrapped in a protective medium—keep this moist. Soak the roots in a bucket of lukewarm water for a few hours before planting. If you need to wait to plant, pot up the roots until you are ready.

Field-dug Perennials

If you handle the root ball carefully, you can move field-dug, mature perennials much later into the growing season than bareroot plants, because the roots are protected by soil. Set the root ball, surrounded by soil, in a firm, wooden flat or sturdy bucket. Cover it with a moist towel, damp peat moss or compost to keep the roots and soil moist. Replant them as soon as you get them home.

WAYS TO BUY PERENNIALS

Container-grown perennials (left) may cost more, but they give your garden an instant effect. Field-dug plants (center) usually adapt quickly to a new site. Bareroot plants (right) take a bit of care but are often less expensive.

FRAGILE HOLLYHOCK

If you start off with healthy young plants they will be less likely to attract pests and develop diseases such as rust.

Preparing the Bed

P reparing the planting bed is critical to the success of your perennial garden. If you do a thorough job here, you will be rewarded by quicker plant establishment and less weeding to do later.

COLORFUL RESULTS
With care, even poor soil can produce good results, such as these *Aster* spp. blooms.

TENDER LOVING CARE
These healthy *Achillea* and *Aster* spp. blooms are the result of a good, granular soil structure. It's worth a little effort to prepare the soil well; your plants will thank you for it.

TIMING
If possible, start digging a season or a year before you plant. That way the soil will have a chance to settle. If spring typically is too wet to work the soil in your area, dig in autumn instead. If you can't prepare the soil ahead of time, you can usually get the bed ready and start planting in the same season.

MAKING NEW BEDS
When you're digging a garden bed in a lawn, strip off the sod with a flat spade by cutting long, spade-width strips across the width of your bed. Slide your spade under the strips to sever them from the soil and remove them. Or kill the grass

by covering it with black plastic, but this can take weeks, depending on the weather—the hotter it is the faster it works. Till in the turf when it decays.

Now break up the soil. If you're making a small bed you can usually loosen the soil to a depth of 6 inches (15 cm)—or 1 foot (30 cm) if you double dig. Add compost before planting and work it into the bed. For a heavy clay or light, sandy loam that is low in organic matter, lay a 4-inch (10-cm) thick layer of compost over the entire area and work it into the top 8 inches (20 cm). Use less to grow perennials that like drier conditions. Add more in warm climates to make up for fast decomposition.

ALL IN THE PREPARATION
With good preparation, you will have a garden full of thriving plants, such as *Dicentra spectabilis* 'Alba' with healthy foliage and an abundance of flowers.

TO PREPARE A NEW BED
1. Outline the edge with rope or string.
2. Use a spade to strip off the sod and expose the soil.
3. If a soil test indicates the site is too acid, apply lime.
4. Spread a layer of compost over the surface and work it into the bed.

Double-Digging

Double-digging is hard work, but it can be worthwhile if you are gardening in heavy, clayey soil or if you want to encourage perennials to root extra deeply in drought-prone areas. Remove the sod and weed roots first. Starting at one end of the bed, dig a trench that is 1 foot (30 cm) wide and as deep as your spade across the width of the bed. Put all of the topsoil you unearth into a wheelbarrow and move it to the far end of the garden. Now loosen up the exposed subsoil with a garden fork or your spade. Then back up to dig the next 1-foot (30-cm) wide strip. Shift that topsoil, with some extra compost or other organic matter, into the first trench and then loosen the new area of subsoil. Continue in this fashion until you reach the far end of the bed. Finish the last strip with the topsoil from your wheelbarrow and rake the bed smooth. Once you've prepared the bed, avoid stepping on it or you'll compact the soil and undo all your hard work. If you can't reach in from the sides to plant, lay a board across the soil and step on that. Remove it when you're finished.

SOIL AMENDMENTS

Wood ash (above left) supplies potassium—it will raise the pH, so don't apply it to acid-loving plants. Gypsum (above right) supplies soil with calcium and sulfur.

POOR-SOIL SOLUTION

In poor soil, double-digging can help give your perennials the best possible conditions for root growth.

Dalmatian bellflower
Campanula portenschlagiana likes
average to rich, well-
drained soil. Test the soil
before you add any extra
nutrients—you may not
need to add anything.

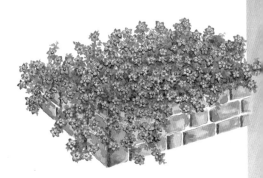

USE COMPOST

If you are preparing a new bed, work compost in as you dig. In an established garden, use compost as a mulch. As a general rule, cover the bed with 2 inches (5 cm) a year to maintain. Use more for moisture-loving perennials or if you want to control weeds. Use less around perennials that prefer drier, less fertile soils. Compost breaks down gradually over the growing season, so add more as needed.

LIKING IT LEAN

Some perennials, such as dyers' chamomile *Anthemis tinctoria*, grow best if the soil isn't too rich.

APPLYING ORGANIC NUTRIENTS

How you actually apply organic nutrients to your garden depends on several quite different factors. If you are starting a new bed, for instance, you can spread compost, fertilizers and other soil amendments (such as lime or sulfur) over the surface and work the materials in before you plant. Once your perennial garden is established, you can supply your plants with nutrients by working fertilizer materials into the soil around the base of each plant and by mulching with organic materials, such as chopped leaves or compost. If they need a mid-summer nutrient boost, you can spray the plants with a liquid fertilizer, such as compost tea or seaweed extract.

Planting

Although you may have been anticipating the moment of planting for months, don't rush it. Planting takes time and a lot of bending. Work slowly to get each plant settled as well as possible.

When to Plant

Once you've prepared your soil, it's time to get your carefully chosen plants in the ground so they can start growing. But planting your perennials at the right time is important to give them a good start.

Time your planting efforts so your new perennials will start growing in a period of abundant rainfall and moderate temperatures—usually spring or autumn. In cool climates, concentrate your planting efforts in spring. Spring planting allows the new plants time to establish strong root systems before winter. You can chance late-summer planting for very hardy or seasonally available perennials. In warmer climates with mild winters, plant in autumn so perennials will be well established before the long, hot summer. In areas where summer isn't too hot and winter isn't too cold, you can plant perennials in autumn or spring. If your climate has periods of drought, plant whenever there is abundant, natural rainfall and temperatures are about 40–70°F (4.4–21.2°C).

GARDEN MUMS
Fibrous-rooted garden mums are fast growing and need to be divided every 1–2 years to keep them vigorous.

EXTREMELY TOLERANT
Blanket flower *Gaillardia* x *grandiflora* is one of the hardiest garden flowers.

UP, UP AND AWAY
Good soil preparation and careful planting will help get your chosen perennials off to a vigorous start for healthy future growth.

Container-grown Perennials

If you are planting a potted perennial, dig deeply enough so the surface of the container soil will be at the top of the hole. Fill the hole with water.

Now, prepare the plant. Slip the roots out of the pot. Break up the edges of the root ball so the roots will have more contact with the surrounding soil. If the roots are wrapped around themselves, you may have to work them loose.

After planting, firm the soil gently around the plant, water it well and mulch. Mulching your bed with organic materials, such as compost, straw or shredded leaves will conserve moisture and reduce weed competition. (New beds are especially weed-prone, since turning the soil exposes weed seeds.)

Field-dug Perennials

Plant field-dug perennials that have a large amount of soil still around the roots

CONTAINER-GROWN

1. Dig a hole larger than the root ball and add water.
2. Slide the plant out of its container and loosen the soil around the roots.
3. Set the plant in the hole, backfill with soil then firm lightly.

SPACING IS EVERYTHING

If you crowd plants, they will grow weakly and be more susceptible to disease. Before you plant, set them in place to see how they look. Leave enough elbow room for difficult-to-move plants to mature to their full size.

When planting, remember to space your plants evenly and give them the room they need to thrive.

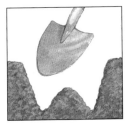

BAREROOT PERENNIALS

1. Dig a hole large enough to hold the roots without bending them, leaving a mound in the center.
2. Set crown in the hole. Spread roots over mound.
3. Backfill with soil, gently firm soil and water well.

in a hole the same size as the root ball. If some soil has fallen off the roots, make the hole slightly larger to allow the roots to be moved into position. Then drench the hole with water and set the plant at the same depth it was growing. Work any exposed roots into the surrounding soil as you refill, then firm the soil.

BAREROOT PLANTING

Bareroot plants take more time to settle. Soak the roots in lukewarm water for a few hours. Identify how deeply the plants had been growing in the nursery. The aboveground portions usually emerge from the root system above the former soil line. Plant so that these stay slightly above the soil in your garden.

Make a hole deep and wide enough to set the plant crown at the soil surface and stretch out the roots. Form a small mound of soil in the bottom of the hole. Set the root clump on it with the crown resting on top. Spread the roots in all directions and fill around them with soil. Firm the soil gently, water and mulch. Keep the soil moist for a few weeks.

Part Four

Maintaining Perennials

Mulch

Mulching is important in almost any climate. It helps keep out weeds by preventing them from getting a foothold and it protects the soil. Organic mulches can add nutrients and organic matter.

Using Mulch

If you use mulch on frozen soil during the winter, it will keep the earth evenly frozen. This helps reduce the rapid freezing-and-thawing cycles that can damage plant roots and push plant crowns out of the soil (a process known as frost heaving). In hot-summer climates, mulch will slow the rapid decay of organic matter in the soil so that each application will last longer. In any climate, if you choose carefully, mulch can work double duty as an attractive background for your perennials.

CONSERVING MOISTURE
Foxgloves like moist soil, so apply a layer of mulch during summer to slow evaporation and keep the soil moist longer after each watering.

KEEPING IT CONSTANT
A generous layer of organic mulch will help moderate soil temperatures and conserve water.

Mulching with compost is a good way to add nutrients to your garden. It may be all you need to fertilize light feeders, such as coreopsis *Coreopsis* spp., yarrow *Achillea* spp. and common thrift *Armeria maritima*. Compost mulch will conserve moisture, but may not do much to eliminate weeds.

CHOOSING A MULCH

Many kinds of organic mulch are available for your perennial garden. Shredded leaves make a useful mulch and they are usually free. Dark-colored, fine-textured, well-decomposed compost gives the soil a rich, healthy look as well as improving soil fertility. Grass clippings or straw may look too utilitarian for most flower gardens and bark or wood chips may be suitable for bold plants, but can dwarf small perennials.

Try to choose a mulch that won't pack down into dense layers. Dense layers of materials such as grass clippings tend to shed water—it runs off the bed instead of into the soil. If you use these kinds of mulches, mix in coarse, fluffy material such as shredded leaves.

WATERING

F ine-tune your watering depending on several factors, including the type of soil you have, the amount of natural rainfall you receive, the plants you grow and the stage of growth the plants are in.

FLOWERS FIRST TO GO
A garden that is actively growing and flowering will need a source of moisture at all times. If water is in short supply, flowers and flower buds are the first to suffer.

SMALL IRRIGATION
Hand watering with a watering can is often the most realistic option for irrigating small gardens.

How Moisture–retentive?
To answer this question, water a portion of the garden thoroughly. After 48 hours, dig a small hole 6 inches (15 cm) deep. If the soil is reasonably water-retentive, the earth at the bottom of the hole will be moist. If it is not, you can improve it by working in lots of compost. This acts like a sponge—if you add a lot of compost or other organic matter, you can water less frequently. But when you do irrigate, water extra thoroughly to saturate the organic matter.

Keeping Track of Rainfall
Monitor your rainfall and vary your watering accordingly. Overwatering can be as disastrous as underwatering, especially in heavy soils. You can tell how much rain has fallen if you leave out a rain gauge. If you don't want to

buy a rain gauge, set a small, clean can in an open part of the garden and use a ruler to measure how much rainwater it collects. Check once a week.

DIFFERENT PLANTS, DIFFERENT NEEDS

Some perennials thrive in moist soils, others grow weakly or rot if water is abundant. Water more often if you grow perennials that need evenly moist soil. These include delphiniums, astilbes and moisture-loving bog plants such as Japanese primroses *Primula japonica*.

Let the soil dry more between waterings for drought-tolerant plants, such as lavender, perennial candytuft *Iberis sempervirens* and torch lilies *Kniphofia* hybrids. These perennials probably need no more than ½ inch (12 mm) of water per week.

Expect to coddle newly planted perennials until their roots spread far enough to support the plants. If the weather is warm and dry, you may have to water daily until a drenching rain comes. If the season is cool and rainy, you can let nature handle the irrigation.

HOW MUCH WATER?

A good rule of thumb is that your perennial garden should get 1 inch (25 mm) of water a week. This wets the soil deeply, encouraging roots to grow farther underground. Of course, some perennials need more moisture and some need less, so you'll have to adjust your supplemental irrigation depending on the needs of all your plants.

WATER OFTEN
Endres cranesbill *Geranium endressii* thrives with evenly moist, humus-rich soil. Water often to keep soil moist.

FERTILIZING

Supplying the nutrients that perennials need is critical to keeping them healthy. How much fertilizer to add to your garden will depend on how fertile the soil is and which plants you're growing.

SOIL AND FERTILIZING

The texture and natural fertility of your soil will have a great impact on how much and how often you need to fertilize. A sandy soil will hold fewer nutrients than a clayey soil or a soil that's high in organic matter, so you'll need to fertilize sandy soil more. If you prepared the soil thoroughly before planting you may not have to fertilize a new perennial garden for a year or more.

VARYING NEEDS

Fertilizer requirements vary widely among different perennials. Some are light feeders, such as common sneezeweed *Helenium autumnale*, sunflower heliopsis *Heliopsis helianthoides* and daisy fleabane *Erigeron speciosus*. A light layer of compost applied once or twice a year should meet their nutrient needs. Other perennials are heavy feeders; these include delphiniums, astilbes and garden phlox *Phlox paniculata*. They need more frequent fertilizing to stay in top form.

You may want to give your plants a fertility boost to encourage new growth or rejuvenation. Fertilize in spring as they begin growing, after planting or dividing, and after deadheading or cutting back.

APPLYING FERTILIZER

Make holes in the soil and fill them with dry fertilizer (top). Or sprinkle dry fertilizer around the base of the plant (center). Liquid fertilizers are easy to mist right onto plant leaves (bottom).

ONCE A YEAR

A yearly application of a light fertilizer will supply all of the nutrients many perennials need to thrive.

COMPOST TEA

If you want to turn your compost from a solid nutrient source into a quick-acting liquid fertilizer, make it into compost tea. Put one or two shovelfuls of compost (or farm manure) into a burlap or woven-mesh bag. Tie the bag securely at the top and submerge it into a large watering can or bucket of water. Let it steep for 1 week, then remove the bag. Dilute the remaining liquid until it is the color of weak tea if you plan to spray or sprinkle it directly on your perennials, or use it full strength to drench the ground around the base of the plants.

APPLYING FERTILIZERS

When you fertilize, you can eliminate deficiencies by applying either liquid or dry fertilizer, or both. If you use a combination, make sure you don't apply more nutrients than your plants need. Remember, too much fertilizer can be as bad as not enough, leading to weak stems, sprawling growth and disease.

Common liquid fertilizers include fish emulsion, liquid seaweed and compost tea. Use a single dose for a quick fix, or apply every 2 weeks for a plant boost. You can spray these directly on the plants, which absorb nutrients through their foliage.

Dry fertilizers are released to plants more slowly. Scratch them into the surface of moist soil in a circle around the perimeter of the plant's foliage, so the nutrients are released gradually. This encourages roots to extend outward.

MAKING AND USING COMPOST

Compost is the key to success in any kind of gardening. Compost is a balanced blend of recycled garden, yard and household wastes that has broken down into dark, crumbly organic matter.

HOT COMPOSTING

Hot composting takes work, but it provides high-quality compost in weeks. There are different systems but they tend to have elements in common. Most require building a pile of different layers of elements, along with soil or finished compost to ensure the right decomposers are present. Turning the pile every few days or weeks is another critical part of encouraging fast breakdown.

To create a hot-compost pile, blend both soft and green (high-nitrogen) plant scraps and tough and brown (high-carbon) scraps. The moist, green items provide the decomposers with nitrogen, which they consume as they break down the high-carbon materials.

Chop up the ingredients and combine about 1 part high-nitrogen elements with 2 parts high-carbon material in a pile about 3 feet (90 cm) high and wide. Add a shovelful of soil or finished compost in between each layer and enough water to keep the pile moist. Turn the pile with a pitchfork every few days to add oxygen. When your compost is fairly cool and most of the original materials are unrecognizable, it is ready to use.

HOT, FAST COMPOST

1. Build your compost with equal amounts of high-carbon and high-nitrogen materials—add in layers or mix them up.

2. As you add new materials, sprinkle them with a watering can to moisten them and encourage decomposition.

3. Aerate the compost pile by turning it once every couple of days using a garden fork. This hastens microbial activity.

Cold Composting

Making cold compost is easier than making hot compost, but it takes longer. (A cold-compost pile won't really feel cold; it just doesn't get as warm as a hot-compost pile does.) Since the decomposition period is extended to up to a year or more, more nutrients can wash away in rainwater. You'll have to leave more space for the slower decomposing piles, and you'll have to wait much longer until it's ready. Cold compost will not heat up enough to kill seeds or disease organisms, so don't add mature weeds or diseased plant material to the pile.

To create a cold-compost pile, choose a shady, well-drained place to drop your scraps. Let them build up to a pile about 3 feet (90 cm) wide by 3 feet (90 cm) high and then begin again in a new location. After a year or so, the original materials should be broken down, although the compost will probably still be fairly lumpy. Use the compost as it is, or screen out the lumps and leave them to break down for a while longer.

HAPPY BELLFLOWERS
The time you spend making compost and applying it to your garden will be more than returned by improved soil and plant health.

MAKE USE OF SCRAPS
Most kinds of kitchen scraps are suitable ingredients for your compost. Remember to avoid bones, meat and fat.

COMPOST BIN
A homemade wire and timber frame keeps the compost heap neat and compact.

SUPPORTING AND TRAINING

Staking, deadheading, pinching and cutting back are all techniques used to produce the most vigorous and beautiful perennials. These are tasks which good gardeners employ to help plants perform.

STAKING SECRETS

Support plants as they grow, don't wait until the stems are sagging—make a note on your calendar to set out your supports as plants emerge. If the foliage of your perennials is not full enough to hide the supports, you can plant low-growing annuals or perennials in the front. They will fill in quickly and hide the staking.

DEADHEADING MADE EASY

You can handle deadheading with a quick snip or a series of calculated cuts. No matter what tools you use, cut back

DROOPY LUPINES
Stakes and string can be used to support bushy lupines *Lupinus* spp.

START EARLY
Put up stakes early in the season so your plants can grow up and through them. For bushy plants, use something the plants can grow up through, which they'll then fill out and hide.

Pruning shears are handy for snipping off spent flowers that have thick or wiry stems.

The following plants may bloom longer or rebloom if you remove faded flowers promptly: baby's breath, bellflowers *Campanula* spp., thread-leaved coreopsis, red valerian *Centranthus ruber*, daylilies, delphiniums, pinks *Dianthus* spp., foxgloves *Digitalis* spp., blanket flowers *Gaillardia* x *grandiflora*, phlox, sages *Salvia* spp., and yarrows.

COLUMBINE HAIRCUT
Columbines *Aquilegia* spp. are beautiful in bloom but decline after flowering. Cut them back to encourage new growth.

to a leaf, bud or another stem. The exceptions are perennials with fine, wiry stems topped with flowers—with these perennials, shear off the top layer with grass clippers when the flowers fade.

PINCHING
By removing the growing tip of the stem, you cut off the source of hormones that make that branch elongate. This frees buds lower on the stem to develop into side branches. It will make leggy perennials more bushy and compact, with better branching and more blooms. Perennials that otherwise need staking may be able to stand on their own if you pinch them back.

CUTTING BACK AND THINNING
You can cut back long or straggly stems to make a plant tidier and produce new growth. Cutting back is like a more radical form of deadheading.

Thinning removes whole stems, improving air circulation around the plant. Remove one-third to one-half of the stem length.

Weeds

W eeds pop up in well-maintained gardens. The trick is to take care of the problem early, before they get large enough to compete with your plants for space, light, water and nutrients.

What Is a Weed?

What separates unwanted weeds from desirable plants is often the speed with which they spread. Removing the roots of perennial weeds as you prepare the soil for planting will help keep them at bay. Mulching and regular weeding help prevent new weeds starting. If perennial weeds get out of control, it's often easiest to start over. Dig up your perennials and set them aside until you can dig through the bed and remove all the roots of the weeds. Annual weeds may not have the invasive roots that perennials do, but they reproduce from seed, often growing fast and spreading far. Remove annual weeds from the garden before they set seed. Cut them off or scrape them out with a hoe or hand weeder.

Pulling gets rid of annual weeds but digging is a slightly better choice for perennial weeds, assuming you get all of the buried portions of the plant. If you don't, they can produce new weeds. When the weeds are too numerous to pull up individually by hand, a sharp hoe is a good solution. In most cases, hoes are best for young or annual weeds, but they can also be used for some established

START EARLY
Removing weeds when they're small or preventing them from sprouting in the first place will make the job of weed control much easier.

SPREADING WEEDS
Many perennial weeds such as bindweed have rhizomes that spread quickly, engulfing desirable plants.

HEAVE HOE

Hoeing flower gardens once or twice early in the season can control weeds until your plants fill in to cover the soil.

DANDELION DANGER

You may need to pour boiling water over hard-to-get weeds, such as these dandelions between paving.

BE WEED WISE

Start while you are preparing your new garden bed. Look for the long, white roots of weeds and remove them completely—if you leave even little pieces, they sprout into new plants. Once your perennials are well established, you can control most weeds if you mulch and weed for the first year or two. By about the third year, there should be little room for weed invasion.

---

perennials by forcing them to use their food reserves to replace the decapitated top growth. Hoe every 7–14 days to cut off the top growth before it starts sending food back to the roots.

One of the most common weed problems in perennial gardens is lawn grass, which will creep in along the edges of beds and borders. You can block invasion of grass by cutting along the garden's edge frequently with a sharp spade or edger and removing the errant sprigs of grass. Or you can take some preventive action when you dig the bed: Add a metal, wood, stone, brick or plastic edging to form a barrier around the perimeter of the garden. Sink the edging at least 4–6 inches (10–15 cm) deep to block creeping grass stems in their underground movement.

Pest and Disease Prevention

Creating and maintaining a naturally healthy garden isn't a simple one- or two-step process. Every decision you make, or don't make, plays a part in the results you get throughout the season.

Steps to a Healthy Garden

Diversity provides habitats for a range of insects and animals, and predators and parasites help to keep pest populations at a relatively constant level.

Good growing conditions give perennials a head start. Before buying new plants, make sure you can supply the conditions they prefer. If you have a struggling plant, move it or replace it.

Healthy soil produces healthy plants. Adding organic matter improves soil and encourages beneficial microorganisms.

TAKE CARE
Hostas are dependable shade perennials, but remember they are prone to snails and slugs, so take precautions before they strike.

REMEMBER
Vigorous plants grown in fertile soil attract fewer pests and are less susceptible to infection by plant pathogens than plants grown in poor soil. Start with a variety of healthy plants, give them the growing conditions they require and keep an eye out for potential problems. These simple steps will go a long way toward producing a successful garden, free from pests and diseases.

BEAUTY IN DIVERSITY
Including a diversity of flowering plants helps attract beneficial insects and makes your garden interesting.

ONLY THE BEST

Monitoring soil fertility will help ensure strong, healthy stems and leaves, vigorous roots and beautiful flowers, such as these *Aster* spp.

Checking your plants at least once a week can help you spot potential problems before they get out of hand.

Become familiar with diseases, pests and beneficials so you'll know which to control and which to leave alone.

Become familiar with available controls before you need to use them.

Keep track of when and where problems occurred and what you did to control them. Write down what worked and what didn't work.

PESTS

Pests are easiest to control if you catch them before they get out of hand. Inspecting your garden regularly helps you spot problems early. Identify the pest before you decide how to treat it.

SOME COMMON PESTS

Aphids are tiny, soft-bodied insects that can cause the plants to twist, pucker or droop. They leave a trail of sugary excrement (honeydew). Japanese beetles are shiny, metallic blue-green beetles. Leafminers are the larvae of small flies. Mites are tiny, spider-like pests that attack, especially when it is hot and dry. Two-spotted mites suck the plant sap from the underside of a leaf. Plant bugs leave irregular holes or sunken brown spots in the middle of leaves. Slugs and snails can be a problem anywhere the soil stays damp. Thrips leave pale, silvery damaged areas.

CONTROLLING PESTS

If you find only a few pests, pick them off the plants by hand and crush them.

Catch pests in traps or deter them with barricades. Yellow sticky traps attract aphids and white traps attract tarnished plant bugs. Trap slugs with a shallow container of beer set in the soil so the top rim is at ground level.

You can use biological weapons such as *Bacillus thuringiensis* (BT), a bacterial disease, to eliminate pests without harming people, animals or beneficial insects. BT will control many caterpillars.

BENEFICIAL LACEWINGS
Adult lacewings feed mostly on nectar and honeydew, but their larvae are voracious predators of pest insects.

APHID INFESTATION
If aphids are out of control and pruning is not an option, try a soap spray.

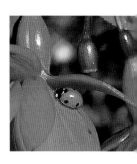

LOOK BEFORE YOU SPRAY
Before spraying, look for beneficial insects such as ladybugs. They may control the problem for you.

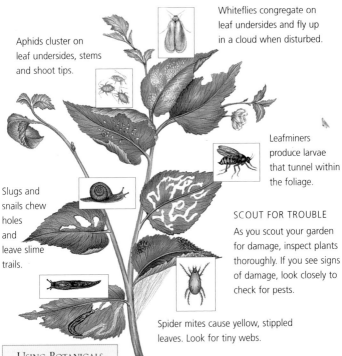

Whiteflies congregate on leaf undersides and fly up in a cloud when disturbed.

Aphids cluster on leaf undersides, stems and shoot tips.

Leafminers produce larvae that tunnel within the foliage.

SCOUT FOR TROUBLE

As you scout your garden for damage, inspect plants thoroughly. If you see signs of damage, look closely to check for pests.

Slugs and snails chew holes and leave slime trails.

Spider mites cause yellow, stippled leaves. Look for tiny webs.

USING BOTANICALS

Botanicals are insecticides derived from plants. Pyrethrins are effective on some beetles, caterpillars, aphids and bugs. Rotenone will control beetles, borers, aphids and two-spotted mites. Ryania is effective on caterpillars and beetles. Sabadilla is a powerful insecticide—use it as a last resort for pests such as thrips.

Botanicals have broad-spectrum activity, meaning that they will harm beneficial as well as pest insects.

In a healthy garden, populations of beneficial insects will go a long way toward keeping pests under control.

If all else fails, try some of the less toxic insecticides. Apply these products according to package directions and apply them at the right time in the pest's life cycle, so they are effective.

Insecticidal soaps will kill soft-bodied insects such as aphids. And you can spray with highly refined horticultural oils to coat plant leaves and to smother insects such as aphids, leafminers, leafhoppers and mites. Read the label carefully and apply only when the weather is cool.

DISEASES

Garden hygiene and proper plant selection go a long way to preventing and controlling diseases. Removing faded foliage and cutting back flowers after they bloom will remove sites of disease.

SOME COMMON DISEASES

Many different fungi attack perennials, causing a variety of symptoms. Rot fun can affect roots, crowns, stems and flowers, turning them soft and mushy. You will see rot most commonly on ro growing in wet, heavy soil or on crowns planted too deeply in the garden. Botrytis blight attacks flowers that open during wet weather, making them blacken and curl downward. Fungal leaf spots disfigure and can cause defoliation.

Rust diseases turn foliage a rusty color, often stunting growth and distorting leaf development.

Bacteria also cause diseases characterized by wilting and rotting. Bacterial blight causes black spots on leaves, flowers and stems. Bacterial crown gall stunts growth and can kill

Viruses can cause leaves or flowers to turn yellow or mottled. They cause stunted growth and poor flowering or sudden wilting and deat

CONTROLLING DISEASES

If soilborne disease is a particular problem in your area, grow perennials in well-drained soil to reduce root diseases. Also, try not to damage the plant roots when you work the soil or weed.

VIRAL ALERT
Viral mosaic can attack pinks *Dianthus* spp. (above), garden mums, delphiniums, peonies and poppies.

POWDERY PROBLEM
Powdery mildew is a fungal disease that forms a furry, white coating on leaves and can cause leaves to drop.

A BREATH OF FRESH AIR
Thin out the stems of bushy perennials such as common sneezeweed *Helenium autumnale* to promote air circulation and good health.

PREVENTION

Antitranspirants (leaf coatings) may reduce fungal disease. To prevent mildew, rust and leaf spots, dust the foliage with powdered sulfur. A baking soda spray (1 teaspoon of baking soda to 1 quart [1 l] water) prevents and controls some problems. Seaweed-based fertilizer sprays and compost tea can also help prevent some diseases. If a disease becomes rampant and sprays do not help, it may be time to replace a plant with one that is not as susceptible—another species or a resistant cultivar.

PUZZLED?

Leaf spots can be caused by either fungi or bacteria. Removing infected foliage may stop the spread. If a plant's disease leaves you stumped, ask for help from your local garden center.

Careful watering can help reduce disease outbreaks. Avoid wetting plant leaves; they stay wet overnight and fungal spores can germinate and attack. Overhead watering and even walking through wet foliage or cultivating soil can transfer disease from plant to plant. Use a ground-level irrigation system and don't work in the garden when plants are wet—and always keep your tools clean.

When a disease does strike, remove damaged parts promptly and throw them away with the household trash. If you have any doubts, consider throwing the whole plant away, or plant it in an isolated spot in the yard. If it seems all right at the end of the season, move it back into the garden. If it's diseased, dispose of it permanently.

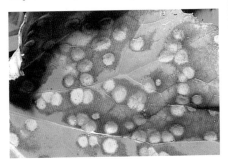

Seed Starting

G rowing your own seedlings allows you to select unusual species and choose varieties that you can't buy at greenhouses and nurseries. Use high-quality seed, and check the use-by date.

Sowing the Seed

Just as wild and self-sowing perennials do naturally, you can sow seed directly outdoors in a well-prepared bed. Cover seed in loose soil to the depth indicated on the package and keep the soil moist until the seedlings emerge.

INDOORS OR OUTDOORS
Sea hollies *Eryngium* spp. can be started from fresh seed outdoors during autumn, or started indoors after stratification.

Although direct sowing is the easiest way, it is not the most dependable. When planted directly into your garden, your seed is very vulnerable. For a better survival rate, start seedlings indoors under fluorescent lights or on a window ledge on the sunny side of the house.

Depending on the size of the seed and the speed of growth, you should start easy-germinating seed indoors 6–12 weeks before the last spring frost. In warm climates, start fast-germinating seed in summer to set out in the cool of autumn and winter.

Other perennials will take much longer to germinate. You may need to expose the seed to a chilling period by placing the seed in the refrigerator for a certain number of weeks (known as stratification). If special treatment is needed, it will be indicated on the seed packet.

PROLIFIC RESEEDERS
Orange coneflowers *Rudbeckia* spp. may reseed prolifically if you don't cut off spent flowers in autumn.

PLANTING SEED

1. Sow seed evenly over a thoroughly moistened, sterile, peat-based mix.
2. Press the seed lightly into the surface—push larger seeds into the soil as deeply as they are wide.
3. Cover the seed according to packet directions and firm slightly.
4. Moisten with a fine mist of water.
5. Label the container.
6. Cover with clear plastic to keep soil evenly moist until the seed begins to germinate.

CARING FOR SEEDLINGS

When seedlings emerge, move them into bright light and remove the plastic. Set the container in a tray of water to soak up moisture, then keep moist.

Move seedlings to pots when they have two sets of true leaves and a bottom set of fleshy seed leaves. You can move most into 4-inch (10-cm) pots if you intend to plant them outdoors soon. If not, move the plants up to larger pots to prevent roots from binding. Feed lightly. If the weather is cold or hot, leave the transplants indoors under lights or near a sunny window. If it is relatively mild, move the plants out into a cold frame or another sheltered area.

POTTING-UP SEEDLINGS

1. Gather your materials and tools together in a clean, shady spot.
2. Put some moist potting mix in the base of a new pot.
3. Gently squeeze the seedling container to loosen roots and to make it easy to remove the plant.
4. Carefully slide the plant from the container, taking care not to harm the roots.
5. Center the plant in the pot and fill in with moist, but not wet, potting mix.

DIVISION

Division is one of the easiest, fastest and most reliable ways to propagate clump-forming perennials. It is also a great way to revive older plants and to keep spreading perennials under control.

WHEN TO DIVIDE

How often you need to divide depends on why you are dividing. If you're using division to propagate, then it depends on how many new plants you want and how fast the plant you are dividing is growing. Divide annually to retard aggressive spreaders such as bee balm *Monarda didyma*, obedient plant *Physostegia virginiana* and yarrows. If you want to rejuvenate perennials, you can divide them whenever flowering starts to decline. To keep performance high, you can divide asters every year or two. Some perennials, such as peonies, daylilies, Siberian irises *Iris sibirica* and astilbes, can go for years without division.

AVOID ROOT DAMAGE
Divide balloon flower *Platycodon grandiflorus* in spring or early autumn. Dig deeply to avoid root damage.

NOTHING TOO BIG
To divide a big clump, try prying it apart with two garden forks. If that doesn't work, try a saw or an ax.

REJUVENATED VIGOR
A mature clump of iris will yield many new, vigorous plants once divided.

How to Divide

Begin by digging up the root system.
Shake off loose soil and remove dead
leaves and stems. You may also want to
wash most of the soil off the roots and
crown to see the roots and buds clearly.

Perennials with fibrous roots, such as
garden mums and asters, are the easiest
to dig and divide. Pull them apart with
your hands or cut them with a spade.
Others, such as daylilies and astilbes, can
grow woody with age. You may have to
pry these roots apart with a crowbar or
two garden forks held back to back or
cut them with a saw or ax. Discard the
woody parts, which will not reroot well.

To renew an existing planting, slice
the plant into halves, thirds or quarters.
Discard old, woody growth from the
center of the clump and replant the
vigorous outer portions.

When you want to build a larger
stock of new plants, divide perennials
into smaller pieces. Just make sure you
keep several buds or growing shoots on
the sections you will replant. Look for
buds growing along the length of the
roots or clustered in a central crown.

Work your compost, and any other
soil amendments, back into the soil
before replanting the division. Reset them
at the same level at which the original
clump was growing.

STEP-BY-STEP DIVISION

1. Divide the clump into
   several pieces.
2. Make sure each new piece
   has its own roots and
   some top growth.
3. Replant the pieces
   immediately, water
   well and apply a light
   layer of mulch.

Cuttings and Layering

Cuttings—small pieces of stem or root—are another way to propagate perennials. Cuttings take more care than layering, which can be done with stems that root while attached to the plant.

ROOT CUTTINGS
Propagate Japanese anemone *Anemone* x *hybrida* by taking root cuttings after plants go dormant in autumn.

TAKING STEM CUTTINGS
1. Select a strong, young shoot and make a clean cut just below the node.
2. Snip the leaves off the bottom half of the cutting, exposing two to three leaf nodes, and insert the bottom half into a container of moist potting mix.
3. Cover with an upended jar to hold in moisture. Set in a bright place out of direct sun.

Taking Cuttings

Take stem cuttings in spring or after flowering. When they shoot, remove the plastic and move them into brighter light. To check if they have rooted, tug gently on the stem—if you meet resistance, they have. Transplant into larger containers.

Take root cuttings from autumn to early spring, while the plant is dormant. Lift the plant from the garden and wash the soil from the roots. Cut off pencil-thick roots close to the crown. Cut them into 2–4-inch (5–10-cm) pieces, making a straight cut at the top and a slanted cut at the bottom. Put into a pot filled with moist, sterile potting mix, so the top of each cutting is level or slightly below the surface. Put in a cold frame until they root then pot them into a larger pot—move them into the garden when ready.

LAYERING WORKS

Good candidates for layering include pinks *Dianthus* spp. (above), wall rock cress and snow-in-summer.

SIMPLE LAYERING

1. Select a flexible stem and bend it down to the soil.
2. Use a wire pin to firmly secure the stem, then cover the pinned stem with soil. Stake the leafy tip of the stem if it needs support.
3. Dig up the newly rooted layer and transplant it to another spot.

LAYERING

Layering takes up space, you won't get many plants and it can take weeks or months—but it is easy and you get exact duplicates of the parent plant.

Leave the top three sets of leaves on the stem, but remove the leaves for 2–7 inches (5–17.5 cm) below the top greenery. Strip leaves from at least two nodes, leaving dormant buds undamaged. Loosen the soil where the stripped area will make contact and water it. Bury it 2–3 inches (5–7.5 cm) deep with the leafy tip exposed and firm the soil.

Keep the area moist and mulched. The easiest way is to leave the plant in place until the following season. If you want faster results, check its progress by uncovering the stem and looking for roots or tugging lightly to see if it has become more secure. Once the roots reach about 1 inch (2.5 cm) long, you can cut the shoot free from the mother plant. Wait several weeks for more rooting, then dig and transplant the new plant.

Part Five

Plant Directory

Acanthus mollis

CLIMATE
Zones 8–10.

HEIGHT AND
SPREAD
2½–4 feet
(75–120 cm) tall.
3 feet (90 cm)
wide. Spreads to
form broad clumps.

FLOWERING TIME
Late spring or
summer. Flowers
open sequentially
up the spike.

BEAR'S BREECHES

USE BEAR'S BREECHES FOR FOUNDATION
PLANTINGS OR AS ACCENTS IN FORMAL OR
INFORMAL GARDENS.

Description A robust plant with
lustrous, deep green leaves 1–2 feet
(30–60 cm) long and edged with
jagged teeth. It grows from a stout
crown with thick, fleshy roots. It
has unusual 1-inch (2.5-cm) flowers
with three white petals and
overarching purple-pink hoods
carried on tall spikes.

Ideal position Full sun to partial
shade. Sensitive to winter frost and
to hot, humid weather. Produces
foliage in colder zones but the
flower buds are usually killed.

Ideal soil conditions Evenly moist,
humus-rich soil. Dry soil will reduce
the size of the leaves.

Cultivation Mulch after the ground
freezes in winter and remove mulch
gradually in spring to protect plants
from heaving. Keep moist.

Propagation Divide plants in spring
when they first emerge or take root
cuttings in spring or late autumn.
Roots left in the ground when
plants are divided will form new
shoots. Or propagate from seed.

Pest and disease prevention Bait
slugs with pans of beer set flush
with the soil surface. Or surround
plants with sharp or irritant products

Acanthus spinosus

such as diatomaceous earth, lime or crushed seashells. If caterpillars are a problem, handpick them or spray them with the biological control BT (*Bacillus thuringiensis*), a bacterial disease of caterpillars. Powdery mildew may be a problem; destroy affected leaves and avoid overhead watering.

Landscape use Good as a specimen plant in wide borders as it can cover large areas of ground when it matures. Good when combined with fine-textured plants such as yarrow for added contrast. A good plant for cutting and drying for flower arrangements. Bear's breeches release compounds that can stunt the growth of cucumbers, radishes and cabbage, so avoid planting near these vegetables.

Other species *A. spinosus* (pictured above) has large, deeply divided leaves, which are narrower than those of *A. mollis*. The flower spikes are similar to those of *A. mollis* and can grow up to 4 feet (1.2 m) tall. Zones 7–10.

Achillea filipendulina

CLIMATE
Zones 3–9.

HEIGHT AND
SPREAD
3–4 feet
(90–120 cm) tall.
3 feet (90 cm)
wide. Forms broad,
tight clumps.

FLOWERING TIME
Summer. Flowers
last for several
weeks. Plants
rebloom if
deadheaded.

FERN-LEAVED YARROW

FERN-LEAVED YARROW IS A TRADITIONAL
BORDER PLANT AND IS PERFECT FOR COTTAGE-
GARDEN AND ISLAND-BED PLANTINGS.

Description This aromatic herb
grows from fibrous roots and has
deeply incised, ferny, olive-green
leaves. It has dozens of tightly
packed, golden yellow flowers
clustered in flat-topped heads
4–5 inches (10–12.5 cm) across.
Flowers are on dozens of tall stems.

Ideal position Full sun to light
shade. Thrives in low to moderate
summer humidity.

Ideal soil conditions Dry to moist,
well-drained soil. Overly rich soil
creates growth but weakens stems.

Cultivation Fern-leaved yarrow is a
tough, easy-care perennial. Plants
spread rapidly and need frequent
division. Lift and divide clumps
every 3 years to keep vigorous.

Propagation Take tip cuttings in
spring or early summer. Divide in
early spring or autumn. Replant
healthy divisions into soil that has
been enriched with organic matter.

Pest and disease prevention Plants
can develop powdery mildew,
especially in areas with warm,
humid nights. Rot causes stems to
blacken and collapse. Destroy all
affected parts and dust with sulfur.
Provide well-drained soil to avoid
powdery mildew and rot.

Common yarrow *Achillea millefolium*

Landscape use Plant at the front or middle of formal perennial borders or with grasses in informal gardens. Plant in casual borders or wild-flower meadows and other informal settings. Use in cutting or herb gardens. Plants rebloom later in the season if first flower flush is trimmed.

Cultivars 'Gold Plate' has 6-inch (15-cm) deep yellow flower heads on 6-foot (1.8-m) stems.

'Parker's Variety' grows 3–4 feet (90–120 cm) tall and has golden yellow flowers held on self-supporting stems.

Other species *A. millefolium*, common yarrow, or milfoil,

(pictured above) offers finely cut, deep green foliage. It has numerous tiny pink, white or red florets in dense, flat clusters 2–3 inches (5–7.5 cm) across that are produced on stout stems. It flowers for several months in summer and grows 1–2½ feet (30–75 cm) tall and 3 feet (90 cm) wide. Plants may spread rapidly and become invasive. Sow seed shallowly indoors in early spring or outdoors in late spring. Divide established plants in early spring or autumn. Choose a named selection such as 'New White', 'Cerise Queen', 'Fire King' or 'Terracotta'. 'Terracotta' (pictured on page 118) has beautiful flowers that begin as rich orange and fade to

Fern–leaved yarrow continued

Common yarrow *Achillea millefolium* 'Terracotta'

yellow. It grows to 2 feet (60 cm) and is drought-tolerant. It prefers a hot, full-sun position.

The closely related Galaxy series of new yarrows arose from hybrids with *A. aegyptiaca* (syn. *A. taygetea*). Plants resemble common yarrow with 2–3-inch (5–7.5-cm) flower heads on sturdy stems. Colors range from creamy yellow to salmon-rose and brick-red. Flowers fade with age, giving them a multicolored appearance.

A. 'Moonshine' is a cultivar of hybrid origin. It grows 1–2 feet (30–60 cm) tall, with soft, blue-gray foliage and sulfur-yellow flowers.

A. 'Coronation Gold' is a cultivar of two species and grows 3 feet (90 cm) tall with stout self-supporting stems, gray-green leaves and 5-inch (12.5-cm) wide clusters of mustard-yellow flowers.

Aconitum carmichaelii

CLIMATE
Zones 3–7.

HEIGHT AND SPREAD
2–3 feet
(60–90 cm) tall.
2 feet (60 cm)
wide. Open and
somewhat vase-
shaped, especially
in shade.

FLOWERING TIME
Late summer and
autumn.

AZURE MONKSHOOD

AZURE MONKSHOOD IS BEST PLANTED NEAR
THE MIDDLE OR REAR OF BORDERS WITH
OTHER AUTUMN-BLOOMING PERENNIALS.

Description A graceful plant with
lush, three-lobed, dissected leaves,
sturdy stems and deep blue hooded
flowers in dense spikes. All parts
of the plant are poisonous.

Ideal position Full sun to light
shade. Afternoon shade in warmer
climates. Prefers cool summer nights
and warm days with low humidity.

Ideal soil conditions Fertile, humus-
rich, moist but well-drained soil.

Cultivation Azure monkshood
dislikes disturbance once it is
established. Space plants 2–3 feet

(60–90 cm) apart with the crowns
just below the surface. Divide if
plants become overcrowded.

Propagation Divide crowns in
autumn or early spring. Replant
strong, healthy divisions into soil
enriched with organic matter.

Pest and disease prevention Crowns
will rot if the soil is wet and if
temperatures are hot. Site plants
properly to avoid problems.

Landscape use Plant with
ornamental grasses or in groups
with fruiting shrubs such as
Viburnum spp.

Actaea alba

CLIMATE
Zones 3–9.

HEIGHT AND
SPREAD
2–4 feet
(60–120 cm) tall.
Mature clumps may
reach 3 feet
(90 cm) across.

FLOWERING TIME
Spring flowers. Late
summer to autumn
berries.

WHITE BANEBERRY

FOR A DRAMATIC ACCENT, PLANT WHITE
BANEBERRY AT THE EDGE OF A PATH IN A
WOODLAND GARDEN OR A SHADY WALK.

Description Mature clumps of white
baneberry in full fruit provide a
stunning highlight in the autumn
garden. The red-stalked berries are
poisonous to people but savored
by birds. It has white flowers
composed of a fuzzy cluster of
broad stamens. The showy, oval
white fruits, for which this plant is
noted, are ¼ inch (6 mm) long and
borne on long stalks.

Ideal position Partial to full shade.
Afternoon shade is ideal for this
plant in warmer climates. Best in
cool, humid conditions.

Ideal soil conditions Moist,
humus-rich soil.

Cultivation Top-dress clumps with
compost or shredded leaves in
spring or autumn. Plants seldom
need division.

Propagation Sow fresh seed
outdoors in early to midautumn,
after removing the pulp from the
ripe berries.

Pest and disease prevention No
serious pests or diseases.

Landscape use Mass plantings of
white baneberry are breathtaking
among ferns. Combine with
common bleeding heart *Dicentra
spectabilis* and violets.

Agapanthus africanus

CLIMATE
Zones 8–10.

HEIGHT AND SPREAD
1½–3 feet
(45–90 cm) tall.
1 foot
(30 cm) across.

FLOWERING TIME
Midsummer to
early autumn.

OTHER COMMON NAMES
Agapanthus.

AFRICAN LILY

AFRICAN LILIES MAKE A STUNNING BACKGROUND FEATURE OR AN EDGING ALONG BORDERS OR DRIVEWAYS.

Description African lilies bear flowers on tall, upright stems. The many-flowered umbels—each separate flower head displays 20–50 individual blossoms—are borne on 3-feet (90-cm) stems and are known to attract bees. Attractive, arching, evergreen, dark green, straplike leaves arise from short rhizomes and fleshy roots. African lilies have pretty pale to deep blue flowers and there are also white cultivars available.

Ideal position Full sun to partial shade. Best in hot, moderately humid conditions. Will tolerate the occasional frost. Needs full sun for best flowering. Plants need protection from cold, winter winds.

Ideal soil conditions Dry to moist, well-drained soil. These plants, with their strong, fleshy root system, are effective for use in binding less than ideal soil on steep banks or other hard-to-cultivate areas in a sunny garden situation.

Cultivation Remove spent flower stems before seeds mature if not wanted for propagating purposes. To ensure the plants remain neat and tidy at all times, trim dead leaves from the base of the plant when they become evident.

African lily continued

Agapanthus campanulatus

To avoid overcrowding, and consequent poor flowering, divide the plants every 4–5 years and prune back overhanging shrubs to prevent excess shade, which can also inhibit flowering.

Propagation Divide in late winter but only after the plant has become rootbound—usually in 4–5 years. Large clumps of roots form a tight network that can be very difficult to cut through. Fresh, ripe seed sown in autumn will give good germination results; indeed, in some more humid areas, these plants will self-sow and become quite invasive. If grown from seed, they may not flower for 3 years.

Pest and disease prevention No serious pests or diseases. Snails and slugs can use these fleshy-leaved plants as camouflage, although they don't seem to eat the leaves themselves. Place some snail baits in the form of beer traps around the plants to lure these pests.

Landscape use African lilies are perfect for grassy or rocky slopes and do well in coastal areas. They are also stunning in large tubs or containers. The flowers can last up to 1 week when cut.

Cultivars 'Loch Hope' is a late-flowering African lily that grows to 4 feet (1.2 m) and has large, dark blue flowers.

Agapanthus praecox subsp. *orientalis* 'Albus'

Hybrid cultivars include 'Irving Cantor' and 'Storm Cloud'.

Headbourne Hybrids are vigorous and hardy, growing to 3 feet (90 cm) with flowers in a wide range of colors.

In keeping with the trend toward smaller gardens, a range of miniature African lilies has been developed. These include 'Baby Blue', which grows to 1½–2 feet (45–60 cm) tall and has dainty, straplike, evergreen leaves and pale blue flowers, and 'Peter Pan', which is a midblue flowering dwarf variety of similar size. White forms are also available in these miniature African lilies. Zones 8–10.

Other species *A. campanulatus* (pictured on page 122) is the most frost-hardy agapanthus. *A. campanulatus* var. *patens* is smaller in both growth and flowering habit.

A. inapertus is a much sought-after deep blue species with distinctive, elongated, bell-shaped flowers, which hang rather than form an open-ball shape. Zones 8–10.

A. praecox has starbursts of trumpet-shaped, rich lavender-blue flowers on large, spherical heads. The densely clumped, evergreen foliage is attractive all year round.

A. praecox subsp. *orientalis* 'Albus' (pictured above) has white flowers.

Ajuga reptans

CLIMATE
Zones 3–9.

HEIGHT AND
SPREAD
4–10 inches
(10–25 cm) tall.
8–10 inches
(20–25 cm) wide.
Clumps may spread
to several feet
across from a
single plant.

FLOWERING TIME
Late spring to early
summer.

OTHER COMMON
NAMES
Ajuga.

COMMON BUGLEWEED

COMMON BUGLEWEED IS A TROUBLE-FREE
GROUNDCOVER THAT IS PERFECT FOR
PLANTING UNDER TREES AND SHRUBS.

Description A low, rosette-forming
groundcover that spreads by
creeping aboveground stems to
form broad, dense mats. The spoon-
shaped leaves are evergreen in mild
climates. It has tiered whorls of
small, intense blue flowers.

Ideal position Full sun to light
shade. Tolerates heat, humidity
and cold.

Ideal soil conditions Average to
humus-rich, moist, but well-drained
soil. Will not tolerate extended
drought or excessive moisture.

Cultivation Plant in spring or
autumn. Spreads rapidly to form a
dense weed-proof groundcover and
may become invasive.

Propagation Propagate by division
anytime during the growing season
or from seed sown in spring.

Pest and disease prevention Provide
good drainage and air circulation to
prevent crown rot and mildew.

Landscape use Use as an edging or
groundcover for islands and beds.

Cultivars 'Catlin's Giant' (pictured
above) has large, bronze leaves.
     'Atropurpurea' has characteristic
bronze-purple leaves.

Alcea rosea

CLIMATE
Zones 2–8.

HEIGHT AND
SPREAD
2–8 feet
(60–240 cm) tall.
2–3 feet
(60–90 cm) wide.

FLOWERING TIME
Summer and
early autumn.
May bloom for
2 months.

HOLLYHOCK

PLANT HOLLYHOCK AT THE BACK
OF BORDERS WHERE THE FOLIAGE IS
OBSCURED BY BUSHY PERENNIALS.

Description A tall, short-lived
perennial with rounded or lobed
foliage. The flowers bloom along
the upper half of the stem. Flowers
range from white and pale yellow
to pink, rose and red.

Ideal position Full sun to partial
shade. Prefers cool nights.

Ideal soil conditions Average to
humus-rich, well-drained soil.

Cultivation Plant in spring or
autumn. Hollyhocks are frost-hardy
but they need staking in areas that
are prone to strong wind.

Propagation Sow seed indoors in
winter for bloom in the summer,
or outdoors in summer for bloom
the following summer.

Pest and disease prevention If
affected by rust, dust the infected
foliage with sulfur. Deter spider
mites by spraying infested plants
with insecticidal soap.

Landscape use Hollyhock is perfect
when planted beside a garden shed,
fence or garage wall.

Cultivars 'Chater's Double' has fully
double flowers in a range of mixed
hues or single colors.
  'Farmyard Strain' has beautiful,
large, single flowers.

Alchemilla mollis

CLIMATE
Zones 2–8.

HEIGHT AND
SPREAD
1–1½ feet
(30–45 cm) tall.
2 feet
(60 cm) wide.

FLOWERING TIME
Summer and early
autumn.

LADY'S MANTLE

THE GREENISH YELLOW FLOWERS OF LADY'S
MANTLE ADD LIGHT AND INTEREST TO
SUMMER EVENINGS IN THE GARDEN.

Description Lady's mantle forms
mounded clumps of pleated foliage.
The 4–6-inch (10–15-cm) pale green
leaves are covered in soft hair that
collects beads of water like jewels
on velvet. It has foamy clusters of
small, greenish yellow flowers.

Ideal position Full sun to partial
shade. Excessive heat and humidity
can damage foliage.

Ideal soil conditions Humus-rich,
evenly moist soil.

Cultivation Set the crowns at soil
surface. Cut old foliage down to the
ground and new leaves quickly
appear. Mulch for evenly moist soil.

Propagation Divide the crowns in
spring or autumn. Sow fresh seed
outdoors in summer. Lady's mantle
often self-sows.

Pest and disease prevention No
serious pests or diseases.

Landscape use Plant at the front
of formal and informal beds and
borders or beside pathways.
Combine lady's mantle with other
plants that enjoy moist soil, such as
Siberian iris *Iris sibirica* and astilbe.

Cultivar 'Auslese' has firm, erect
flower stems.

Allium christophii

CLIMATE
Zones 4–8.

HEIGHT AND
SPREAD
1–1½ feet
(30–45 cm) tall.
1 foot
(30 cm) wide.

FLOWERING TIME
Early to
midsummer.

STAR OF PERSIA

PLANT STAR OF PERSIA BULBS AT THE FRONT OF BORDERS WHERE THEIR STALKS EXPLODE INTO BLOOM IN SUMMER.

Description Star of Persia produces 1½-foot (45-cm) upright leaves arching out from the bulbs. Metallic, lilac-pink flowers in 10-inch (25-cm) heads radiate from stalk tops.

Ideal position Full sun.

Ideal soil conditions Humus-rich, well-drained soil.

Cultivation New bulbs planted in autumn multiply slowly to form spectacular flowering clumps. Plants become dormant after flowering.

Propagation Divide in mid- to late summer as plants go dormant.

Sow ripe seed outdoors in summer or autumn.

Pest and disease prevention No serious pests or diseases. Mulch with organic matter to keep the soil evenly moist.

Landscape use Combine with shrubs or overplant with a groundcover. Plant with mounding plants such as cranesbills *Geranium* spp.

Other species *A. giganteum*, giant onion, grows 3–5 feet (90–150 cm) tall, with 5-inch (12.5-cm), rounded heads of deep purple flowers. Zones 4–9.

Alstroemeria aurea

CLIMATE
Zones 7–10.

HEIGHT AND SPREAD
2–3 feet
(60–90 cm) tall.
2 feet
(60 cm) wide.

FLOWERING TIME
Summer.

PERUVIAN LILY

PERUVIAN LILY IS EXCELLENT FOR CUTTING GARDENS. PLANT IT IN BEDS AND BORDERS FOR A SUMMER SUPPLY OF CUT FLOWERS.

Description Peruvian lily has tall, leafy stems crowned by open clusters of orange or yellow flowers with brownish purple flares on the upper petals. The gray-green leaves are narrow and pointed. Plants grow from thick, fibrous roots.

Ideal position Full sun to partial shade. Thrives in a range of temperatures but needs protection from strong winds.

Ideal soil conditions Moist, humus-rich soil.

Cultivation Plant dormant roots in early spring or autumn. Growth begins early in the season and plants may be damaged by late frost. Mulch with organic matter in autumn to avoid frost damage. Achieves best performance after the third year.

Propagation Divide clumps in early spring or autumn. Sow fresh seed indoors after 4–6 weeks of cold (35°–40°F [4°–5°C]), moist stratification.

Pest and disease prevention No serious pests or diseases.

Landscape use Plant in partial shade with ferns or in containers.

Alstroemeria Ligtu Hybrids

Other species *A. haemantha*, herb lily. This has flower stems to 3 feet (90 cm) tall. The flowers are red and the plant spreads by rhizomes. Zones 7–9.

A. psittacina. This Brazilian native has narrow, red and green, bell-shaped blooms in early summer. It can spread easily from tuberous roots and can prove somewhat invasive in humid, warm climates. Zones 8–10.

Cultivars Dr Salter's Hybrids. This group of hybrid cultivars comes in a wide variety of colors and the flower heads are slightly compact and heavily marked. Zones 7–9.

Dutch Hybrids. These hybrid cultivars (pictured on page 128) are very popular in the flower trade. The flowers are broad petaled with compact umbels. They are heavily marked with stunning contrasting colors. Zones 8–10.

Ligtu Hybrids (pictured above). These popular hybrids were developed in the 1920s. The colors range from cream to yellow to orange and red. The plants die down after flowering. Zones 7–9.

Amsonia tabernaemontana

CLIMATE
Zones 3–9.

HEIGHT AND
SPREAD
1–3 feet
(30–90 cm) tall.
3 feet
(90 cm) wide.

FLOWERING TIME
Spring, with some
secondary shoots
blooming in early
summer.

OTHER COMMON
NAMES
Willow amsonia.

WILLOW BLUE STAR

USE THE SHRUBBY CLUMPS OF WILLOW BLUE
STAR TO ADD STRUCTURE AND INTEREST TO
YOUR SPRING GARDEN.

Description A tough, shrubby plant
with lance-shaped leaves, stout
stems and terminal clusters of tiny,
steel-blue, ½-inch (12-mm), starry
flowers. Plants grow from a woody,
fibrous-rooted crown.

Ideal position Full sun to partial
shade. Heat- and cold-tolerant.

Ideal soil conditions Average to
humus-rich, moist, well-drained soil.

Cultivation Will reach shrublike
proportions with age. Plants in
shade may be floppy. If necessary,
prune stems back to 6–8 inches

(15–20 cm) after flowering. New
shoots will form an attractive,
compact mound. Leaves turn bright
orange to golden yellow in autumn.

Propagation Divide plants in early
spring or autumn. Take 4–6-inch
(10–15-cm) stem cuttings in early
summer. Sow ripe seed outdoors
in autumn or indoors after soaking
in hot water for several hours.

Pest and disease prevention No
serious pests or diseases. Mulch
with organic matter to keep soil
evenly moist.

Landscape use Grow either alone as
a mass planting or combined with
other perennials.

Anaphalis triplinervis

CLIMATE
Zones 3–8.

HEIGHT AND SPREAD
1–1½ feet (30–45 cm) tall.
1 foot (30 cm) wide.

FLOWERING TIME
A profusion of flowers in mid- to late summer.

THREE-VEINED EVERLASTING

THE PAPERY WHITE FLOWERS AND SOFT LEAVES OF THREE-VEINED EVERLASTING ADD BRIGHTNESS TO THE LATE-SUMMER GARDEN.

Description Unlike most silver-leaved plants, three-veined everlasting grows well in moist soil. It has white, double flowers with dark centers borne in open, flattened clusters. The flowers dry on the plant and persist for weeks.

Ideal position Full sun to partial shade.

Ideal soil conditions Moist, average to humus-rich soil.

Cultivation Spreads to form large clumps in moist soil. Divide the vigorous clumps every 2–4 years to control their spread.

Propagation Cuttings root freely during early summer.

Pest and disease prevention No serious pests or diseases.

Landscape use Grow three-veined everlasting in the front or middle of beds and borders or in informal and meadow gardens. Combine with Siberian iris *Iris sibirica* or sweet flag *Acorus calamus*. Ornamental grasses also make excellent companion plants, as do astilbes, daylilies and garden phlox *Phlox paniculata*.

Anchusa azurea

CLIMATE
Zones 3–8.

HEIGHT AND
SPREAD
2–5 feet
(60–150 cm) tall.
2 feet
(60 cm) wide.

FLOWERING TIME
Late spring.

ITALIAN BUGLOSS

FOR A STUNNING SPRING DISPLAY, PLANT
ITALIAN BUGLOSS AMONG SUCH FLOWERS AS
SHASTA DAISIES AND YARROWS.

Description Italian bugloss has lush,
oblong leaves covered in stiff hair.
Long branches bear terminal
clusters of brilliant blue, ¾-inch
(18-mm), five-petaled flowers. It
may reach 5 feet (1.5 m) in height.

Ideal position Full sun to light
shade. Best when grown in cool,
humid conditions.

Ideal soil conditions Humus-rich,
well-drained soil.

Cultivation Seed-grown plants may
be short-lived; choose a named
cultivar for better performance.

Cut plants back after blooming to
encourage flowers. Divide every
2–3 years to keep plants vigorous.

Propagation Divide clumps after
flowering. Replant strong, healthy
divisions into soil enriched with
organic matter. Take root cuttings in
early spring. Plants freely self-sow.

Pest and disease prevention No
serious pests or diseases.

Landscape use Use in mass
plantings with flowering shrubs.

Cultivars 'Dropmore' is a compact,
4-foot (1.2-m) selection with deep
blue flowers.
'Loddon Royalist' is 3 feet (90 cm)
tall with gentian-blue flowers.

Anemone blanda

CLIMATE
Zones 5–8.

HEIGHT AND
SPREAD
6 inches
(15 cm) tall.
4–6 inches
(10–15 cm) wide.

FLOWERING TIME
Spring.

GRECIAN WINDFLOWER

THE DELICATE FLOWERS OF GRECIAN
WINDFLOWER LOOK STUNNING WHEN
ALLOWED TO NATURALIZE UNDER TREES.

Description Grecian windflower
blooms in mid- to late spring in
most areas. In warmer gardens, it
may appear in late winter or early
spring. It has daisy-like blue, pink
or white flowers, which grow to
2 inches (5 cm) across.

Ideal position Full sun to partial
shade.

Ideal soil conditions Average to
moist, well-drained soil.

Cultivation Buy and plant tubers
in late spring through early autumn.
Soak them overnight before

planting, and set them in individual
holes or larger planting areas dug
about 2 inches (5 cm) deep. If you
can see a shallow depression on
one side, plant with that side up.
Otherwise, plant the tubers on their
sides or simply drop them into the
hole. Space them 4–6 inches
(10–15 cm) apart. Grecian
windflowers propagate themselves
by spreading and self-sowing.

Propagation Dig and divide the
tubers in spring, before replanting.

Pest and disease prevention No
serious pests or diseases.

Landscape use Grecian windflower
combines well with daffodils.

Anemone coronaria

CLIMATE
Zones 7–8 with mulch. Zones 9–10 without mulch.

HEIGHT AND SPREAD
1½ feet (45 cm) tall. 4–6 inches (10–15 cm) wide.

FLOWERING TIME
Midspring.

FLORIST'S ANEMONE

COMBINE FLORIST'S ANEMONE WITH OTHER ANEMONE SPECIES AND BULBS FOR A SPECTACULAR SPRING FLOWER DISPLAY.

Description A tuberous-rooted anemone that bears beautiful blue, pink, red and white flowers in spring. The flowers are solitary and poppy-like, 1–1½ inches (2.5–3.5 cm) in diameter on stalks 9–18 inches (22.5–45 cm) long. Pick the flowers when buds show plenty of color and are about to burst open. The black stamens contrast with the color of the petals. They last about 4 weeks.

Ideal position Full sun. Tolerates summer drought, but keep moist during autumn and spring.

Ideal soil conditions Average to moist, well-drained soil.

Cultivation In autumn, plant tubers 3 inches (7.5 cm) deep and provide a sunny exposure. Soak them overnight before planting. After the foliage matures, dig the tubers and store them through the winter in moist peat moss or vermiculite.

Propagation Division of tuberous rhizomes.

Pest and disease prevention No serious pests or diseases.

Landscape use Ideal for rock and wall gardens, beds, borders and woodland gardens.

Anemone nemorosa

CLIMATE
Zones 4–7.

HEIGHT AND
SPREAD
6 inches
(15 cm) tall.
4–6 inches
(10–15cm) wide.

FLOWERING TIME
Spring.

WOOD ANEMONE

WOOD ANEMONE MAKES AN EFFECTIVE
WOODLAND GROUNDCOVER. PLANT WHERE
ITS DAINTY FLOWERS CAN BE ADMIRED.

Description Wood anemone is a
very pretty, low-growing, spreading
anemone with fine, creeping
rhizomes. It has white (creamy)
flowers with yellow stamens.

Ideal position Moist, shaded
woodland conditions.

Ideal soil conditions Moist, humus-
rich, well-drained soil. Will tolerate
slightly drier conditions during
summer when dormant.

Cultivation These plants form a
mat about 4 inches (10 cm) high
and are best left alone in their
humus-rich position where they will
form a good groundcover dotted
with flowers in spring.

Propagation Can be divided or
sown with fresh seed.

Pest and disease prevention If the
conditions are suitable, no serious
pests or diseases.

Landscape use Wood anemone is
best planted in a large mass where
it won't be overwhelmed by more
vigorous plants.

Hybrids 'Rosea' has pink flowers in
bud, aging to deep pink.

Anemone x hybrida

CLIMATE
Zones 5–8.

HEIGHT AND
SPREAD
3–5 feet
(90–150 cm) tall.
2–3 feet
(60–90 cm) wide.

FLOWERING TIME
Late summer and
autumn.

JAPANESE ANEMONE

JAPANESE ANEMONE LIGHTS UP THE AUTUMN
GARDEN WITH CLOUDS OF DELICATELY
COLORED FLOWERS ON TALL STEMS.

Description Japanese anemone
produces single or double flowers
on slender stems. The deeply
divided, hairy leaves are mostly
basal. Plants grow from tuberous
roots. Flower color is from white
to pink and rose.

Ideal position Full sun to light
shade. Protect from hot afternoon
sun in warmer zones.

Ideal soil conditions Humus-rich,
evenly moist soil.

Cultivation Spreads by creeping
underground stems to form broad
clumps once established. Thin
overgrown clumps in spring if
blooms wane. Replant into humus-
rich soil and mulch in colder zones.

Propagation Take root cuttings after
plants go dormant in autumn. Sow
fresh seed outdoors in summer or
autumn. Divide in early spring.

Pest and disease prevention No
serious pests or diseases.

Landscape use Group with other
late-season perennials and
ornamental grasses. Combine with
shrubs or ferns in open shade.

Cultivars 'Honorine Jobert' bears
pure white single blooms on stems
3–4 feet (90–120 cm) tall.

Angelica archangelica

CLIMATE
Zones 4–9.

HEIGHT AND SPREAD
5–6 feet
(1.5–1.8 m) tall.
1 foot
(30 cm) wide.

FLOWERING TIME
Summer.

OTHER COMMON NAMES
Wild celery and wild parsnip.

EUROPEAN ANGELICA

USE EUROPEAN ANGELICA FOR ITS UNUSUAL HONEY-SCENTED FOLIAGE IN YOUR HERB OR SCENTED GARDEN.

Description This tall, sweet-scented herb resembles its close relatives, parsley and coriander. It has unusual, palmlike leaves and pale green flowers on tall stems. The seeds and dried root can be infused as a tea.

Ideal position Partial shade.

Ideal soil conditions Moist, well-drained rich soil.

Cultivation European angelica can only be propagated from seed, which germinates poorly if sown too deeply. Best sown *in situ* in late spring. Seedlings do not transplant well, so ideally sow three to four seeds in a cluster at stations about 3 feet (90 cm) apart and thin to the strongest seedling. If sown in a heated greenhouse in early spring, an earlier crop can be expected.

Propagation Will self-sow or can be propagated from seed.

Pest and disease prevention Wash aphids from seed heads with a spray of water.

Landscape use European angelica is a medicinal herb and is excellent in herb gardens and perfumed gardens. Plant it near a gate so you can enjoy the scent.

Antennaria dioica

CLIMATE
Zones 4–7.

HEIGHT AND SPREAD
Height of foliage to 10 inches (25 cm). Spreads over a wide area in time. Flower height to 1 foot (30 cm).

FLOWERING TIME
Early summer.

PUSSY TOES

PUSSY TOES IS A CHARMING LITTLE GROUND-COVER FOR A DRY, SUNNY SITE. THE TINY FLOWERS DRY WELL FOR WINTER BOUQUETS.

Description Pussy toes has rosettes of hairy, silver-green, 1-inch (2.5-cm) wide leaves, which are topped with off-white, pink-tipped flowers in early summer. It gets its name from the tiny flowers that resemble a cat's foot.

Ideal position Full sun.

Ideal soil conditions Dry, sandy, poor soil.

Cultivation Set plants 6 inches (15 cm) or more apart in light soil in spring or autumn. Plants are generally maintenance-free, but they self-sow readily and tend to become invasive, so cut off the flowers before they form seed if you wish to prevent spreading.

Propagation Sow seed or divide in spring.

Pest and disease prevention No serious pests or diseases.

Landscape use Pussy toes will spread to form a good cover for hot, dry spots in sunny, wild areas or rock gardens.

Cultivars 'Rosea' has rosy pink flower heads and whitish leaves.

Anthemis tinctoria

CLIMATE
Zones 4–10.

HEIGHT AND SPREAD
Mounds to 2–3 feet
(60–90 cm).
2–3 feet
(60–90 cm) wide.

FLOWERING TIME
Late spring and
summer.

OTHER COMMON NAMES
Golden marguerite.

DYERS' CHAMOMILE

DYER'S CHAMOMILE PRODUCES A BRILLIANT DISPLAY OF GOLDEN FLOWERS, WHICH ARE LONG-LASTING WHEN CUT.

Description Dyer's chamomile is a hardy, mounding plant with aromatic, fernlike foliage. It has tiny, golden, daisy-like flowers.

Ideal position Thrives in full sun.

Ideal soil conditions Average, well-drained soil and dry, poor soil.

Cultivation Cut back in autumn, after flowering, to ensure a tidy, well-shaped plant.

Propagation Prolific self-seeder. Take cuttings during summer or divide in autumn or spring.

Pest and disease prevention No serious pests or diseases.

Landscape use Use in mixed borders or as edgings in island beds. Also ideal for rock gardens, sloping banks, cutting gardens and herb gardens.

Cultivars 'Alba' has cream-colored petals and golden centers.
'E.C. Buxton' has soft yellow flowers, perfect for informal gardens among fine-leaved plants.

Other species *A. cretica* has white flowers with yellow centers on stems up to 1 foot (30 cm) tall. Zones 5–9.

Aquilegia canadensis

CLIMATE
Zones 3–8.

HEIGHT AND SPREAD
1–3 feet
(30–90 cm) tall.
1 foot
(30 cm) wide.

FLOWERING TIME
Early spring to
midspring.

WILD COLUMBINE

WILD COLUMBINE IS WONDERFULLY ALLURING
WHEN PLANTED IN A GROUP IN BEDS,
BORDERS, WOODLANDS AND MEADOWS.

Description Wild columbine may be
short-lived in the garden, but self-
sown seedlings are plentiful and
will replenish your plantings. The
red-and-yellow blooms of these
wildflowers nod atop delicate stalks
with divided, gray-green leaflets.

Ideal position Full sun to partial
shade. Drought-tolerant.

Ideal soil conditions Plant in poor to
average, well-drained soil.

Cultivation Set out young plants in
spring or autumn.

Propagation Divide or sow seed in
autumn or spring. Self-seed readily.

Pest and disease prevention Wild
columbines are plagued by
leafminers. Remove and destroy
affected foliage. In severe cases,
spray weekly with insecticidal soap.

Landscape use Use as a mass
planting with flowering shrubs and
small trees. Combine with ferns and
woodland wildflowers such as wild
ginger *Asarum canadense* and
foamflower *Tiarella cordifolia*.
In sunny meadows, plant them
with wild geranium *Geranium
maculatum* and ornamental grasses.

Aquilegia hybrids

CLIMATE
Zones 3–9.

HEIGHT AND
SPREAD
2–3 feet
(60–90 cm) tall.
1–2 feet
(30–60 cm) wide.

FLOWERING TIME
Spring and early
summer.

HYBRID COLUMBINES

HYBRID COLUMBINES ARE GRACEFUL PLANTS
WITH CURIOUS-LOOKING NODDING FLOWERS.
THEY LOOK BEST IN GROUPS OR DRIFTS.

Description Plants grow from a
thick taproot. They have single- or
bicolored variable flowers. Each
flower has five spurred petals
surrounded by five petal-like sepals.
The spurs may be ½–4 inches
(12–100 mm) long. Yellow, red,
blue, purple, pink and white
flowers are common.

Ideal position Full sun to partial
shade.

Ideal soil conditions Light, average
to humus-rich, well-drained soil.

Cultivation Hybrid columbines may
be short-lived even under the best
garden conditions. They generally
live from 2–4 years, rewarding
the gardener with a month or more
of blooming. Plants self-sow
prolifically and new plants are
always developing.

Propagation Sow seed outdoors in
spring or summer. Sow indoors in
winter after dry-storing seed in a
refrigerator for 4–6 weeks. Plants
develop quickly.

Pest and disease prevention The
leaves are attacked by leafminers.
Destroy damaged foliage. In severe
cases, spray weekly with insecticidal

Hybrid columbines continued

Hybrid columbines often reseed themselves with variable results.

soap. Borers also attack hybrid columbines, causing the plants to collapse dramatically. Remove and destroy all affected parts.

Landscape use Plant with spring and early-summer perennials and bulbs. Combine with wildflowers, ferns and hostas in light shade. Try them along stone walls or in rock gardens.

Cultivars Biedermeier Hybrids come in mixed colors. Plants are only 1 foot (30 cm) tall.

'Crimson Star' grows to 2½ feet (75 cm) tall and has crimson-and-white flowers.

Dragonfly Hybrids are 10–12 inches (25–30 cm) tall and come in mixed colors.

McKana is a strain of large-flowered hybrids in mixed colors.

'Nora Barlow' has double flowers in red, white and green combinations.

Other species *A. caerulea*, Rocky Mountain columbine, has graceful, upfacing, blue-and-white flowers with long spurs. Zones 3–8.

A. chrysantha, golden columbine, has huge, 2–3-inch (5–7.5-cm), yellow flowers with 4-inch (10-cm) spurs. Zones 3–9.

A. flabellata, fan columbine, has showy, blue-green foliage and short-spurred, deep blue or white flowers. Zones 3–9.

Arabis caucasica

CLIMATE
Zones 3–7.

HEIGHT AND
SPREAD
6–10 inches
(15–25 cm) tall.
1–1½ feet
(30–45 cm) wide.

FLOWERING TIME
Late winter and
early spring.

WALL ROCK CRESS

ATTRACTIVE WALL ROCK CRESS LOOKS GREAT
TUMBLING OVER A STONE WALL OR CREEPING
THROUGH A ROCK GARDEN.

Description Wall rock cress is an
evergreen groundcover 4–6 inches
(10–15 cm) high. The 1-inch
(2.5-cm) leaves are clothed in soft
hair and are often obscured by the
spring pink or white flowers.

Ideal position Full sun to partial
shade. Plants will languish in
warmer zones.

Ideal soil conditions Tolerates a
range of soil moisture and fertility.

Cultivation Spreads quickly to form
loose mats of foliage. Cut plants
back after flowering to encourage

new shoots and to keep them neat.
Divide every 2–4 years to keep
plants healthy.

Propagation Take cuttings in spring.
Layer by burying 6 inches (15 cm)
of a low-growing stem and leaving
the leafy tip exposed. Divide in
spring or autumn.

Pest and disease prevention No
serious pests or diseases.

Landscape use Interplant with
spring bulbs and early perennials
along borders.

Cultivars 'Rosabella' has rose-pink
flowers.
   'Snow Cap' is a robust plant with
profuse white flowers.

Arenaria montana

CLIMATE
Zones 4–8.

HEIGHT AND
SPREAD
2–4 inches
(5–10 cm) tall,
6 inches
(15 cm) tall
in flower.
10–12 inches
(25–30 cm) wide.
Larger with age.

FLOWERING TIME
Spring and early
summer.

MOUNTAIN SANDWORT

MOUNTAIN SANDWORT IS A VERY HANDY
GROUNDCOVER. YOU CAN EVEN USE IT TO
PLANT BETWEEN PAVERS IN WALKWAYS.

Description Mountain sandwort is
a dense, mat-forming groundcover
with tiny, needle-like leaves and
flat, white, five-petaled flowers.
Plants grow from thin, fibrous roots.

Ideal position Full sun.

Ideal soil conditions Average sandy
or loamy, well-drained soil. Plants
dislike acid soil.

Cultivation Spreads slowly to form
low, mosslike mats of foliage. It is
very shallow-rooted, so keep moist
during dry spells.

Propagation Divide in spring or
autumn. Sow seed outdoors in
autumn or inside in early spring.

Pest and disease prevention No
serious pests or diseases.

Landscape use Plant among rocks in
loosely constructed walls. Excellent
in rock gardens and perfect for pot
or trough culture.

Arisaema triphyllum

CLIMATE
Zones 3–9.

HEIGHT AND
SPREAD
1–3 feet
(30–90 cm) tall.
1–1½ feet
(30–45 cm) wide.

FLOWERING TIME
Spring.

JACK–IN–THE–PULPIT

JACK-IN-THE-PULPIT IS A SPRING-FLOWERING
WILDFLOWER THAT IS PERFECT FOR PLANTING
AMONG LOW-GROWING WILDFLOWERS.

Description The unusual green
flowers, striped with yellow or
purple, are hidden beneath single
or paired leaves, each with three
broad leaflets. Plants grow from a
button-like tuber. Glossy, red
berries ripen in late summer.

Ideal position Partial to full shade.

Ideal soil conditions Evenly moist,
humus-rich soil. Tolerates wet soil.

Cultivation Easy to grow and long-
lived. Clumps grow slowly from
offsets or seed.

Propagation Remove the pulp
from ripe berries and sow the
seed outdoors in spring or autumn.
Seedlings develop slowly and
may take several years to bloom.
Propagate from natural offsets
in spring.

Pest and disease prevention No
serious pests or diseases.

Landscape use Combine with
fringed bleeding heart *Dicentra
spectabilis*, bloodroot *Sanguinaria
canadensis*, hostas and ferns. Plant
under shrubs or flowering trees.

Armeria maritima

CLIMATE
Zones 4–8.

HEIGHT AND
SPREAD
10–14 inches
(25–35 cm) tall.
8–10 inches
(20–25 cm) wide.

FLOWERING TIME
Late spring and
summer.

OTHER COMMON
NAMES
Sea pink.

THRIFT

THRIFT, WITH ITS PINK, BALL-SHAPED
FLOWERS, LOOKS STUNNING AGAINST A
WALL OR PLANTED IN ROCK GARDENS.

Description Forms dense tufts of
grasslike, gray-green, evergreen
leaves. The bloom stalks arise from
the centers of the rosettes. Small,
pink flowers are crowded into
rounded 1-inch (2.5-cm) heads.

Ideal position Full sun. Prefers cool
nights and low humidity.

Ideal soil conditions Average to
humus-rich, moist, well-drained soil.

Cultivation Drought-tolerant once
established, it will grow in rock
crevices where water is scarce.
It tolerates air- and soilborne salt.

Propagation Divide clumps of thrift
in early spring or autumn. Sow
seed indoors in winter on a warm
(70°F [21°C]) seedbed.

Pest and disease prevention No
serious pests or diseases.

Landscape use Combine with low
plants such as snow-in-summer
Cerastium tomentosum.

Cultivars 'Alba' has white flowers
on 5-inch (12.5-cm) stems.
　'Dusseldorf Pride' has attractive
wine-red flowers on 6–8-inch
(15–20-cm) stems.
　'Robusta' has 3-inch (7.5-cm),
pink flower heads on 1–15-inch
(30–37.5-cm) stems.

Artemisia absinthium

CLIMATE
Zones 3–9.

HEIGHT AND SPREAD
2–3 feet
(60–90 cm) tall.
2 feet
(60 cm) wide.

FLOWERING TIME
Late summer and autumn.

COMMON WORMWOOD

THE SOFT GRAY-GREEN FOLIAGE OF COMMON WORMWOOD IS LOVELY WITH ORNAMENTAL GRASSES OR IN FRONT OF CONIFERS.

Description Common wormwood is a stout, shrubby perennial with stems that become woody with age. Soft hair on the deeply lobed, aromatic foliage gives the plant a muted gray-green tone. Inconspicuous yellow flowers are borne in terminal clusters.

Ideal position Full sun.

Ideal soil conditions Average sandy or loamy, well-drained soil.

Cultivation Thrives in all but the most inhospitable garden spots. Overly rich soils result in weak growth. Encourage compact growth by pruning back untidy plants by at least half.

Propagation Grow from stem cuttings taken in late summer or spring. Dust the cut surfaces with a rooting hormone to speed production of new roots.

Pest and disease prevention No serious pests or diseases.

Landscape use Use in dry-soil gardens. Combine with other drought-tolerant perennials.

Cultivars 'Lambrook Silver' has deeply cut, silver-gray foliage.

Artemisia lactiflora

CLIMATE
Zones 5–8.

HEIGHT AND
SPREAD
4–6 feet
(1.2–1.8 m) tall.
Up to 4 feet
(1.2 m) wide.

FLOWERING TIME
Late summer.

WHITE MUGWORT

WHITE MUGWORT HAS A SPECTACULAR
SHOW OF WHITE FLOWERS THAT IS STUNNING
AS A BACKDROP FOR A FLOWER BED.

Description Unlike its silver-leaved
relatives, white mugwort can take
light shade. It bears graceful, 2-foot
(60-cm) long plumes of fragrant,
white flowers in late summer.

Ideal position Does best in full sun
but will tolerate light shade.

Ideal soil conditions Light, moist,
fertile soil.

Cultivation Give plenty of space
when planting seedlings. Fertilize
lightly in spring and prune back
minimally to stimulate growth.
Water during drought.

Propagation Propagate by cuttings
in summer or by division in spring.

Pest and disease prevention No
serious pests or diseases.

Landscape use White mugwort
makes a nice background plant in
a flower border, especially when
highlighted by lower-growing
coneflowers *Rudbeckia* spp.,
daylilies or asters.

Aruncus dioicus

CLIMATE
Zones 3–7.

HEIGHT AND
SPREAD
3–6 feet
(90–180 cm) tall.
3–5 feet
(90–150 cm) wide.

FLOWERING TIME
Late spring and
early summer.

GOAT'S BEARD

SHRUBLIKE GOAT'S BEARD MAKES A
STUNNING ACCENT WHEN PLANTED WITH
SPRING- AND SUMMER-FLOWERING SHRUBS.

Description A showy perennial with large, three-lobed leaves and airy plumes of flowers. It has creamy white flowers with small petals. Male and female flowers are borne on separate plants.

Ideal position Full sun (in cooler zones) to partial shade. Avoid areas with hot nights.

Ideal soil conditions Moist, humus-rich soil.

Cultivation Plant 4–5 feet (1.2–1.5 m) apart to allow for the plants' impressive mature size. The tough rootstocks are difficult to move once established. Divide plants only if necessary to revitalize the clumps. Lift in early spring and replant strong, healthy divisions into soil enriched with organic matter.

Propagation Sow seed outdoors in summer or inside on a warm (70°F [21°C]) seedbed.

Pest and disease prevention No serious pests or diseases.

Landscape use Use goat's beard with ferns, wildflowers and hostas in a lightly shaded woodland garden. It combines well with other perennials in beds and borders.

CLIMATE
Zones 4–8.

HEIGHT AND
SPREAD
6–12 inches
(15–30 cm) tall.
1 foot
(30 cm) wide.

FLOWERING TIME
Spring.

EUROPEAN WILD GINGER

THE GLOSSY, EVERGREEN LEAVES OF
EUROPEAN WILD GINGER REFLECT LIGHT
AND BRIGHTEN SHADED GARDENS.

Description A slow-creeping, evergreen groundcover. The aromatic rhizomes creep at or just below the soil surface. The glossy, kidney-shaped leaves are mottled along the veins. Juglike, dull brown flowers are usually hidden under the foliage. The plant forms broad clumps with age.

Ideal position Partial to full shade. Drought-tolerant once established but best when moisture is adequate.

Ideal soil conditions Moist, humus-rich soil.

Cultivation Clumps spread steadily to form tight mats of weed-proof foliage. Divide crowded plants in early spring or autumn.

Propagation Divide in spring or autumn. Sow fresh seed outdoors in summer.

Pest and disease prevention No serious pests or diseases.

Landscape use European wild ginger is an exceptional groundcover. Plant along the garden path with ferns and wildflowers or in a shaded rock garden.

Aster novae-angliae

CLIMATE
Zones 3–8.

HEIGHT AND SPREAD
3–6 feet
(90–180 cm) tall.
3 feet
(90 cm) wide.
Matures into broad clumps.

FLOWERING TIME
Late summer through autumn.

NEW ENGLAND ASTER

NEW ENGLAND ASTER IS IDEAL FOR PLANTING AT THE BACK OF A BORDER IN INFORMAL AND FORMAL GARDENS.

Description A tall, stately plant with hairy stems and clasping, lance-shaped leaves. It has lavender to purple, 1½–2-inch (3.5–5 cm) flowers with yellow centers. Flowers may vary in color from white to pink and rose.

Ideal position Full sun to light shade.

Ideal soil conditions Moist, humus-rich soil.

Cultivation Clumps will become quite large with age. Divide every 3–4 years in spring. Plants may need staking.

Propagation Take 4–6-inch (10–15-cm) stem cuttings in late spring or early summer. Divide in early spring or autumn.

Pest and disease prevention Powdery mildew turns leaves dull gray. Thin stems to promote air circulation. Dust affected plants with sulfur.

Landscape use Plant with autumn perennials such as sunflowers *Helianthus* spp., Japanese anemone *Anemone* x *hybrida* and ornamental grasses.

Aster novi–belgii

CLIMATE
Zones 3–8.

HEIGHT AND
SPREAD
Depending on the
cultivar, 1–6 feet
(30–180 cm) tall.
1–3 feet
(30–90 cm) wide.

FLOWERING TIME
Late summer and
early autumn.

NEW YORK ASTER

LATE-BLOOMING NEW YORK ASTER IS A
COLORFUL ADDITION TO THE AUTUMN
GARDEN, ESPECIALLY IN MASS PLANTINGS.

Description This plant is one of the
most useful for a perennial border.
It has pretty white, blue, purple
or pink single or double flowers,
1¼–2½ inches (3–6 cm) wide, with
bright yellow centers.

Ideal position Full sun to
light shade.

Ideal soil conditions Moist, well-
drained soil of moderate fertility.

Cultivation Pinch asters once or
twice before midsummer to make
them bushier and promote strong
stems so they are less likely to need
staking. Divide clumps every
1–2 years to renew the plant and
keep it vigorous. Mulch during
winter in Zone 4.

Propagation Divide in early spring.

Pest and disease prevention Don't
overcrowd. This plant needs plenty
of fresh air to avoid mildew.

Landscape use Use in clumps
or masses in flower or mixed
borders. New York asters look good
with garden mums *Dendranthema*
spp. and goldenrods *Solidago* spp.

Aster x *frikartii*

CLIMATE
Zones 5–8.

HEIGHT AND
SPREAD
2–3 feet
(60–90 cm) tall.
2–3 feet
(60–90 cm) wide.

FLOWERING TIME
Midsummer
through autumn.

FRIKART'S ASTER

FRIKART'S ASTER COMBINES WELL WITH
LATE-SUMMER- AND AUTUMN-FLOWERING
PERENNIALS AND ORNAMENTAL GRASSES.

Description Plant grows from short,
slow-creeping rhizomes with fibrous
roots. It produces open clusters of
2½-inch (6-cm), lavender-blue
flowers, with bright yellow centers,
on loosely branched stems.

Ideal temperature Full sun to
light shade.

Ideal soil conditions Moist but
well-drained soil. Plants will rot in
sodden soil, especially in winter.

Cultivation Frikart's aster may be
short-lived. Clumps spread slowly.
Divide as necessary in spring or
autumn. Does well in Zone 4 with
mulch or consistent winter snow.

Propagation Take stem cuttings
in spring. Divide in early spring
or autumn.

Pest and disease prevention A well-
drained position will deter root rot.

Landscape use Combine Frikart's
aster with garden phlox *Phlox
paniculata* and coneflowers
Rudbeckia spp. It also grows
well in containers in Zones 6–8.

Cultivars 'Monch' has erect stems
and deep lavender-blue flowers.
'Wonder of Staffa' is more open
in habit with paler flowers.

Astilbe x arendsii

ASTILBE

ASTILBE LOOKS SPECTACULAR BY STREAMS OR PONDS WHERE THE PLUMES OF SHOWY FLOWERS ARE REFLECTED IN THE WATER.

Description Astilbe has ferny, dissected leaves with shiny, broad leaflets. The emerging spring shoots are often tinged with red. Upright, often-plumed flower clusters bear tightly packed, fuzzy blooms in shades of red, pink, rose, lilac, cream and white.

Ideal position Full to partial shade. Astilbe tolerates more sun in cool-summer areas.

Ideal soil conditions Moist, slightly acid, humus-rich soil. Dry soil will result in shriveled foliage.

Cultivation Astilbes are heavy feeders and benefit from an annual application of balanced organic fertilizer. Top-dress with compost or lift and replant the clumps if crowns rise above the soil. Divide clumps every 3–4 years and replant into soil that has been enriched with organic matter. Keep plants well watered.

Propagation Propagate the true species by sowing fresh seed outdoors in summer or early autumn. Propagate cultivars by division in spring or autumn.

Pest and disease prevention Spider mites may be a problem for astilbe in warm areas. Spray with insecticidal soap as necessary.

Astilbe continued

CLIMATE
Zones 3–9.

HEIGHT AND
SPREAD
2–4 feet
(60–120 cm) tall.
2–3 feet
(60–90 cm) wide.
Leafy clumps
spread steadily
outward. Each
clump maintains a
distinct crown.

FLOWERING TIME
Spring and early
summer.

OTHER COMMON
NAMES
False spirea.

Astilbe is perfect for planting in a moist shade garden or beside a stream.

Control root rot with good drainage and good air circulation.

Landscape use In beds or borders, plant astilbes at front or toward center, depending on their size. Combine with hostas, lungworts *Pulmonaria* spp. and wildflowers.

Cultivars 'Amethyst' is an early bloomer with lilac-purple flowers on 1½–2-foot (45–60-cm) stems.

'Bridal Veil' has open, drooping clusters of creamy white flowers.

'Fanal' has deep red flowers on 1–1½-foot (30–45-cm) plants.

'Cattleya' is a midseason bloomer with lilac-pink flowers on 3-foot (90-cm) tall stems.

'Glut' is a late-flowering red plant with long 1½–2-foot (45–60-cm) stems.

Other species *A. chinensis* is a creeping plant with rose-pink, late-summer flowers. 'Pumila' is a low-growing groundcover. *A. chinensis* var. *taquetti*, autumn astilbe, is similar to *A. chinensis* but is 3–4 feet (90–120 cm) tall.

A. japonica, Japanese astilbe. This is an early-blooming species with glossy leaves.

A. simplicifolia, star astilbe. This is a dwarf species with glossy, deeply lobed leaves and open, drooping flower clusters.

Astrantia major

CLIMATE
Zones 4–7.

HEIGHT AND
SPREAD
2–3 feet
(60–90 cm) tall.
1–2 feet
(30–60 cm) wide.

FLOWERING TIME
Early to late
summer.

MASTERWORT

MASTERWORT IS A TROUBLE-FREE PERENNIAL
WITH BOLD FOLIAGE AND UNUSUAL FLOWERS
THAT COMPLEMENT PERENNIALS AND SHRUBS.

Description Masterwort has deeply
lobed, palmate leaves on a stout,
fibrous-rooted crown. Leafy,
branched flower stalks rise from the
center. It has creamy white, button-
like flower heads surrounded by a
whorl of starry, pointed bracts. The
stiff bracts remain after the flowers
fade, prolonging the display.

Ideal position Full sun to partial
shade. Intolerant of high
temperatures, especially at night.

Ideal soil conditions Evenly moist,
humus-rich soil. Tolerates wet soil.

Cultivation Clumps become quite
large with age. Divide to control
their size and spread.

Propagation Divide plants in
autumn or early spring or remove
runners from the main clump. Sow
fresh seed outdoors in late summer.

Pest and disease prevention No
serious pests or diseases.

Landscape use Plant along borders
or combine with airy meadow rues
Thalictrum spp., ornamental grasses
and spiky mulleins *Verbascum* spp.
Or plant by ponds with irises
and ferns.

Cultivars 'Rosea' has pink flowers
and bracts.

Aubrieta deltoidea

CLIMATE
Zones 4–8.

HEIGHT AND SPREAD
6–8 inches
(15–20 cm) tall.
8–12 inches
(20–30 cm) wide.

FLOWERING TIME
Early spring.

ROCK CRESS

ROCK CRESS IS AT HOME IN THE CRACKS AND CREVICES OF WALLS OR AMONG ROCKS IN SUNNY ROCK GARDENS.

Description A low, mounding, spring-blooming plant with weak stems clothed in sparsely toothed, evergreen leaves. It spreads by rhizomes to form broad clumps and has four-petaled, ¾-inch (18-mm) flowers in white, rose or purple.

Ideal position Full sun to light shade. Grows best with moderate summer humidity and temperatures.

Ideal soil conditions Well-drained, sandy or loamy, neutral soil.

Cultivation Plants tend to flop after flowering. Shear clumps to promote compact growth and to encourage repeat bloom.

Propagation Divide in autumn. Take stem cuttings after flowering. Sow seed indoors or outdoors from spring to autumn.

Pest and disease prevention Plant in well-drained soil to avoid root rot, especially where night temperatures are high.

Landscape use Plant at the edge of walks or at the front of beds and borders with spring bulbs, coral bells *Heuchera* spp., sedums, red valerian *Centranthus ruber* and basket of gold *Aurinia saxatilis.*

Aurinia saxatilis

CLIMATE
Zones 3–7.

HEIGHT AND
SPREAD
10–12 inches
(25–30 cm) tall.
1 foot
(30 cm) wide.

FLOWERING TIME
Early spring.

BASKET OF GOLD

GIVE BASKET OF GOLD SUN AND GOOD
DRAINAGE, AND IT WILL PRODUCE MASSES
OF BRILLIANT YELLOW BLOOMS.

Description Produces mounds of
6-inch (15-cm), oblong, gray-green
leaves from a thick crown. Hairy
leaves and deep roots help the
plant endure dry soil and warm
temperatures. It has brilliant yellow
flowers, which have four rounded
petals and are carried in upright,
branched clusters.

Ideal position Full sun. Avoid
excessively hot and humid climates.
Tolerates hot, dry conditions.

Ideal soil conditions Average,
well-drained, loamy or sandy soil.

Cultivation Clumps spread by
creeping stems and may flop after
flowering. Cut stems back by two-
thirds after flowering to encourage
compact growth.

Propagation Divide in autumn.
Take stem cuttings in spring or
autumn. Sow seed in autumn.

Pest and disease prevention Heavy
moist soils and high humidity will
encourage root rot. Plant in
well-drained soils only.

Landscape use Basket of gold lends
color to rock walls, rock gardens
and walkways.

Baptisia australis

CLIMATE
Zones 3–9.

HEIGHT AND
SPREAD
2–4 feet
(60–120 cm) tall.
3–4 feet
(90–120 cm) wide.

FLOWERING TIME
Late spring and
early summer.

OTHER COMMON
NAMES
Baptisia.

BLUE FALSE INDIGO

SPECTACULAR BLUE FALSE INDIGO LOOKS
EQUALLY ATTRACTIVE IN FORMAL BORDERS
OR INFORMAL MEADOW PLANTINGS.

Description Mature plants form
dense, rounded mounds of three-
lobed, blue-green leaves. Deep blue
1-inch (2.5-cm) flowers are carried
in narrow, open clusters and
resemble lupines. The dried gray
pods are showy during autumn
and winter.

Ideal position Full sun to partial
shade. Tolerant of heat and cold.

Ideal soil conditions Average to
humus-rich, moist, well-drained soil.

Cultivation Grows slowly until its
taproot establishes. Mature plants
have massive, tough root systems
that resent disturbance. Space
young plants 3–4 feet (90–120 cm)
apart. Division is seldom necessary.

Propagation Take cuttings after
flowering or sow fresh seed
outdoors in autumn. Treat stored
seed by pouring near-boiling water
over it and soaking for 12–24 hours
before sowing. Divide clumps in
autumn, late winter or early spring.

Pest and disease prevention No
serious pests or diseases.

Landscape use Plant toward the
rear of the border with Siberian iris
Iris sibirica, peonies and other
bold-textured plants.

Begonia Tuberhybrida Group

CLIMATE
Hardy in Zone 10.
Elsewhere, grown
as annuals or
stored indoors
in winter.

HEIGHT AND
SPREAD
1½ feet
(45 cm) tall.
1–1½ feet
(30–45 cm) wide.

FLOWERING TIME
Summer through
autumn.

HYBRID TUBEROUS BEGONIAS

HYBRID TUBEROUS BEGONIAS HAVE
GORGEOUS FLOWERS IN A WIDE RANGE OF
COLORS AND ARE PERFECT FOR CONTAINERS.

Description These bushy plants
produce an abundance of single
or double flowers up to 4 inches
(10 cm) wide in almost every color
except blue, and many are edged
with other colors.

Ideal position Partial shade.

Ideal soil conditions Evenly moist
but well-drained soil that has been
enriched with added organic matter.

Cultivation Buy thick tubers
1½–2 inches (3.5–5 cm) across. Start
growing indoors about 4 weeks
before your last frost date. Give

developing plants bright light and
keep the soil evenly moist. Set
plants out when night temperatures
stay above 50°F (10°C). Water and
mulch to keep the soil evenly
moist. Fertilize several times during
the season. Pinch off spent flowers
to keep plants tidy.

Propagation Divide tubers in
spring, after bringing them out
of winter storage.

Pest and disease prevention Prevent
powdery mildew by giving plants a
site with good air circulation.

Landscape use Plant in shaded
beds, borders and hanging baskets.

Begonia Rex-cultorum Group

Other species This is a large genus of plants with many hybrids of mixed parentage, which have been placed into specific groups, including the bedding or wax begonia *B.* Semperflorens-cultorum Group. These are often used as annual bedding plants in colder areas but in more temperate areas can overwinter for a couple of years. They combine glossy, colorful foliage with myriads of pink, red or white flowers, which are held on the plants for months at a time.

Another group with hundreds of named cultivars of mixed parentage, known as rex begonias or beefsteak geranium *B.* Rex-cultorum Group, (pictured above) is grown mainly for its colorful leaves because the flowers are generally inconspicuous. Zones 6–10.

While there are many other begonias, a lot are considered to be shrubs rather than perennials. One exception is the winter-flowering begonia *B.* x *hiemalis* with fibrous root systems, which in the past has tended to die while dormant. Newer cultivars have now been bred to overcome this drawback.

Belamcanda chinensis

IRIDACEAE

CLIMATE
Zones 4–10.

HEIGHT AND SPREAD
2–4 feet
(60–120 cm) tall.
1–2 feet
(30–60 cm) wide.

FLOWERING TIME
Mid- to late
summer.

BLACKBERRY LILY

PLANT BLACKBERRY LILY WITH PLANTS THAT
HAVE LARGE FLOWERS, TO CONTRAST WITH
ITS SMALL, STARRY FLOWERS.

Description Produces showy, curved
fans of foliage that resemble irises.
Branched clumps grow from
creeping rhizomes. Its six-petaled,
2-inch (5-cm), orange flowers are
speckled with red.

Ideal position Full sun to light
shade. Afternoon shade can prolong
the life of flowers. Provide winter
protection in colder areas.

Ideal soil conditions Average to
humus-rich, well-drained soil.

Cultivation Plants spread by
creeping rhizomes to form dense

clumps. Divide as necessary to
control spread. Self-sown seedlings
often appear.

Propagation Divide in late summer
or sow fresh seed in spring.

Pest and disease prevention No
serious pests or diseases.

Landscape use Combine blackberry
lily with garden phlox *Phlox
paniculata* and daylilies for formal
borders and informal gardens.

Other species The closely related
B. flabellata grows 1–2 feet
(30–60 cm) tall and has pretty,
yellow flowers.

Bergenia cordifolia

CLIMATE
Zones 3–9.

HEIGHT AND
SPREAD
1 foot
(30 cm) tall.
1 foot
(30 cm) wide.

FLOWERING TIME
Late winter and
early spring.

HEART-LEAVED BERGENIA

USE HEART-LEAVED BERGENIAS AS ACCENTS
IN BEDS AND BORDERS AND AT THE BASE OF
ROCK WALLS OR ALONG GARDEN PATHS.

Description Heart-leaved bergenia
is a long-lived, handsome plant with
broad, oval, leathery, evergreen
foliage. The 10–12-inch (25–30-cm)
leaves emerge in a whorl from a
stout, creeping rhizome. Nodding,
pink or rose flowers are carried
above the foliage on thick stems.

Ideal position Full sun to partial
shade. Provide afternoon shade in
warmer zones to protect leaves
from burning.

Ideal soil conditions Moist,
humus-rich soil.

Cultivation These plants creep
slowly from rhizomes. As clumps
age, they become bare in the
center. Lift in spring and remove
old portions of the rhizome. Replant
in humus-rich soil. Mulch in winter.

Propagation Divide in spring. Sow
ripe seed indoors on a warm
(70°F [21°C]) seedbed. Leave the
seed uncovered. Young plants will
develop slowly.

Pest and disease prevention Exclude
slugs with barrier strips of wood
ashes or sand.

Landscape use Plant under shrubs
for a glossy, green groundcover. Or
use them in borders or containers.

Boltonia asteroides

CLIMATE
Zones 3–9.

HEIGHT AND SPREAD
4–6 feet
(1.2–1.8 m) tall.
4 feet
(1.2 m) wide.

FLOWERING TIME
Late summer
through autumn.

OTHER COMMON NAMES
False chamomile.

BOLTONIA

CHOOSE BOLTONIA FOR THE REAR OF
FORMAL BEDS OR BORDERS OR INFORMAL
PLANTINGS AND COTTAGE GARDENS.

Description Boltonia is a tall, late-season perennial with lovely, gray-green, willow-like foliage. It has a profusion of 1-inch (2.5-cm) white daisies with bright yellow centers carried in open clusters.

Ideal position Full sun to light shade.

Ideal soil conditions Moist, humus-rich soil. Dry soil will produce smaller plants.

Cultivation These easy-to-grow plants form sturdy, dense stems that seldom need staking.

Propagation Divide oversized clumps in spring. Take cuttings in early summer. Seed collected from cultivars will produce seedlings.

Pest and disease prevention No serious pests or diseases.

Landscape use Combine with autumn-blooming perennials such as asters, Japanese anemones *Anemone* x *hybrida*, goldenrods *Solidago* spp. and Joe-Pye weeds *Eupatorium* spp.

Cultivars 'Pink Beauty' sports soft pink flowers in open clusters. Cool summers produce brighter colors.
    'Snowbank' is a compact selection with bright white flowers.

Brunnera macrophylla

CLIMATE
Zones 3–8.

HEIGHT AND
SPREAD
1–1½ feet
(30–45 cm) tall.
2 feet (60 cm)
wide. Foliage
reaches mature size
in summer.

FLOWERING TIME
Early spring.
Flowering often
continues for
3–4 weeks.

SIBERIAN BUGLOSS

SIBERIAN BUGLOSS HAS BOLD SUMMER
FOLIAGE, A PERFECT FOIL FOR FINE-TEXTURED
PLANTS SUCH AS ASTILBES AND FERNS.

Description The 8-inch (20-cm),
heart-shaped leaves rise in a mound
from a short, fibrous-rooted
rhizome. The ¼-inch (6-mm), pale
blue flowers cover plants before
leaves emerge, and whiten with age.

Ideal position Partial to full shade,
full sun in cooler zones. Tolerates
short, dry spells once established.

Ideal soil conditions Evenly moist,
humus-rich soil.

Cultivation Plants are tough,
increase slowly and seldom need
division. Self-sown seedlings appear

regularly. Keep moist, as plants will
go dormant during drought.

Propagation Divide clumps in early
spring or autumn. Take 3–4-inch
(7.5–10-cm) root cuttings in autumn
or early winter. Transplant self-sown
seedlings to desired position.

Pest and disease prevention No
serious pests or diseases.

Landscape use Plant as a
groundcover under trees or shrubs
with bulbs, wildflowers and ferns.

Cultivars 'Hadspen Cream' has
leaves with creamy white borders.
'Langtrees' has spaced, silver
blotches near the leaf margins.

Caladium bicolor

CLIMATE
Hardy in Zone 10.
Elsewhere, grown
as annuals or
stored indoors
for winter.

HEIGHT AND
SPREAD
1–2 feet
(30–60 cm) tall.
2 feet
(60 cm) wide.

FLOWERING TIME
Late spring until
frost.

CALADIUM

CALADIUM IS GROWN FOR ITS SHOWY
LEAVES. PINCH OFF ANY OF THE SMALL,
HOODED FLOWERS THAT APPEAR IN SUMMER.

Description This shade-loving plant
thrives in heat and humidity. It
produces bushy clumps of, usually,
heart-shaped leaves that are shaded
and veined with combinations of
green, white, pink and red.

Ideal position Partial shade.

Ideal soil conditions Moist but
well-drained soil. Plants will rot in
sodden soil, especially in winter.

Cultivation Start tubers indoors in
early spring. Set them with the
knobby side up in pots of moist
potting mix and cover with 2 inches

(5 cm) of mix. Keep in a warm,
bright spot with moist soil. Move to
the garden when night temperatures
stay above 60°F (16°C). Keep soil
moist until late summer. When
leaves die, dig up the tubers and
store them in a warm place.

Propagation Divide tubers in
spring, after bringing them out
of winter storage.

Pest and disease prevention No
serious pests or diseases.

Landscape use Caladiums provide
summer color in shady beds and
borders, especially in warm- and
hot-summer areas.

CLIMATE
Zones 2–8.

HEIGHT AND
SPREAD
1–2 feet
(30–60 cm) tall.
Up to 2 feet
(60 cm) wide.

FLOWERING TIME
Early to midspring.

OTHER COMMON
NAMES
Cowslip.

MARSH MARIGOLD

MARSH MARIGOLD GROWS IN MOIST SOIL
AND SHALLOW WETLANDS. IT IS THE PERFECT
PLANT FOR WATER GARDENS.

Description Marsh marigold
produces yellow spring flowers over
mounds of rounded leaves from a
thick crown with fleshy, white
roots. Butter-yellow, 1½-inch
(3.5-cm) flowers have five shiny
petals in open clusters.

Ideal position Full sun to partial
shade. Grows even when covered
with 1–4 inches (2.5–10 cm) of
water. Once flowering is complete,
moisture is less critical.

Ideal soil conditions Wet,
humus-rich or loamy soil.

Cultivation Divide overgrown plants
1 month after flowering.

Propagation Divide in summer. Sow
fresh seed outdoors immediately
upon ripening. Plants will not
germinate until the following spring.

Pest and disease prevention No
serious pests or diseases.

Landscape use Plant with primroses,
irises and ferns in bog gardens.

Cultivars 'Flore Pleno' ('Multiplex')
has fully double flowers that last for
1 week or more.

Campanula carpatica

CLIMATE
Zones 3–8.

HEIGHT AND SPREAD
9 inches (22.5 cm) tall and a slightly wider spread.

FLOWERING TIME
Early summer.

OTHER COMMON NAMES
Carpathian bellflower.

CARPATHIAN HAREBELL

ADAPTABLE CARPATHIAN HAREBELL PRODUCES A LIVELY DISPLAY OF FLOWERS AND IS PERFECT FOR BORDER PLANTINGS.

Description Spreads to form tidy mounds of dark green leaves topped with cup-shaped, blue-purple or white flowers.

Ideal position Full sun, light shade in hotter sites.

Ideal soil conditions Well-drained, moist, fertile soil.

Cultivation Mulch with compost during summer. Water in drought.

Propagation Short-lived unless you divide and renew plants every couple of years. Deadhead for an extended bloom period or leave a few flowers on so plant can self-sow. Mulch to keep the roots cool in warm climates.

Pest and disease prevention Exclude snails and slugs with barrier strips of diatomaceous earth, wood ashes or sand. Alternatively, bait them with shallow pans of beer set flush with the soil surface.

Landscape use Set Carpathian harebell in clumps or rows at the front of a shrub or flower border. Or use plants individually in a rock garden or beside a stone patio.

Cultivars 'Alba' displays a show of pure white flowers.

Campanula glomerata

CLIMATE
Zones 3–8.

HEIGHT AND SPREAD
1–3 feet
(30–90 cm) tall.
1 foot
(30 cm) wide.

FLOWERING TIME
Late spring or early summer.

CLUSTERED BELLFLOWER

ROBUST CLUSTERED BELLFLOWER IS THE
PERFECT SHADED-GARDEN, BORDER
AND BED PLANT.

Description Erect, leafy, flowering
stems and hairy, 5-inch (12.5-cm)
oval leaves. It grows from slow-
creeping rhizomes with fibrous
roots and has purple to blue-violet
flowers in tiered clusters.

Ideal position Full sun to partial
shade.

Ideal soil conditions Moist, humus-
rich soil. Tolerates alkaline soil.

Cultivation Cut back flowering
stems after blossoms fade. Divide
overgrown clumps.

Propagation Divide in autumn or
early spring. Sow seed indoors.
Self-sown seedlings will appear.
Take cuttings after flowering.

Pest and disease prevention Exclude
slugs with barrier strips of wood
ashes or sand.

Landscape use Plant with Siberian
iris *Iris sibirica* and leopard's bane
Doronicum spp.

Cultivars 'Crown of Snow' has large
clusters of white flowers.
'Joan Elliot' is a delicate,
floriferous selection with deep
blue-violet flowers.
'Superba' grows to 2½ feet
(75 cm) with violet flowers.

Campanula persicifolia

CLIMATE
Zones 3–8.

HEIGHT AND
SPREAD
1–3 feet
(30–90 cm) tall.
2 feet
(60 cm) wide.

FLOWERING TIME
Summer.

PEACH-LEAVED BELLFLOWER

PEACH-LEAVED BELLFLOWER HAS SHOWY
FLOWERS AND COMBINES WELL WITH
YARROW AND OTHER FINE-TEXTURED PLANTS.

Description Produces mounds of
narrow, 8-inch (20-cm), evergreen
leaves from a fibrous-rooted crown.
Has open, bell-shaped, lavender-
blue flowers. The summer blooms
make long-lasting cut flowers.

Ideal position Full sun to partial
shade. Protect from hot afternoon
sun in warmer zones. Prefers cooler
summer temperatures.

Ideal soil conditions Moist but
well-drained, humus-rich soil.

Cultivation Peach-leaved bellflower
is a tough, easy-care plant that

spreads slowly by sideshoots from
the central crown.

Propagation Take tip cuttings in
early summer. Divide clumps
in early spring.

Pest and disease prevention Exclude
slugs with barrier strips of wood
ashes or sand.

Landscape use Plant in the middle
or rear of borders. Or use them in
drifts as an accent.

Cultivars 'Alba' displays a show of
pure white flowers.
  'Grandiflora' has 2-inch (5-cm),
blue flowers.
  'Telham Beauty' has pale blue
flowers on 3-foot (90-cm) stems.

Canna x generalis

CLIMATE
Usually hardy in
Zones 7–10.
Elsewhere, they
grow as annuals.

HEIGHT AND
SPREAD
2–6 feet
(60–180 cm) tall.
1–2 feet
(30–60 cm) wide.

FLOWERING TIME
Mid- to late
summer.

CANNA

MASS PLANTINGS OF SHOWY, STURDY
CANNA MAKE A DRAMATIC AND EYE-
CATCHING SUMMER BORDER OR BED DISPLAY.

Description Canna grows from thick
rhizomes. It produces tall stems
with large, oval, green or reddish
purple leaves from spring until
frost. Clusters of broad-petaled
flowers up to 5 inches (12.5 cm)
across bloom in shades of pink,
red, orange, yellow and as bicolors.

Ideal position Full sun to partial
shade.

Ideal soil conditions Average to
moist, well-drained, humus-rich soil.

Cultivation Start rhizomes indoors
about 1 month before your last frost
date. Set out 2–3 weeks after the
last frost date. Or plant rhizomes
directly into the garden at that time,
setting them 3–4 inches (7.5–10 cm)
deep and 1–1½ feet (30–45 cm)
apart. Cannas are drought-tolerant,
but mulch and water during dry
spells. Pinch off spent flowers to
prolong blooming.

Propagation Divide clumps in
spring. Divide rhizomes into pieces
about 6 inches (15 cm) long.

Pest and disease prevention No
serious pests or diseases.

Landscape use Use canna alone
in masses or with annuals and
perennials in beds and borders.

Catananche caerulea

CLIMATE
Zones 4–9.

HEIGHT AND SPREAD
1½–2 feet (45–60 cm) tall.
10–12 inches (25–30 cm) wide.

FLOWERING TIME
Summer.

CUPID'S DART

THE STRAWLIKE FLOWERS OF CUPID'S DART LOOK GREAT IN THE SUMMER GARDEN AND DRY EASILY FOR FLOWER ARRANGEMENTS.

Description Cupid's dart produces tufts of narrow, woolly leaves from a fibrous rootstock. Its blue 2-inch (5-cm) flowers resemble asters and are carried singly on wiry stems.

Ideal position Full sun. Heat-tolerant.

Ideal soil conditions Light, well-drained, humus-rich soil. Good drainage for healthy growth.

Cultivation Plants may be short-lived, especially in heavy soil. Divide each year for longevity.

Propagation Divide in autumn. Take 2–3-inch (5–7.5-cm) root cuttings in autumn or winter. Sow seed indoors in early spring. Plants will bloom the first year.

Pest and disease prevention No serious pests or diseases.

Landscape use Use in mass plantings in rock gardens or at the front of a dry, sunny perennial garden. Combine with yarrows and sundrops *Oenothera* spp.

Cultivars 'Blue Giant' is a stout cultivar with dark blue flowers.
'Major' has lavender-blue flowers on 3-foot (90-cm) stems.

Centaurea dealbata

CLIMATE
Zones 3–7.

HEIGHT AND
SPREAD
1½–2½ feet
(45–75 cm) tall.
1½ feet
(45 cm) wide.

FLOWERING TIME
Late spring and
early summer.

OTHER COMMON
NAMES
Persian cornflower.

KNAPWEED

KNAPWEED IS A GREAT COTTAGE GARDEN
PLANT AND IS PERFECT FOR ANY INFORMAL
SETTING AS WELL AS MEADOW PLANTINGS.

Description Knapweed has lobed
leaves with eight to 10 woolly
divisions. The leaves clothe thick,
weakly upright stems over fibrous-
rooted crowns. Fringed, pink
flowers have broad, white centers.
They resemble the annual
bachelor's buttons *Centaurea
cyanus* and are borne one to a
stem. Use the blooms as fresh, cut
flowers or cut them for drying.

Ideal position Full sun.

Ideal soil conditions Moist but
well-drained, humus-rich soil.

Cultivation Remove flower heads as
they fade to promote rebloom. Cut
plants back to remove floppy stems
when flower production wanes.
Divide clumps every 2–3 years to
keep plants vigorous.

Propagation Divide in spring or
autumn. Sow seed outdoors in
autumn or indoors in late winter.

Pest and disease prevention No
serious pests or diseases.

Landscape use Combine knapweeds
with ornamental grasses, orange
coneflowers *Rudbeckia* spp. and
yarrows in informal settings.

Knapweed continued

Dusty miller *Centaurea cineraria*

Cultivars 'Steenbergii' is a long-flowering, compact selection with rose-pink flowers. Zones 4–9.

Other species *C. cineraria*, dusty miller (pictured above). This shrubby plant has beautiful silvery gray, finely cut leaves. It is grown mainly for its foliage and has small, thistle-like, lilac-pink flower heads. It is drought-tolerant and needs fertile, well-drained soil. To propagate, take cuttings, sow seed or divide in spring or autumn. Mix dusty miller with flowers of contrasting colors and foliage textures. Zones 7–10.

C. hypoleuca. This spreading, clump-forming perennial has fragrant pink to red flowers. Flower stems can be up to 2 feet (60 cm) tall and the plant forms a clump up to 1½ feet (45 cm) wide. 'John Coutts' has rosy purple flowers. Zones 5–9

C. macrocephala, globe cornflower. This yellow-flowering species has foliage similar to that of a large dandelion. It grows up to 3 feet (90 cm) tall. Zones 4–9.

C. montana, perennial cornflower. This plant grows to 2½ feet (75 cm) tall with beautiful violet, lacy flowers in early summer. Zones 5–9.

Centranthus ruber

CLIMATE
Zones 4–8.

HEIGHT AND
SPREAD
1–3 feet
(30–90 cm) tall.
2 feet
(60 cm) wide.

FLOWERING TIME
Spring and
summer.

OTHER COMMON
NAMES
Jupiter's beard.

RED VALERIAN

THE STRIKING, BRIGHT RED FLOWERS OF RED
VALERIAN ADD VIBRANT COLOR TO THE
SPRING AND SUMMER BORDER.

Description Red valerian is an
upright perennial with opposite,
gray-green oval leaves. Plants grow
from a fibrous-rooted crown. Small
red flowers are carried in domed,
branched clusters. Rose, pink and
white selections are also available.

Ideal position Full sun. Best in cool-
summer areas. Grows readily in
rock crevices where soil is limited.

Ideal soil conditions Average, sandy
or loamy, neutral or alkaline soil.

Cultivation Plants may become
floppy after blooming. Shear them
back to promote compact growth
and reblooming.

Propagation Sow seed outdoors
in summer. Plants often self-sow
prolifically. To reproduce plants
of a specific color, remove basal
shoots and treat them like cuttings.

Pest and disease prevention No
serious pests or diseases.

Landscape use Perfect for wall and
rock gardens. The red flowers
combine well with the neutral
colors of stone.

Varieties *C. ruber* var. *albus* has
white flowers and var. *coccineus*
has deep red flowers.

Cerastium tomentosum

CLIMATE
Zones 2–7.

HEIGHT AND SPREAD
6–10 inches
(15–25 cm) tall.
1–3 feet
(30–90 cm) wide.

FLOWERING TIME
Late spring and
early summer.

SNOW-IN-SUMMER

SNOW-IN-SUMMER'S PROFUSION OF FLOWERS IS A BRIGHT ADDITION TO THE SPRING GARDEN DISPLAYING LATE BULBS.

Description A low-mounding plant with small, woolly leaves and clusters of white flowers on wiry stems. Snow-white ½–1-inch (12–25-mm) flowers have five deeply notched petals that give the impression of a 10-petaled flower. Plants grow from a dense tangle of fibrous roots.

Ideal position Full sun.

Ideal soil conditions Average, sandy or loamy, well-drained soil.

Cultivation Shear after flowering to promote fresh, compact growth.

Clumps spread easily and may overgrow their position.

Propagation Divide in spring or autumn and replant vigorous portions. Take tip cuttings during early summer or take rooted cuttings in spring.

Pest and disease prevention May suffer from fungal rots. Remove and destroy infected foliage.

Landscape use Use snow-in-summer for cascading over a wall, planting in a rock garden or for edging.

Cultivars 'Silver Carpet' is a compact selection.

Ceratostigma plumbaginoides

CLIMATE
Zones 5–9.

HEIGHT AND
SPREAD
6–12 inches
(15–30 cm) tall.
1–1½ feet
(30–45 cm) wide,
wider with age.

FLOWERING TIME
Mid- to late
summer, often into
autumn.

OTHER COMMON
NAMES
Leadwort.

PLUMBAGO

PLUMBAGO WORKS WELL AS A GROUND-
COVER UNDER FLOWERING SHRUBS OR AT
THE FRONT OF THE PERENNIAL GARDEN.

Description A creeping, semiwoody
perennial with russet stems and
sparse wedge-shaped leaves. Plants
die back to the ground each year.
Deep gentian-blue flowers are
carried in clusters at the tips of
the stems.

Ideal position Full sun to partial
shade. Plants will survive on dry,
sunny banks or under shrubs, but
not in the dense, dry shade of large
trees. Quite heat-tolerant.

Ideal soil conditions Average to
humus-rich, moist well-drained soil.

Cultivation Prune stems back to
the ground in autumn or spring and
prune out winter-damaged stems by
late spring, at which time new
growth emerges. Foliage often turns
orange in autumn.

Propagation Divide in early spring.
Take tip cuttings in early summer.

Pest and disease prevention No
serious pests or diseases.

Landscape use Interplant the
creeping stems with spring- and
autumn-flowering bulbs such as
crocuses, miniature daffodils, spider
lilies *Lycoris* spp. and autumn
crocuses *Colchicum* spp. Plant as
a groundcover in rock walls.

Chelone lyonii

CLIMATE
Zones 3–8.

HEIGHT AND
SPREAD
1–3 feet
(30–90 cm) tall.
1–2 feet
(30–60 cm) wide.

FLOWERING TIME
Late summer into
autumn.

PINK TURTLEHEAD

PINK TURTLEHEAD DIVIDES EASILY AND
MAKES A STRIKING DISPLAY IN A VARIETY
OF PERENNIAL SETTINGS.

Description A bushy perennial with
leafy stems from a stout, fibrous-
rooted crown. The 4–7-inch
(10–17.5-cm) leaves are broadly
ovate with toothed margins. Pink,
inflated, tubular flowers resemble
a turtle's head with jaws open.

Ideal position Full sun to partial
shade. Intolerant of excessive heat.

Ideal soil conditions Evenly moist,
humus-rich soil. Tolerates drier soil.

Cultivation Divide the crowns to
increase vigor and reduce size of
large clumps in more mature plants.

Propagation Divide in spring or
after flowering. Take stem cuttings
in early summer. Remove any
flower buds. Sow seed outdoors in
autumn or indoors in late winter
after stratification. To stratify, mix
seed with moist peat moss or seed-
starting medium in a plastic bag.
Close bag with a twist-tie and
refrigerate for 4–6 weeks. Then sow
mixture as you would normal seed.

Pest and disease prevention No
serious pests or diseases.

Landscape use Combine with asters,
phlox and goldenrods *Solidago* spp.
for late-summer color.

Cimicifuga racemosa

CLIMATE
Zones 3–8.

HEIGHT AND
SPREAD
4–7 feet
(1.2–2.1 m) tall.
3–4 feet
(90–120 cm) wide.

FLOWERING TIME
Early to
midsummer.

OTHER COMMON
NAMES
Black cohosh and
bugbane.

BLACK SNAKEROOT

COMBINE BLACK SNAKEROOT IN THE
WOODLAND GARDEN WITH FERNS, HOSTAS
AND WILDFLOWERS.

Description The wandlike spires of
black snakeroot wave above an
open cluster of large compound
leaves with toothed leaflets. Plants
grow from a stout, fibrous-rooted
crown. The small, ½-inch (12-mm),
creamy white flowers have a dense
whorl of fuzzy stamens (male
reproductive structures) and no
petals. They are carried on tall,
sparsely branched spikes.

Ideal position Full sun to partial
shade. Protect from afternoon sun
in warmer zones. Dense shade may
produce sparse flowers.

Ideal soil conditions Moist,
humus-rich soil.

Cultivation Black snakeroot is an
extremely long-lived perennial.
Young plants take several years
to reach flowering size. Clumps
increase each year and may have
10–15 bloom stalks at maturity.

Propagation Divide clumps in
autumn or spring. Leave at least
one bud per division. Sow fresh
seed outdoors in autumn.

Pest and disease prevention No
serious pests or diseases.

Landscape use Place at the rear
of borders with bold flowers such
as phlox and daylilies.

THREAD-LEAVED COREOPSIS

USE THREAD-LEAVED COREOPSIS IN A MASS
PLANTING WITH SHRUBS OR COMBINE THEM
WITH ORNAMENTAL GRASSES.

Description An airy, rounded plant
with threadlike, three-lobed leaves
and bright, summer, starry flowers
from butter to golden yellow. Plants
grow from a fibrous-rooted crown.

Ideal position Full sun or light
shade. Drought-tolerant.

Ideal soil conditions Average to rich,
moist but well-drained soil.

Cultivation This plant is easy-care,
demanding little attention once
established. Plants eventually die
out at the center. Divide old
clumps. Replant in rich soil.

Propagation Divide in spring or
autumn. Take stem cuttings in
early summer.

Pest and disease prevention No
serious pests or diseases.

Landscape use Perfect for the front
of the border with cranesbills
Geranium spp., yarrows, daylilies
and coneflowers *Rudbeckia* and
Echinacea spp.

Cultivars 'Golden Showers' grows
2 feet (60 cm) tall with golden
yellow flowers.
 'Moonbeam' is a spreading plant
from 1–2 feet (30–60 cm) wide with
pale yellow flowers.

Coreopsis auriculata

CLIMATE
Zones 3–9.

HEIGHT AND
SPREAD
1–3 feet
(30–90 cm) tall.
2–3 feet
(60–90 cm) wide.

FLOWERING TIME
Throughout
summer.

Other species *C. auriculata* (pictured above) is a relatively short-lived perennial with masses of single yellow flowers produced throughout summer. The species grows to around 1½ feet (45 cm); however, its compact cultivar 'Nana' grows to a height of only 6 inches (15 cm) and makes a colorful addition to the front row border, while 'Perry's Variety', with its semidouble flowers, adds extra interest. Zones 3–9.

C. grandiflora has clear, yellow, single flowers topping pale green foliage and is one of the easiest species to grow. A native of the southern and eastern United States, it does well in warmer climates.

There are many choices of cultivars available, including the semidouble 'Early Sunrise' and the tall-growing 'Mayfield Giant', which has flower stems up to 3 feet (90 cm) tall carrying bright yellow single blooms. Zones 6–9.

C. lanceolata is the parent of many cultivars with additional coloring to the blooms, including 'Rotkehlchen', which has brown splashes across yellow flowers, and 'Sternataler', with interesting brown rings. Zones 3–9.

Corydalis flexuosa

CLIMATE
Zones 3–9.

HEIGHT AND
SPREAD
1–3 feet
(30–90 cm) tall.
2–3 feet
(60–90 cm) wide.

FLOWERING TIME
Throughout
summer.

CORYDALIS

CORYDALIS IS IDEAL FOR PROVIDING A SEA
OF VIVID BLUE IN THE SHADE OF EMERGING
SPRING GROWTH IN A WOODLAND GARDEN.

Description Corydalis has a mass of
blue, long-spurred, tubular flowers
that are about 1 inch (2.5 cm) long.
It is the amazing color of these
flowers, set over pale green fern
foliage, that makes corydalis so
popular with gardeners and a
welcome choice as a perennial.

Ideal position Cool, shady, fairly
moist position.

Ideal soil conditions Moist but
well-drained soil.

Cultivation Grow corydalis in
partial shade such as that provided

in a woodland garden where
deciduous trees provide a
continuing supply of humus.
They can be easily naturalized
in moderate climates and they
self-seed freely.

Propagation Either by seed or
by division.

Pest and disease prevention No
serious pests or diseases.

Landscape use Corydalis is perfect
for mass plantings, especially in a
woodland garden.

Cultivars 'Purple Leaf' forms an
8-inch (20-cm) mound with purplish
leaves and dark blue flowers.

Yellow corydalis *Corydalis lutea*

Other species *C. lutea*, yellow corydalis (pictured above). Yellow corydalis is the easiest corydalis to grow and has one of the longest blooming seasons. It is a mound-forming, rhizomatous plant with attractive, soft, bright green foliage. It grows to about 1 foot (30 cm) tall and 1½ feet (45 cm) wide. The lovely foliage is topped with bright yellow flowers from spring through to autumn if growing conditions are to its liking. It will grow happily in walls, between paving stones and in rockeries, and it makes a colorful groundcover. It grows best where drainage is good but can be used in alkaline soils. Zones 6–9.

C. ochroleuca. This white-flowering corydalis prefers partial shade to full sun and dry soil. Zones 5–9.

C. solida, fumewort. This solid-tuberous corydalis has pink to dark purple flowers in spring. It requires full sun. 'George Baker' has rich red flowers. 'Beth Evans' has pretty pale pink flowers. Zones 6–9.

C. wilsonii. This low-growing species has pale, blue-green foliage and yellow flowers in spring. It grows to 8 inches (20 cm) tall and 8 inches (20 cm) wide.

Cyclamen coum

CLIMATE
Zones 5–7.

HEIGHT AND
SPREAD
6 inches
(15 cm) tall.
1½ feet
(45 cm) wide.

FLOWERING TIME
Spring.

CYCLAMEN

CYCLAMEN IS PERFECT AS A GROUNDCOVER
WHEN ITS INTERESTING FOLIAGE CAN BE SEEN
TO BEST ADVANTAGE.

Description A hardy, tuberous
perennial with attractive silver-
marked leaves and early spring
flowers. Colors range from creamy
white to pale and deep pink.

Ideal position Best in partial shade.

Ideal soil conditions Provide good
drainage in moist position with
ample humus added.

Cultivation Plant the tuber at
a depth of about 2 inches (5 cm).
Once the plants have become
established, leave them alone.
A winter mulch is strongly
recommended in zones colder than
Zone 5.

Propagation Best results by planting
fresh seed. Soaking seed for up to
24 hours may help germination,
which can be erratic. Plant into a
moist medium and keep in a warm
position. Keep potting mix moist.

Pest and disease prevention No
serious pests or diseases.

Landscape use An attractive groundcover near dormant trees or shrubs

Cultivars Many cultivars exist with
flowers in white or shades of pink
as well as those in the Pewter-
leaved Group selected for their
foliage colors and markings.

Cyclamen hederifolium

CLIMATE
Zones 5–9.

HEIGHT AND SPREAD
Height and spread of flowers and foliage 4–6 inches (10–15 cm).

FLOWERING TIME
Early autumn.

HARDY CYCLAMEN

HARDY CYCLAMEN IS A GREAT CHOICE FOR COOL, SHADY AREAS AND PARTNERS WELL WITH A VARIETY OF FERNS.

Description A tuberous perennial, which blooms in early autumn. Handsome, heart-shaped, silver-marked, green leaves emerge shortly after the blooms finish. Leafless flower stalks are topped with pink or white nodding flowers that have upward-pointing petals.

Ideal position Partial shade.

Ideal soil conditions Average, well-drained soil.

Cultivation Set plants into the garden in spring or summer, or plant dormant tubers shallowly in summer. Make sure the smooth, unmarked side of the tuber is on the bottom. Top-dress with a thin layer of compost in late summer.

Propagation Divide tubers in summer or grow from seed. Soak the seed overnight, then sow ¼ inch (6 mm) deep in a pot. Enclose the pot in a plastic bag, then place it in a dark place.

Pest and disease prevention No serious pests or diseases.

Landscape use Use hardy cyclamen in shady spots with ferns and hellebores *Helleborus* spp.

Cyclamen persicum

CLIMATE
Zones 8–9.

HEIGHT AND SPREAD
Up to 1 foot (30 cm) tall and wide.

FLOWERING TIME
Winter.

FLORIST'S CYCLAMEN

FLORIST'S CYCLAMEN IS IDEAL TO BRIGHTEN UP AN INDOOR SETTING WITH ITS COLORFUL BLUSH OF EYE-CATCHING BLOOMS.

Description A tuberous perennial herb with thick, slender-stalked, rounded and heart-shaped, finely toothed, variegated leaves. Stems grow to 1 foot (30 cm) and carry fragrant, single, five-parted flowers in pink, rose, white, red and purple.

Ideal position Indoor plant. Humid.

Ideal soil conditions Evenly moist soil. Don't let plant sit in water.

Cultivation Florist's cyclamen is a hobby plant requiring knowledge and experience. It needs a dormant period after flowering. Begin watering and fertilizing when new growth appears.

Propagation Best results gained from fresh seed. Soaking seed for up to 24 hours may help sometimes erratic germination. Plant into moist medium and keep in warm position. Keep potting mix moist.

Pest and disease prevention Root rot is a danger. Don't let sit in water. Cyclamen mites may trouble this plant. Buy only non-infected plants. Wash, apply miticide and isolate.

Landscape use Primarily for indoors.

Cultivars 'Giganteum' has very large flowers. There are many cultivars with a wide range of colors.

Delphinium Elatum Group

CLIMATE
Zones 4–7. Many hybrids are hardy to Zone 3.

HEIGHT AND SPREAD
4½–6 feet (1.35–1.8 m) tall. 2–3 feet (60–90 cm) wide.

FLOWERING TIME
Late spring through summer, depending on the hybrid group. Plants may rebloom in autumn.

HYBRID DELPHINIUMS

HUNDREDS OF HYBRID DELPHINIUMS ARE AVAILABLE AND OFFER A VAST ARRAY OF SHADES TO ADD COLOR AND CONTRAST.

Description Stately border plants with dense flower clusters atop tall stems with deeply cut, palmately lobed leaves. Plants grow from stout crowns with thick, fleshy roots. The showy flowers of the various hybrids range in color from white to all shades of true blue to lavender and into purple. Five petal-like sepals surround two to four small, true petals that are often called the "bee."

Ideal position Full sun. Hybrid delphiniums are particularly sensitive to high night temperatures.

Ideal soil conditions Evenly moist but well-drained, fertile, humus-rich soil. A neutral to slightly acid soil is best. Add ground limestone to raise the pH if necessary.

Cultivation Often short-lived in warm climates. Delphiniums are heavy feeders and benefit from an annual spring topdressing of a balanced organic fertilizer or well-rotted manure. Set out new plants in spring. Mature plants produce many stems. Thin the clumps to three to five stems as they emerge. Cut off old flowering stems below the foliage. New shoots often emerge from the crown. When they develop, cut the old shoots to the

The ruffled flowers of delphiniums are a natural choice for a cottage garden.

ground. Divide overgrown plants and replant into soil enriched with organic matter.

Propagation Divide plants in spring. Sow fresh seed in summer or autumn. Take cuttings in spring from new shoots. Use stems from thinning clumps for propagation.

Pest and disease prevention Exclude slugs with a ring of diatomaceous earth, wood ashes or sand around the clumps. Dust parts affected with powdery mildew with sulfur.

Landscape use Plant at the rear of borders where their showy spires will tower over other summer-blooming perennials such as phlox,

lilies, lupines and bellflowers *Campanula* spp.

Hybrids A few popular selections are listed here. Blackmore and Langdon hybrids are a seed-grown strain of mixed colors. Mid-Century hybrids are mildew-resistant selections. Pacific Hybrids have 1½–2-inch (3.5–5-cm) single or semidouble flowers. 'Astolat' is lavender with a dark center.

Other species *D.* Belladonna Group hybrids are hardy, heat-resistant, compact plants. 'Bellamosum' has deep blue flowers on 4-foot (1.2-m) stalks. 'Clivedon Beauty' has sky blue flowers. All this group of delphiniums are hardy to Zone 3.

Dendranthema x grandiflorum

CLIMATE
Zones 3–9. Vary in hardiness.

HEIGHT AND SPREAD
1½–5 feet (45–150 cm) tall. 1–3 feet (30–90 cm) wide.

FLOWERING TIME
Late summer through autumn.

OTHER COMMON NAMES
Florist's chrysanthemum, hardy chrysanthemum, hardy mum, mum.

GARDEN MUM

GARDEN MUMS IN FLOWER ARE A FAMILIAR SIGHT IN LATE SUMMER AND ARE IDEAL FOR ADDING COLOR TO AN AUTUMN DISPLAY.

Description Hardy garden mums have stout stems clothed in lobed leaves. They grow from creeping stems with tangled fibrous roots and bloom in a wide variety of colors from white to pale pink, rose, burgundy, red, golden brown, gold, yellow and cream. Flower shapes range from button-like heads to pompons (double ball-shaped flowers), cushions (flat, fully double flowers) and decoratives (large double to semidouble heads). There are even novelty hybrids with spider-like heads (pictured on page 190) and those with spoon-shaped petals. Flower sizes range from 1–6 inches (2.5–15 cm).

Ideal position From full sun to light shade.

Ideal soil conditions Light, humus-rich, well-drained soil.

Cultivation Many garden mums tend to sprawl in summer. Pinch the stems once or twice in spring and early summer to promote compact growth. Stop pinching altogether in summer or you will sacrifice bloom. To encourage larger flowers, remove axillary buds (those surrounding the largest main bud). This process, called disbudding,

Garden mum continued

Mixed colors of the spider form

allows the stem to direct its energy into producing one large flower. Garden mums spread outward from the center by creeping stems. Divide the fast-growing clumps every 1–2 years to keep them healthy and vigorous.

Propagation Divide in spring. Tip cuttings taken in late spring or early summer root quickly.

Pest and disease prevention Aphids may attack young shoots. Spider mites may cause stippling and leaf curl. Spray with insecticidal soap or a botanical insecticide.

Landscape use Use to brighten annual displays or mix with asters and anemones for autumn color.

Cultivars The array of garden mums available is astounding. Since they vary in hardiness and bloom time, consult your local garden center for recommendations.

Other species *D.* x 'Mei-kyo' is an old-fashioned hybrid with double rose-pink flowers with yellow centers. Zones 6–9.

D. zawadskii var. *latilobum* is an early-blooming hardy mum with deeply lobed leaves and 2-inch (5-cm), single flowers.

Dianthus plumarius

CLIMATE
Zones 3–9.

HEIGHT AND SPREAD
1½–2 feet
(45–60 cm) tall.
1 foot
(30 cm) wide.

FLOWERING TIME
Early to
midsummer.

COTTAGE PINK

COTTAGE PINK GROWS VERY WELL IN SUNNY ROCK GARDENS OR CASCADING OVER WALLS.

Description Broad, mounded plants with dense clusters of 3-inch (7.5 cm), blue-green, grasslike leaves and fragrant, white or pink flowers in open clusters on wiry stems. *D. plumarius* (pictured above) is the parent of many cultivars.

Ideal position Full sun. Tolerates extreme heat and cold.

Ideal soil conditions Average, well-drained, sandy or loamy soil. Should be neutral or slightly acid for best growth. Can tolerate alkaline soil.

Cultivation Plants may be short-lived, especially in warmer zones. Divide clumps every 2–3 years to keep them vigorous. Remove flowers as they fade to promote continued blooming.

Propagation Layer or take stem cuttings from the foliage rosettes in summer. Strip leaves from the lower third of a 2–3-inch (5–7.5-cm) cutting. Place in a medium of one part vermiculite and two parts sand or perlite to allow excellent drainage and good air circulation.

Pest and disease prevention Rust causes yellow blotches on the upper surface of the leaves and raised orange spots on the lower

Cottage pink continued

Maiden pink *Dianthus deltoides*

surface. To discourage rust, thin clumps for better air circulation and dust with sulfur. Watch for aphids, thrips and caterpillars.

Landscape use Plant at the front of borders or use as an edging along paths.

Cultivars 'Essex Witch' has rose-pink flowers.

'Helen' has lovely, double salmon-pink flowers.

'Mrs Sinkins' has fragrant, double white flowers.

'Spring Beauty' is a seed-grown strain with clove-scented semi-double to double flowers in white, pink, rose and red.

Other species *D. alpinus*, alpine pink. This clump-forming pink has 1½-inch (3.5-cm), single pink flowers. Zones 4–7.

D. barbatus, sweet William. This slow-growing biennial or short-lived perennial forms tufts of deep green, lance-shaped leaves and dense, rounded clusters of 1-inch (2.5-cm) bicolored pink, rose or white flowers. Sweet William self-sows and grows to 1½ feet (45 cm), ideal for massed plantings. Zones 3–9.

D. caryophyllus, wild carnation. This summer-flowering plant has perfumed purple, pink or white flowers. It grows to 2½ feet (75 cm) tall and 9 inches (23 cm) wide. Zones 8–10.

Cheddar pink *Dianthus gratianopolitanus*

D. deltoides, maiden pink (pictured on page 192). A mat-forming pink with a mass of single rose-colored flowers borne one to a stem. Zones 3–9.

D. gratianopolitanus, cheddar pink (pictured above). Cheddar pink bears sweet-scented flowers you'll enjoy outdoors in the garden or indoors as cut flowers. This spring-blooming pink has 1-inch (2.5-cm), fragrant white, rose or pink flowers borne singly or in pairs. It grows well in sunny rock gardens or cascading over walls. As an alternative, combine with other front-of-the-border plants such as sedum, thyme and lamb's ears *Stachys byzantina*. Interplant them with spiky foliage such as yuccas and grasses.

Many varieties and cultivars are available. 'Bath's Pink' has fringed soft-pink flowers. 'Splendens' has deep red flowers. 'Tiny Rubies' has deep pink double flowers.

D. gratianopolitanus var. *grandiflorus* has 1½-inch (3.5-cm) rose-pink flowers. Zones 3–9.

D. superbus, lilac pink. This stunning pink has deeply fringed pink, lavender or white flowers borne in open clusters on wiry stems. Zones 4–8.

Dicentra spectabilis

COMMON BLEEDING HEART

PLANT COMMON BLEEDING HEART WITH
SPRING BULBS, PRIMROSES AND WILDFLOWERS
FOR A STRIKING SPRING DISPLAY.

Description A beloved, traditional
perennial with strings of heart-
shaped flowers held above deeply
divided blue-green foliage. Plants
grow from thick, fleshy roots. Bright
pink, heart-shaped flowers consist
of two reflexed lobes with a central
column that resembles a dangling
drop of blood.

Ideal position Partial shade.
Common bleeding heart tolerates
full sun in cooler zones. Extremely
tolerant of heat and cold. Mulch in
winter in colder zones.

Ideal soil conditions Evenly moist,
humus-rich soil.

Cultivation Common bleeding
hearts will bloom for 4–6 weeks in
spring. In warm climates or if the
soil is dry, plants will become
dormant after blooming. Top-dress
with well-rotted manure in early
spring to maintain soil fertility.
If plants lose their vigor, lift and
divide clumps and replant them into
soil that has been enriched with
organic matter.

Propagation Divide clumps in
autumn or as they go dormant. Sow
fresh seed outdoors in summer.
Take root cuttings in late summer.

Western bleeding heart *Dicentra formosa*

CLIMATE
Zones 2–9.

HEIGHT AND
SPREAD
1–2½ feet
(30–75 cm) tall.
2–3 feet
(60–90 cm) wide.

FLOWERING TIME
Early spring to
early summer.

Pest and disease prevention No serious pests or diseases.

Landscape use In warm zones combine with hostas or groundcovers that will fill the void left by the declining foliage.

Other species *D. eximia,* fringed bleeding heart. Fringed bleeding heart blooms mostly in spring, but flowers can appear at any time during the growing season. The ferny foliage looks great from spring through autumn. Plant in formal and informal gardens, in rockeries or in masses along garden paths. The flowers and foliage of fringed bleeding heart are exquisite and delicate, so place them where they are easy to admire. Zones 3–9.

D. formosa, Western bleeding heart (pictured above). This is a spreading evergreen perennial with pink and red flowers in summer and autumn. It grows to 1–1½ feet (30–45 cm) tall and 1½ feet (45 cm) wide. Likes full sun to shade. 'Alba' has pure white flowers. Zones 3–9.

Dictamnus albus

CLIMATE
Zones 3–8.

HEIGHT AND
SPREAD
1–4 feet
(30–120 cm) tall.
1–3 feet
(30–90 cm) wide.

FLOWERING TIME
Late spring or early
summer.

OTHER COMMON
NAMES
Dittany.

GAS PLANT

GAS PLANTS ARE EXQUISITE AND DELICATE
IN FOLIAGE AND FLOWER, SO PLACE THEM
WHERE THEY ARE EASY TO ADMIRE.

Description Forms shrublike clumps
of stout stems with deep green,
pinnately lobed leaves and erect
flower spikes. Plants grow from
thick, woody crowns with fibrous
roots. The 1-inch (2.5-cm), showy,
white flowers have five starry petals
and 10 long, curled stamens (male
reproductive structures). The seed
capsules are attractive in summer.

Ideal position Likes full sun to
light shade.

Ideal soil conditions Well-drained,
average to humus-rich soil.

Cultivation Gas plants are long-
lived, trouble-free perennials that
are slow to establish and resent
disturbance once planted.

Propagation Sow seed outdoors in
late summer. Seedlings appear next
season but grow slowly. Transplant
to permanent position after 3 years.

Pest and disease prevention No
serious pests. Avoid soggy soils,
which will encourage root rot.

Landscape use Combine with other
perennials that need good drainage,
such as oriental poppy *Papaver
orientale* and yarrow.

Cultivars 'Purpureus' has dark-
veined, violet-purple flowers.

Digitalis x *mertonensis*

CLIMATE
Zones 3–8.

HEIGHT AND SPREAD
3–4 feet
(90–120 cm) tall.
1 foot
(30 cm) wide.

FLOWERING TIME
Plants flower during late spring and summer.

STRAWBERRY FOXGLOVE

STRAWBERRY FOXGLOVE IS A POPULAR, EASY-CARE PERENNIAL THAT BLOOMS TIRELESSLY. PERFECT FOR MASS PLANTINGS.

Description Strawberry foxglove has fuzzy, broad, lance-shaped leaves. Rosettes of foliage form at the base of the flowering stems and persist over winter. The 2–3-inch (5–7.5-cm), tubular flowers are flushed with pink, rose or purple on the outside and spotted with dark purple or brown on the inside. Some selections are pure white.

Ideal position Likes full sun to partial shade.

Ideal soil conditions Moist but well-drained, humus-rich soil.

Cultivation Divide overgrown clumps by removing new rosettes from the bloom stalk and replant into soil that has been enriched with organic matter. Set out new plants in spring for bloom the same season or in autumn for bloom the following year. Remove spent bloom stalks to promote rebloom. Leave one stalk to self-sow.

Propagation Divide in spring or autumn. Sow fresh seed outdoors in autumn. Seedlings emerge the next spring and will bloom in the second year.

Pest and disease prevention No serious pests or diseases.

Strawberry foxglove continued

Common foxglove *Digitalis purpurea*

Landscape use Plant at the middle or rear of perennial gardens. In informal gardens, combine them with ferns and ornamental grasses. Use mass plantings along a wall or fence, or in combination with flowering shrubs.

Other species *D. ferruginea*, rusty foxglove, grows to 4–5 feet (1.2–1.5 m) tall, with narrow spikes of 1-inch (2.5-cm), rusty brown-and-white flowers. Zones 4–7.

D. grandiflora, yellow foxglove, has 2-inch (5-cm) soft yellow flowers on 1–3-foot (30–90-cm) stalks. The lush foliage is also attractive. Zones 3–8.

D. lutea has small, creamy yellow flowers on narrow, 2–3-foot (60–90-cm) spikes. Zones 4–8.

D. purpurea, common foxglove (pictured above), is a biennial or short-lived perennial with 2–5-foot (60–150-cm) spikes of purple, rose, pink or white flowers. *Digitalis purpurea* f. *albiflora* has white flowers that are often lightly spotted brown inside the blooms. Excelsior Hybrids have dense spikes in a variety of colors. Zones 3–8.

Doronicum orientale

CLIMATE
Zones 3–8.

HEIGHT AND
SPREAD
1–2 feet
(30–60 cm) tall.
1 foot
(30 cm) wide.

FLOWERING TIME
Spring and early
summer.

LEOPARD'S BANE

BRIGHTLY COLORED LEOPARD'S BANE IS
AN EASY-CARE DAISY, PERFECT FOR
SPRING FLOWER GARDENS.

Description Has deep green,
triangular leaves in open clusters
from a fibrous-rooted crown.
Dozens of 1–2-inch (2.5–5-cm)
bright yellow, single daisies are
borne on slender, leafless stems.

Ideal position Sun to partial shade.

Ideal soil conditions Moist, humus-
rich soil. Soil should not dry out
while plant is actively growing.

Cultivation Leopard's banes emerge
early in spring and may be
damaged by late frosts. Plants go
dormant after flowering in warmer

zones. In colder zones, the foliage
remains all season, so moist soil is
imperative. Mulch will help keep
the soil cool. Divide clumps every
2–3 years to keep them vigorous.

Propagation Divide in spring or
autumn. Sow seed indoors in late
winter or early spring.

Pest and disease prevention No
serious pests or diseases.

Landscape use Combine with
clustered bellflower *Campanula
glomerata*, Virginia bluebells
Mertensia pulmonarioides, spring
bulbs and wildflowers.

Cultivars 'Magnificum' has showy
2-inch (5-cm) flowers.

CLIMATE
Zones 3–8.
Extremely heat-
tolerant.

**HEIGHT AND
SPREAD**
2–4 feet
(60–120 cm) tall.
1–2 feet
(30–60 cm) wide.

FLOWERING TIME
Mid- to late
summer.

PURPLE CONEFLOWER

PURPLE CONEFLOWERS ARE SHOWY, SUMMER
DAISIES THAT COMBINE WELL WITH MOST
PERENNIALS AND ORNAMENTAL GRASSES.

Description Purple coneflowers
have sparse, 6-inch (15-cm) oval or
broadly lance-shaped leaves on
stout, hairy stems. Plants grow from
thick, deep taproots. Red-violet to
rose-pink flowers have broad,
drooping rays (petal-like structures)
surrounding raised, bristly cones.

Ideal position Full sun. Drought-
tolerant once established.

Ideal soil conditions Average to
humus-rich, moist, well-drained soil.

Cultivation Plants increase
from basal buds to form broad,
long-lived clumps. Division is
seldom necessary and is not
recommended.

Propagation Sow seed outdoors in
autumn or indoors after stratification.
Take root cuttings in autumn.

Pest and disease prevention No
serious pests or diseases.

Landscape use Plant in formal
perennial gardens or meadow and
prairie gardens.

Cultivars 'Alba' has creamy white
daisy flowers.
      'Bright Star' has flat, rose-pink
daisy flowers.
      'Magnus' has huge, flat, rose-
purple daisy flowers.

Epimedium x *versicolor*

CLIMATE
Zones 5–8.

HEIGHT AND
SPREAD
10–12 inches
(25–30 cm) tall.
1 foot
(30 cm) wide.

FLOWERING TIME
Early to midspring.

OTHER COMMON
NAMES
Bicolor barrenwort.

PERSIAN EPIMEDIUM

PERSIAN EPIMEDIUM IS A WOODLAND GROUNDCOVER THAT COMBINES WELL WITH HOSTAS AND FERNS.

Description Has semi-evergreen leaves divided into glossy, heart-shaped leaflets. The wiry, trailing stems have matted, fibrous roots. The unusual flowers have eight yellow, petal-like sepals and four spurred petals that are tinged with red. They are held above the new leaves as they emerge.

Ideal position Partial to full shade. Avoid waterlogged soil, especially during winter.

Ideal soil conditions Moist, humus-rich soil.

Cultivation Persian epimediums thrive for years with little attention. They perform well under adverse conditions, even in the dry shade of mature trees. Mulch plants in winter. Cut foliage to the ground to allow the flowers to emerge freely.

Propagation Divide overgrown clumps in late summer or spring.

Pest and disease prevention No serious pests or diseases.

Landscape use Combine with bulbs, hellebores, ferns and hostas.

Cultivars 'Neosulphureum' has yellow flowers with short spurs.
'Sulphureum' has very pretty, two-toned, yellow flowers.

Eremurus stenophyllus

CLIMATE
Zones 5–9.

HEIGHT AND
SPREAD
2–3 feet
(60–90 cm) tall.
2 feet
(60 cm) wide.

FLOWERING TIME
Spring and
summer.

FOXTAIL LILY

FOXTAIL LILY IS A ROBUST, STATELY
PERENNIAL. ITS ELEGANT FLOWER SPIKES
LOOK STUNNING PLANTED AGAINST A WALL.

Description These perennials have
tall flower spikes and clumps of
straplike foliage. Plants grow from
a thickened crown with brittle,
spreading roots. Starry, 1-inch
(2.5-cm), six-petaled flowers are
crowded on tall, pointed spikes.

Ideal position Full sun to light
shade. Avoid positions with soggy
soil, which promotes root rot.

Ideal soil conditions Moist but
well-drained, humus-rich soil.

Cultivation Plant crowns 4–6 inches
(10–15 cm) deep. Don't allow them

to dry out. Mulch to protect from
late frosts. Divide clumps if they
become crowded or bloom wanes.

Propagation Divide in autumn. Sow
fresh seed outdoors in autumn or
indoors after stratification.

Pest and disease prevention No
serious pests or diseases.

Landscape use Plant among
perennials or against a wall or a
hedge. Surround with bold poppies
Papaver spp., daylilies *Hemerocallis*
spp. and irises.

Cultivars Shelford Hybrids is
a hybrid group with 5–6-foot
(1.5–1.8-m) spikes of white, yellow
or pink flowers.

Erigeron glaucus

CLIMATE
Zones 3–9.

HEIGHT AND
SPREAD
10 inches
(25 cm) tall.
8 inches
(20 cm) wide.

FLOWERING TIME
Spring through
summer.

OTHER COMMON
NAMES
Beach aster.

SEASIDE DAISY

AS THE NAME SUGGESTS, SEASIDE DAISY
MAKES A GOOD GROUNDCOVER IN SEASIDE
AREAS. IT'S ALSO GREAT IN ROCK GARDENS.

Description Low-growing, clump-forming plant. It forms a dense mat of gray-green foliage topped by pale lilac daisy flowers with yellow centers typical of the daisy family, in spring though summer.

Ideal position Full sun.

Ideal soil conditions Sandy, well-drained soil.

Cultivation Seaside daisy is hardy and will thrive with little water. Space plants 8–10 inches (20–25 cm) apart when planting. Cut back after flowering to encourage compact growth and discourage self-seeding.

Propagation Sow seed or divide mature plants in spring.

Pest and disease prevention No serious pests or diseases.

Landscape use Plant in rock gardens or on dry banks.

Cultivars 'Alba' has white flowers.
    'Elstead Pink' has lovely dark pink flowers.
    'Roseus' has pink flowers.

Erigeron karvinskianus

CLIMATE
Zones 6–10.

HEIGHT AND SPREAD
6–10 inches (15–25 cm) tall, with an indefinite spread.

FLOWERING TIME
Spring until late summer.

FLEABANE

FLEABANE CAN BE INVASIVE. IT RESEEDS HEAVILY. IT WILL TOLERATE DROUGHT BUT LOOKS BETTER WITH OCCASIONAL WATERING.

Description Fleabane bears many tiny, dainty, daisy-type flowers. In warm climates they flower all year round. Masses of small, 1-inch (2.5-cm), daisy-type flowers with yellow centers open white, then age to shades of pink and purple.

Ideal position Full sun.

Ideal soil conditions Moderately fertile, well-drained, dry soil.

Cultivation Fleabane is hardy and will thrive with little water. Space plants 8–10 inches (20–25 cm) apart when planting. Cut back after flowering to encourage compact growth and also to discourage self-seeding.

Propagation Sow seed or divide mature plants in spring.

Pest and disease prevention No serious pests or diseases.

Landscape use Plant in rock gardens or on dry banks.

Erigeron speciosus

CLIMATE
Zones 2–9.

HEIGHT AND
SPREAD
1½–2½ feet
(45–75 cm) tall.
1–2 feet
(30–60 cm) wide.

FLOWERING TIME
Early to
midsummer, with
the occasional
rebloom.

DAISY FLEABANE

DAISY FLEABANE IS LOVELY WITH LOW
GRASSES IN DRY MEADOWS. THE BLOOMS
MAKE LONG-LASTING CUT FLOWERS.

Description Has leafy clumps of
hairy, 6-inch (15-cm), lance-shaped
leaves that spring from fibrous-
rooted crowns. The 1½-inch
(3.5-cm) aster-like flowers of daisy
fleabane have white, pink, rose or
purple rays surrounding bright
yellow centers.

Ideal position Full sun to light
shade. Tolerant of heat and cold.

Ideal soil conditions Moist but well-
drained, average to humus-rich soil.

Cultivation Fleabanes are long-lived
perennials. Divide every 2–3 years.

Propagation Divide in autumn.
Take cuttings in spring before buds
form. Sow seed outdoors in autumn
or indoors in spring.

Pest and disease prevention No
serious pests or diseases.

Landscape use Plant at the front of
borders with summer-blooming
perennials such as cranesbills
Geranium spp., cinquefoils
Potentilla spp. and phlox.

Hybrids Many cultivars are from
crosses with *E. speciosus*.
    'Azure Fairy' has semidouble,
lavender-blue flowers.
    'Foerster's Darling' has reddish
pink flowers.

Eryngium giganteum

CLIMATE
Zones 2–8.

HEIGHT AND SPREAD
3–4 feet
(90–120 cm) tall.
1–2½ feet
(30–75 cm) wide.

FLOWERING TIME
Summer.

OTHER COMMON NAMES
Miss Willmott's Ghost

SEA HOLLY

THE ROUNDED FLOWER CLUSTERS AND SILVERY GREEN BRACTS OF SEA HOLLY ADD EXCITEMENT TO ANY PERENNIAL PLANTING.

Description Sea holly is an architectural plant with stiff flowering stems and mostly basal, pinnately divided leaves. Plants grow from thick taproots. Small, steel-blue, globose flower heads are surrounded by prickly bracts.

Ideal position Full sun. Extremely drought-tolerant once established.

Ideal soil conditions Average, well-drained soil.

Cultivation Set plants in permanent location while young. Older plants resent disturbance.

Propagation Sow fresh seed outdoors in autumn or indoors after stratification. Sow the mixture as you would normal seed.

Pest and disease prevention No serious pests or diseases.

Landscape use Plant in the middle of borders with goldenrods *Solidago* spp., asters, phlox and ornamental grasses.

Other species *E. alpinum*, alpine sea holly, is similar but has larger, showier flowers and lobed leaves. Zones 3–8.

E. x *zabelii*, zabel eryngo, is a showy hybrid with large, blue-violet flowers. Zones 4–8.

Eupatorium maculatum

CLIMATE
Zones 2–8.

HEIGHT AND
SPREAD
4–6 feet
(1.2–1.8 m) tall.
3–4 feet
(90–120 cm) wide.

FLOWERING TIME
Mid- to late
summer.

SPOTTED JOE-PYE WEED

SPOTTED JOE-PYE WEED IS A TALL, STATELY
PERENNIAL THAT'S PERFECT FOR MOIST
BORDERS AND MEADOW PLANTINGS.

Description The showy terminal
flower clusters of spotted Joe-Pye
weed are domed to rounded and
consist of hundreds of small, fuzzy,
rose-purple flowers.

Ideal position Full sun or
light shade.

Ideal soil conditions Moist,
humus-rich soil.

Cultivation Plants take 2–3 years to
mature, so leave ample room when
planting small transplants.

Propagation Divide plants in early
spring or autumn, or take stem
cuttings in early summer.

Pest and disease prevention
Leafminers may cause large, pale
patches on the leaves; remove and
destroy the affected foliage.

Landscape use Choose spotted Joe-
Pye weeds for the middle or back
of the border for a bold accent.
Plant them as a screen with
ornamental grasses. Combine with
tall perennials, such as asters, rose
mallow *Hibiscus* spp., ironweed
Vernonia spp., goldenrods *Solidago*
spp. and grasses.

Euphorbia amygdaloides

CLIMATE
Zones 3–7.

HEIGHT AND SPREAD
3–3½ feet
(90–105 cm) tall.
3–3½ feet
(90–105 cm) wide.

FLOWERING TIME
Spring to summer.

WOOD SPURGE

WOOD SPURGE IS A DELIGHTFUL SPRING-FLOWERING SUCCULENT PERENNIAL. USE IT WHEREVER YOU WANT SPRING COLOR.

Description An erect perennial with dark green leaves. It grows from fleshy, fibrous roots. Grown for its flowers, which are surrounded by prominent, yellowish green bracts.

Ideal position Full sun or part shade.

Ideal soil conditions Moist, well-drained soil.

Cultivation Wood spurge is an easy-care plant. Divide when necessary.

Propagation Take cuttings or divide in spring or summer. Sow seed in autumn or spring.

Pest and disease prevention No serious pests or diseases.

Landscape use Plant at the front of the border, in a sunny rock garden or in a rock wall. Combine with tall, spring-flowering perennials.

Cultivars 'Rubra' (pictured above) has a more bushy habit with stems and foliage, which are often purplish, offset against bright green bracts.

'Variegata' has very pretty, yellow-edged leaves.

Varieties *E. amygdaloides* var. *robbiae* has dark green leaves held in distinctive rosettes on the non-flowering stems. It grows to 2 feet (60 cm) high.

Euphorbia myrsinites

CLIMATE
Zones 5–9.

HEIGHT AND SPREAD
6–10 inches
(15–25 cm) tall.
1–2 feet
(30–60 cm) wide.

FLOWERING TIME
Spring.

MYRTLE EUPHORBIA

PLANT MYRTLE EUPHORBIA IN A SUNNY ROCK GARDEN, IN A ROCK WALL OR AT THE FRONT OF BORDERS.

Description Myrtle euphorbia is a creeping plant with thick stems and succulent, blue-gray, wedge-shaped leaves. It grows from fleshy, fibrous roots and is a striking addition to the spring garden. Unusual flower heads have tiny, yellow flowers surrounded by showy, funnel-shaped, yellow bracts.

Ideal position Full sun to light shade.

Ideal soil conditions Average to humus-rich, well-drained soil. Plants will grow in poor, gravelly soils.

Cultivation Myrtle euphorbias are long-lived, easy-care perennials. They thrive on neglect. Divide the clumps when necessary.

Propagation Take stem cuttings after flowering in spring. Place the cuttings in a well-drained medium after sealing cut ends in lukewarm water. Divide mature plants in spring or autumn. Sow seed outdoors in autumn or spring, or indoors in early spring.

Pest and disease prevention No serious pests or diseases.

Landscape use Combine with rock cresses *Arabis* and *Aubrieta* spp., phlox and bulbs.

Euphorbia polychroma

CLIMATE
Zones 3–8.

HEIGHT AND SPREAD
6–10 inches
(15–25 cm) tall.
1–2 feet
(30–60 cm) wide.

FLOWERING TIME
Spring.

CUSHION SPURGE

CUSHION SPURGE BLOOMS AT THE SAME TIME AS TULIPS, SO YOU CAN CREATE MANY STRIKING COLOR COMBINATIONS.

Description The plants are long-lived garden residents that need little care. The unusual flower heads consist of tiny, yellow flowers surrounded by showy, funnel-shaped, yellow bracts.

Ideal position Full sun or light shade.

Ideal soil conditions Average to rich, well-drained soil. Plants will grow in poor, gravelly soil.

Cultivation Divide the congested clumps of cushion spurge if they overgrow their position.

Propagation Take stem cuttings in summer. Quickly place the cuttings in a well-drained medium, after sealing cut ends in lukewarm water.

Pest and disease prevention No serious pests or diseases.

Landscape use Plant at the front of the border, in a sunny rock garden or in a rock wall. Combine with early-blooming perennials such as columbines *Aquilegia* spp., rock cress *Arabis* and *Aubrieta* spp., creeping phlox *Phlox stolonifera* and daisy fleabane *Erigeron speciosus*. For striking color, use them with bulbs such as ornamental onions *Allium* spp., fritillaries *Fritillaria* spp. and daffodils.

Filipendula rubra

CLIMATE
Zones 3–9.

HEIGHT AND SPREAD
4–6 feet
(1.2–1.8 m) tall.
2–4 feet
(60–120 cm) wide.

FLOWERING TIME
Late spring and early summer.

QUEEN-OF-THE-PRAIRIE

MATURE CLUMPS OF QUEEN-OF-THE-PRAIRIE MAKE AN ARRESTING DISPLAY IN BLOOM. COMBINE THEM WITH DAYLILIES AND PHLOX.

Description Queen-of-the-prairie is a towering perennial with huge flower heads on stout, leafy stalks. The showy, 1-foot (30-cm) leaves are deeply lobed and starlike. Plants grow from creeping stems. Small, five-petaled, pink flowers are crowded into large heads that resemble cotton candy.

Ideal position Full sun to light shade. Plants will not tolerate prolonged dryness.

Ideal soil conditions Evenly moist, humus-rich soil.

Cultivation If leaves become tattered after bloom, cut plants to the ground; new leaves will emerge. Plants spread quickly in moist soil. Divide every 3–4 years to keep them from taking over.

Propagation Lift clumps in spring or autumn, or dig crowns from the edge. Sow seed indoors in spring.

Pest and disease prevention No serious pests or diseases.

Landscape use Plant queen-of-the-prairie at the rear of borders or use them beside ponds with ferns.

Cultivars 'Venusta' has deep rose-pink flowers, but seed-grown plants may vary in color.

Gaillardia x *grandiflora*

CLIMATE
Zones 4–9.

HEIGHT AND
SPREAD
2–3 feet
(60–90 cm) tall.
2 feet
(60 cm) wide.

FLOWERING TIME
Throughout
summer.

BLANKET FLOWER

GIVE BLANKET FLOWER A SUNNY, WELL-
DRAINED SPOT, AND IT WILL BEAR DAZZLING
ORANGE-AND-YELLOW BLOOMS ALL SUMMER.

Description The blooms are held
on loose stems with hairy, lobed
leaves. Plants grow from fibrous-
rooted crowns and may be short-
lived. Ragged yellow-and-orange,
daisy-like flowers have single or
double rows of toothed, petal-like
rays surrounding a yellow center.

Ideal position Full sun.

Ideal soil conditions Average to
poor, well-drained soil. Rich, moist
soil causes overgrowth and flopping.

Cultivation Blanket flowers are
drought-tolerant and thrive in
seaside conditions. Divide every
2–3 years to keep them vigorous.

Propagation Divide in early spring.
Sow seed outdoors in autumn or
indoors in spring after stratification.
Seedlings often bloom the first year.

Pest and disease prevention No
serious pests or diseases.

Landscape use Use for rock gardens,
borders or seaside gardens.

Cultivars 'Baby Cole' is a dwarf
8-inch (20-cm) selection with
orange-centered, yellow flowers.
    'Bremen' has copper-red,
yellow-tipped flowers.
    'Kobold' (pictured above) has
red-and-yellow flowers.

Gaura lindheimeri

CLIMATE
Zones 5–9.

HEIGHT AND SPREAD
3–4 feet
(90–120 cm) tall.
3 feet
(90 cm) wide.

FLOWERING TIME
Throughout summer.

WHITE GAURA

WHITE GAURA IS PERFECT FOR INFORMAL GARDENS. ITS FLOWER CLUSTERS LOOK LIKE A SWIRL OF DANCING BUTTERFLIES.

Description A shrubby perennial with airy flower clusters on wiry stems and small, hairy leaves. It grows from a thick, deep taproot. Unusual white flowers, tinged with pink, have four triangular petals and long, curled stamens (male reproductive structures) on spikes.

Ideal position Full sun. Extremely heat-tolerant.

Ideal soil conditions Moist, well-drained, average to rich soil.

Cultivation White gaura is an easy-care perennial that thrives for years with little attention. Plants bloom non-stop all summer despite high heat and humidity. Remove old bloom stalks to make way for the new ones.

Propagation Sow seed outdoors in spring or autumn. Self-sown seedlings are likely to appear.

Pest and disease prevention No serious pests or diseases.

Landscape use Combine them with low-mounding perennials such as verbenas *Verbena* spp., cranesbills *Geranium* spp. and sedums. In late summer they are beautiful with tawny ornamental grasses.

Gentiana asclepiadea

CLIMATE
Zones 5–7.

HEIGHT AND SPREAD
1½–2 feet
(45–60 cm) tall.
2–3 feet
(60–90 cm) wide.

FLOWERING TIME
Late summer and autumn.

WILLOW GENTIAN

CHOOSE WILLOW GENTIAN TO PLANT IN BORDERS OR USE WITH FERNS AND WILDFLOWERS IN THE WILD GARDEN.

Description Willow gentian is a late-blooming perennial with leafy, arching stems that grow from a crown with thick, fleshy roots. The lance-shaped, opposite leaves have prominent veins. Deep blue flowers are carried in pairs along the arching stems. Each one is tubular, with five flaring, starry lobes.

Ideal position Full sun to partial shade. Provide willow gentian with shade from hot afternoon sun to avoid leaf browning, especially in the warmer zones.

Ideal soil conditions Evenly moist, humus-rich soil.

Cultivation Gentians are long-lived perennials that thrive with little care. Plants seldom need division and dislike root disturbance.

Propagation Divide carefully in spring. Sow fresh seed outside in late autumn or indoors in late winter after stratification.

Pest and disease prevention No serious pests or diseases.

Landscape use Combine them with asters, goldenrods *Solidago* spp. and other autumn-blooming plants.

Geranium endressii

CLIMATE
Zones 4–8.

HEIGHT AND
SPREAD
1–1½ feet
(30–45 cm) tall.
1½ feet
(45 cm) wide.

FLOWERING TIME
Early to
midsummer.

OTHER COMMON
NAMES
Pyrenean
cranesbill,
Endres cranesbill.

CRANESBILL

CRANESBILL IS PERFECT PLANTED AT THE FRONT OF BORDERS TO TIE PLANTINGS TOGETHER OR AS AN EDGING ALONG WALKS.

Description A mounding plant with deeply cut, five-lobed leaves arising from a slow-creeping, fibrous-rooted crown. Pink flowers appear from early to midsummer. Soft pink saucer-shaped, five-petaled flowers are carried in sparse clusters.

Ideal position Full sun to partial shade. Protect from hot afternoon sun in warmer zones.

Ideal soil conditions Evenly moist, humus-rich soil.

Cultivation Heat slows blooming. In cooler zones, plants may bloom all summer. Divide crowded plants and replant into enriched soil.

Propagation Divide in autumn or spring. Sow seed outdoors in autumn or indoors in spring. Take stem cuttings in summer.

Pest and disease prevention No serious pests or diseases.

Landscape use Use with ferns and wildflowers in the wild garden.

Other species *G. argenteum* (pictured on page 216) is an alpine perennial with a silver sheen to the leaves. It has sparse, purple flowers. Zones 5–8.

G. cinereum, gray-leaved cranesbill, is a low, spreading plant

Cranesbill geranium *Geranium argenteum* cultivar

with small, deeply incised leaves and saucer-shaped, pink flowers veined with violet. They are best suited to the rock garden. 'Ballerina' (pictured on page 217) is a cultivar with lilac-pink flowers with striking veins and purple eyes. 'Splendens' has pink flowers with dark eyes. Zones 4 (with protection) or 5–8.

G. clarkei, Clark's geranium, is a floriferous species with white, pink or lilac dark-veined flowers. The rounded leaves are deeply divided. 'Kashmir Purple' has purple-blue flowers. 'Album' has white flowers. Zones 4–8.

G. dalmaticum, Dalmatian cranesbill, is a low, rounded plant with small, curly, lobed leaves and 1-inch (2.5-cm) mauve flowers. Plants spread rapidly by creeping stems. The variety 'Album' has white flowers. 'Biokovo' is a cultivar with pale pink flowers. Zones 4–8.

G. himalayense, lilac cranesbill, is a mounding plant with deeply incised leaves and 2-inch (5-cm) violet-blue flowers. 'Gravetye' is a compact grower with violet-centered, blue flowers. Zones 4–8.

G. ibericum, Caucasus cranesbill, is a robust plant with large seven-to nine-lobed leaves and 2-inch (5-cm) purple-blue flowers on stout stems. Zones 3–8.

G. macrorrhizum, bigroot cranesbill, is fast spreading with fragrant, seven-lobed leaves and

Gray-leaved cranesbill *Geranium cinereum* 'Ballerina'

bright pink flowers. 'Album' has white flowers with pink sepals. 'Ingwersen's Variety' has light pink flowers and glossy leaves. Zones 3–8.

G. maculatum, wild cranesbill, is a woodland plant with five-lobed leaves and tall, sparsely flowering stalks of clear-pink or white flowers. Zones 4–8.

G. x *oxonianum* 'A.T. Johnson' has dozens of silvery pink flowers. 'Claridge Druce' has lilac-pink flowers. 'Wargrave Pink' has pure pink flowers. Zones 4–8.

G. pratense, meadow cranesbill, has deeply incised leaves and 1½-inch (3.5-cm) purple flowers with red veins. 'Mrs. Kendall Clarke' has lilac-blue flowers. Zones 3–8.

G. sanguineum, blood red cranesbill, is a low, wide-spreading plant with deeply cut, starry leaves and flat, magenta flowers held just above the foliage. 'Shepherd's Warning' is low growing with deep rose-pink flowers. *G. sanguineum* var. *Striatum* (also sold as *G. s.* 'Lancastriense') is prostrate with pale pink, rose-veined flowers. Zones 3–8.

G. sylvaticum, wood cranesbill, is an early-spring bloomer with lobed leaves and pink or white flowers. Zones 3–8.

Gypsophila paniculata

CLIMATE
Zones 3–9.

HEIGHT AND
SPREAD
3–4 feet
(90–120 cm) tall.
2–3 feet
(60–90 cm) wide.

FLOWERING TIME
Summer.

BABY'S BREATH

BABY'S BREATH LOOKS GREAT WITH
PERENNIALS THAT HAVE SPIKY LEAVES OR
FLOWERS, SUCH AS FOXGLOVES AND YUCCAS.

Description Baby's breath is an
old-fashioned perennial with sparse,
smooth, blue-green foliage. The
stems and basal leaves grow from
a thick, deep taproot. Small, single
or double white flowers are carried
in large, domed, airy clusters.

Ideal position Full sun to light
shade. Heat- and cold-tolerant.

Ideal soil conditions Near-neutral to
alkaline, moist, humus-rich soil.

Cultivation Set out in spring. Don't
disturb the crowns once the plants
are established. Good drainage is
essential for longevity. Tall cultivars
may need support.

Propagation Take cuttings in
summer. Sow seed outdoors
during spring or autumn or
indoors during spring.

Pest and disease prevention No
serious pests or diseases.

Landscape use Use the airy sprays
to hide the yellowing foliage of
bulbs and perennials such as
oriental poppy *Papaver orientale*
that go dormant in summer.

Cultivars 'Bristol Fairy' has double
flowers on compact plants.
   'Pink Fairy' has beautiful,
double, pink flowers.

Helenium autumnale

CLIMATE
Zones 3–8.

HEIGHT AND
SPREAD
3–5 feet
(90–150 cm) tall.
2–3 feet
(60–90 cm) wide.

FLOWERING TIME
Late summer and
autumn.

COMMON SNEEZEWEED

PLANT COMMON SNEEZEWEED WITH OTHER
LATE-SUMMER PERENNIALS AT THE MIDDLE OR
REAR OF THE BORDER OR IN MASS PLANTINGS.

Description A showy, late-season
perennial with tall, leafy stems that
spring from a fibrous-rooted crown.
The hairy, lance-shaped leaves are
edged with a few large teeth. The
2-inch (5-cm), yellow, daisy-like
flowers have broad, petal-like rays.

Ideal position Full sun or light shade.

Ideal soil conditions Evenly moist,
humus-rich soil. Tolerates wet soil.

Cultivation Either stake or pinch
the stem tips in early summer to
promote compact growth. Divide
clumps every 3–4 years.

Propagation Divide in spring or
autumn. Take stem cuttings in early
summer. Sow seed of the species
outdoors in spring or autumn.

Pest and disease prevention No
serious pests or diseases.

Landscape use Common
sneezeweed offers late-season
color. Combine it with asters,
goldenrods *Solidago* spp. and
garden phlox *Phlox paniculata*.

Cultivars 'Butterpat' has bright
yellow flowers.
'Riverton Beauty' has stunning,
golden-yellow flowers with
bronze-red centers.

Helianthus decapetalus

CLIMATE
Zones 4–8.

HEIGHT AND SPREAD
4–5 feet
(1.2–1.5 m) tall.
2–3 feet
(60–90 cm) wide.

FLOWERING TIME
Mid- to late summer.

THIN-LEAVED SUNFLOWER

THIN-LEAVED SUNFLOWER ADDS BOLD SPLASHES OF COLOR TO THE SUMMER-FLOWERING PERENNIAL GARDEN.

Description Stout stems clothed in wide, 8-inch (20-cm), wedge-shaped leaves. Plants grow from stout, fibrous-rooted crowns. The 2–3-inch (5–7.5-cm) daisy-like flowers have bright yellow, petal-like rays and yellow centers.

Ideal position Full sun.

Ideal soil conditions Moist, average to humus-rich soil. Plants will tolerate wet soil.

Cultivation Thin-leaved sunflowers are easy to grow but need room to spread. Divide them every 3–4 years. The stems are usually self-supporting, except when plants are grown in partial shade.

Propagation Divide in autumn. Take stem cuttings in early summer or sow seed outdoors in autumn.

Pest and disease prevention No serious pests or diseases.

Landscape use Combine with garden phlox *Phlox paniculata*, asters, goldenrods *Solidago* spp., sedums and ornamental grasses.

Other species *H.* x *multiflorus*, perennial sunflower, is a hybrid from *H. decapetalus* and the annual, *H. annuus*. Many double cultivars exist, including 'Loddon Gold'.

Heliopsis helianthoides

CLIMATE
Zones 3–9.

HEIGHT AND SPREAD
3–6 feet
(90–180 cm) tall.
2–4 feet
(60–120 cm) wide.

FLOWERING TIME
Early to
midsummer.

SUNFLOWER HELIOPSIS

A BRIGHT, SUMMER DAISY, SUNFLOWER HELIOPSIS COMBINES WELL WITH SUMMER PERENNIALS AND ORNAMENTAL GRASSES.

Description Has 5-inch (12.5-cm) triangular leaves covering a tall, bushy plant that grows from a fibrous-rooted crown. The golden yellow, 2–3-inch (5–7.5-cm) flowers have broad, petal-like rays and yellow centers that brown with age.

Ideal position Full sun to light shade.

Ideal soil conditions Average to humus-rich, moist, well-drained soil.

Cultivation In rich soils, these plants spread quickly. Divide them every 2–3 years. May need staking.

Propagation Divide in spring or autumn. Take stem cuttings in late spring or early summer. Sow seed outdoors in autumn or spring.

Pest and disease prevention No serious pests or diseases.

Landscape use Plant with garden phlox *Phlox paniculata*, gayfeathers *Liatris* spp. and asters.

Cultivars 'Golden Plume' has double flowers on compact 3–3½-foot (90–105-cm) plants.
'Karat' has 3-inch (7.5-cm) single flowers on 4-foot (1.2-m) stems.
'Summer Sun' has lovely, 4-inch (10-cm) flowers on 2–3-foot (60–90-cm) stems.

Helleborus niger

CLIMATE
Zones 3–8.

**HEIGHT AND
SPREAD**
1–1½ feet
(30–45 cm) tall.
1–2 feet
(30–60 cm) wide.

FLOWERING TIME
Early winter
through spring.

CHRISTMAS ROSE

CHRISTMAS ROSE'S LOVELY FOLIAGE IS
ATTRACTIVE ALL SEASON. USE THIS PERENNIAL
IN SHADE GARDENS OR IN SPRING BORDERS.

Description Has deeply lobed,
leathery leaves growing from a stout
crown with fleshy roots. The
flowers open white and turn pink
with age. They have five petal-like
sepals surrounded by leafy bracts.

Ideal position Light to partial shade.
Established plants tolerate dry soil
and deep shade.

Ideal soil conditions Evenly moist,
humus-rich soil.

Cultivation In spring, remove any
damaged leaves from the plant.
Plants take 2–3 years to become

established and resent disturbance.
Divide only to propagate.

Propagation Lift the clumps after
flowering in spring and separate
the crowns. Replant the divisions
immediately. Sow seed outdoors
in spring or early summer.

Pest and disease prevention No
serious pests or diseases.

Landscape use Combine with early-
spring bulbs, wildflowers and ferns.

Other species *H. argutifolius*,
Corsican hellebore, has green
flowers. Zones 6–8.
    H. orientalis, lenten rose, is
similar to *H. niger* but has pink, red
or white flowers. Zones 4–9.

Hemerocallis Hybrids

CLIMATE
Zones 3–9 for
most hybrids.

**HEIGHT AND
SPREAD**
1–5 feet
(30–150 cm) tall.
2–3 feet
(60–90 cm) wide.
There are miniature
and standard sizes
as well as extremely
tall kinds.

FLOWERING TIME
Late spring through
summer.

DAYLILY

STUNNING DAYLILY HYBRIDS ARE AMONG
THE MOST POPULAR PERENNIALS—THEY
ARE LONG-LIVED, EASY-CARE PLANTS.

Description Each flower only lasts
a day but a profusion of new buds
keeps the plants in bloom for
1 month or more. Daylily flowers
vary in color and form. The majority
of the wild species are orange or
yellow with wide petals and
narrow, petal-like sepals. Modern
hybrids come in many colors.

Ideal position Full sun to light
shade. Most modern hybrids need
at least 8 hours of direct sun to
flower well. Some of the older
selections and the species will
bloom in partial shade.

Ideal soil conditions Evenly moist,
average to humus-rich soil.

Cultivation Plant container-grown
or bareroot plants in spring or
autumn. Place the crowns just
below the soil surface. Plants take
a year to become established and
then spread quickly to form dense
clumps. Most hybrids and species
can remain in place for many years
without disturbance. Some have so
many bloom stalks that the flowers
crowd together and lose their
beauty—divide these every 3 years.
Deadhead regularly to keep them
looking their best. The foliage of
most daylilies remains nice all
season. If leaves are yellow, grasp

Daylily continued

Thousands of daylily cultivars are available in a dizzying range of colors.

them firmly and give them a quick tug to remove them from the base.

Propagation Hybrids are propagated by division only in autumn or spring. Seed-grown plants are often inferior to the parent plant.

Pest and disease prevention Aphids and thrips may attack foliage and flower buds. Wash off aphids with a stream of water or spray them with insecticidal soap. Thrips make small white lines in the foliage and may deform flower buds if damage is severe. Spray with insecticidal soap or a botanical insecticide such as pyrethrin. Deter slugs and snails with shallow pans of beer set flush with the soil surface.

Landscape use Perfect for mass plantings. Combine with summer-blooming perennials and grasses.

Cultivars Thousands of cultivars are available in a full range of colors. Buy plants after you see them in flower to make sure they are the size and color you want. A few old favorites are listed below.

'Catherine Woodbery' is shell-pink with a yellow throat.

'Chicago Royal' is purple with a green throat.

'Hyperion' has very pretty, fragrant, yellow flowers.

'Ice Carnival' is nearly white.

'Mary Todd' has delightful, fluffy, yellow flowers.

Heuchera sanguinea

CLIMATE
Zones 3–8.

HEIGHT AND
SPREAD
1–2½ feet
(30–75 cm) tall.
1–2 feet
(30–60 cm) wide.

FLOWERING TIME
Late spring through
summer.

CORAL BELLS

THE AIRY BLOOMS OF CORAL BELLS DANCE IN THE WIND OVER ROUNDED LEAVES. THEY ARE GREAT FOR THE WOODLAND GARDEN.

Description Forms neat clumps of scalloped leaves. The small, fringed, nodding flowers are carried in slender, branching clusters. The flower colors range from white through shades of pink and red.

Ideal position Full sun or partial shade. In warmer zones, provide protection from hot afternoon sun.

Ideal soil conditions Moist but well-drained, humus-rich soil.

Cultivation Remove old flower stalks to promote reblooming. As plants grow, they rise above the soil on woody crowns. Lift plants every 3–4 years and replant the crowns in amended soil. Do not crowd the plants by packing too many in a small space or they will lose their vigor and bloom less.

Propagation Divide plants in autumn or plant seed in spring. Cultivars will need to be propagated by division as they do not come true from seed.

Pest and disease prevention No serious pests or diseases.

Landscape use Plant coral bells at the front of the border, as an edging for beds, along walkways or in a lightly shaded rock garden.

Coral bells continued

Coral bells *Heuchera sanguinea*

They respond well to container culture. Combine with cranesbills *Geranium* spp., catmints *Nepeta* spp., ornamental onions *Allium* spp., sundrops *Oenothera* spp. and columbines *Aquilegia* spp.

Hybrids Hybrid coral bells including *H.* x *brizoides* (pictured on page 225) are attractive in foliage and in flower. The evergreen leaves may be deep green, gray-green or mottled with silver. Plants grow from woody, fibrous-rooted crowns to produce mounds of rounded, lobed leaves. Mounds are about 1 foot (30 cm) tall and flower stems rise another 1 foot (30 cm). Small, dainty, fringed flowers are carried in slender, branching clusters. Colors vary from white through shades of pink and red. Flowers from late spring to summer—variable depending on the cultivar.

'Chatterbox' has wonderfully large, rose-pink flowers.

'Coral Cloud' is coral-pink.

'June Bride' has stunning, large white flowers.

'Mt St Helens' is brick-red.

Hibiscus moscheutos

CLIMATE
Zones 5–10.

HEIGHT AND
SPREAD
4–8 feet
(1.2–2.4 m) tall.
3–5 feet
(90–150 cm) wide.

FLOWERING TIME
Throughout
summer.

COMMON ROSE MALLOW

COMMON ROSE MALLOW'S PROFUSION OF SHOWY FLOWERS MAKES IT PERFECT FOR PROVIDING A BOLD DASH OF COLOR.

Description A shrublike plant that grows from a thick, woody crown. The broad, oval leaves have three to five shallow lobes. The 6–8-inch (15–20-cm) flowers have five pleated, white petals that surround a central, fuzzy column, which bears the male and female reproductive structures. The flowers have bright red centers.

Ideal position Full sun to light shade.

Ideal soil conditions Evenly moist, humus-rich soil. Tolerant of wet soil.

Cultivation Space young plants 3–4 feet (90–120 cm) apart. Clumps dislike disturbance.

Propagation Take cuttings in summer. Remove the flower buds and cut the leaves back by one-half to reduce water loss. Seeds from the parent plant are variable. Sow fresh seed outdoors in autumn.

Pest and disease prevention Japanese beetles may skeletonize the leaves. Pick them off and drop them in a pail of soapy water.

Landscape use They make great accent plants and are lovely in borders with ornamental grasses and airy summer perennials.

Hosta hybrids

CLIMATE
Zones 3–8.
Some selections are
hardy to Zone 2.

HEIGHT AND
SPREAD
6–36 inches
(15–90 cm) tall.
6–60 inches
(15–150 cm) wide.

FLOWERING TIME
Summer or autumn
depending on
hybrid and origin.

HOSTA

HOSTAS MAKE EXCELLENT COMPANIONS FOR
SPRING BULBS BECAUSE THE LEAVES FILL THE
SPACE LEFT WHEN BULBS FINISH FLOWERING.

Description Hostas are indispensable
foliage plants for shaded gardens.
Their thick, pleated or puckered
leaves grow from stout crowns with
thick, fleshy roots. Lavender, purple
or white flowers are carried on
slender spikes. Individual flowers
have three petals and three
petal-like sepals.

Ideal position Light to full shade.
Adaptable to both dry and wet soil
conditions. Filtered sun encourages
the best leaf color in the gold- and
blue-leaved forms. All hostas need
protection from hot afternoon sun,
especially in warm zones.
Variegated and yellow-leaved
cultivars are particularly susceptible
to burning.

Ideal soil conditions Evenly moist,
humus-rich soil.

Cultivation Hostas take several
years to reach mature form and
size, especially the large-leaved
cultivars. Allow ample room when
planting to accommodate their
ultimate size. New shoots are slow
to emerge in spring, so take care
not to damage them during spring
cleanup. Plant small bulbs such as
snowdrops *Galanthus* spp. and
squills *Scilla* spp. around the
clumps to mark their location.

Hostas come in a range of leaf and flower colors.

Propagation Divide in late summer.

Pest and disease prevention Set shallow pans of beer flush with the soil surface to drown slugs and snails. Or use a barrier of diatomaceous earth, wood ashes or sand around each plant.

Landscape use Use the smaller cultivars to edge beds or as a groundcover under shrubs and trees. Choose giants for creating drama in a mixed planting or alone as an accent. Plant hostas with wildflowers, ferns, sedges *Carex* spp. and shade perennials.

Cultivars Hundreds of cultivars of this popular foliage plant are available; only a few of those available are listed below.

'Antioch' is a medium to large plant with creamy edged leaves.

'August Moon' has large, golden-yellow leaves.

'Francee' is medium-sized with white-edged, deep green leaves.

'Golden Tiara' is small to medium with gold-edged leaves.

'Honeybells' has fragrant, white flowers tinged with violet and large, glossy, green leaves.

'Royal Standard' has medium-sized, glossy, green leaves and fragrant, white flowers.

'Sum and Substance' has huge, golden yellow leaves.

CLIMATE
Zones 3–9.

HEIGHT AND
SPREAD
6–12 inches
(15–30 cm) tall.
1–2 feet
(30–60 cm) wide.

FLOWERING TIME
Early spring.

PERENNIAL CANDYTUFT

GIVE CANDYTUFT WELL-DRAINED SOIL AND IT WILL REWARD YOU WITH MOUNDS OF STUNNING, WHITE FLOWERS IN EARLY SPRING.

Description A semiwoody subshrub with persistent stems tightly clothed in 1½-inch (3.5-cm), narrow, deep green leaves. Plants grow from fibrous-rooted crowns. The tight, rounded clusters consist of many ¼-inch (6-mm), four-petaled flowers.

Ideal position Full sun to light shade.

Ideal soil conditions Average to humus-rich, well-drained soil.

Cultivation Space plants 1–1½ feet (30–45 cm) apart in informal plantings or 6 inches (15 cm) apart in edgings. Shear after flowering to promote compact growth. Mulch in Zones 3–4 in winter.

Propagation Layer or take cuttings in early summer. Sow seed outdoors in spring or autumn.

Pest and disease prevention No serious pests or diseases.

Landscape use Use to edge formal plantings, walks or walls. Plant in rock gardens or with spring bulbs and early-blooming perennials.

Cultivars 'Autumn Snow' has large, white flowers.

'Snowflake' has delightfully large, white flower clusters on 8–10-inch (20–25-cm) stems.

Impatiens New Guinea Hybrids

CLIMATE
Zones 5–10.

HEIGHT AND SPREAD
1–2 feet
(30–60 cm) tall.
1–1½ feet
(30–45 cm) wide.

FLOWERING TIME
Early summer until frost.

NEW GUINEA IMPATIENS

NEW GUINEA IMPATIENS DO NOT USUALLY BLOOM AS MUCH AS THEIR SHADE-LOVING RELATIVES. SO ENJOY THE LOVELY FOLIAGE.

Description Upright, mounded plants. Their pointed, green leaves can be brilliantly variegated in red, cream or bronze. The 2-inch (5-cm) wide, flat flowers come in a variety of colors, including orange, red, purple, pink and lavender. They are perennial in frost-free areas and elsewhere are annuals.

Ideal position Full sun to partial shade.

Ideal soil conditions Average to moist, well-drained soil with added organic matter.

Cultivation Provide a sheltered position and ample moisture. Tip-prune young plants to form neat, well-rounded, shrubby growth.

Propagation Sow seed indoors 6–8 weeks before your last frost date. Set plants out 1–1½ feet (30–45 cm) apart 12 weeks after your last frost date. Take cuttings in late summer and pot up rooted cuttings in autumn; keep in a sunny window until the following spring.

Pest and disease prevention No serious pests or diseases.

Landscape use Enjoy the showy leaves and jewel-like flowers in beds, borders and containers.

Impatiens walleriana

BALSAMINACEAE

CLIMATE
Zones 5–10.

HEIGHT AND
SPREAD
6–24 inches
(15–60 cm) tall.
6–24 inches
(15–60 cm) wide.

FLOWERING TIME
Early summer until
frost.

OTHER COMMON
NAMES
Busy Lizzie,
patient Lucy,
patience, sultana.

IMPATIENS

IMPATIENS ARE POPULAR FOR POTS, PLANTERS,
WINDOW BOXES AND HANGING BASKETS
AND ADD COLOR TO SHADY AREAS.

Description Impatiens are tender
perennials also grown as tender
annuals. Plants form neat, shrubby
mounds of well-branched, succulent
stems. The lance-shaped, green or
bronze-brown leaves have slightly
scalloped edges. The plants are
covered with flat, spurred flowers
over a long period.

Ideal position Shade.

Ideal soil conditions Average to
moist, well-drained soil with added
organic matter.

Cultivation Keep well watered and
tip-prune young plants to produce
well-rounded, bushy plants.

Propagation Cuttings strike easily in
warmer months. Sow seed indoors
8–10 weeks before your last frost
date. Enclose the pot in a plastic
bag and store in a warm place until
seedlings appear. Set transplants out
2 weeks after your last frost date.

Pest and disease prevention No
serious pests or diseases.

Landscape use Impatiens are the
stars of shady gardens. Mix them
with other annuals and perennials
in beds and borders.

Incarvillea delavayi

BIGNONIACEAE

CLIMATE
Zones 5–8.

HEIGHT AND
SPREAD
1½–2 feet
(45–60 cm) tall.
1½ feet
(45 cm) wide.

FLOWERING TIME
Spring and early
summer.

HARDY GLOXINIA

COMBINE HARDY GLOXINIA WITH
GROUNDCOVER PLANTS SUCH AS ROCK
CRESS, CANDYTUFT AND SEDUM.

Description Showy plants with
1-foot (30-cm), pinnately divided
leaves. They are slow to emerge in
spring. The 2–3-inch (5–7.5-cm),
tubular, rose-pink flowers have flat,
five-petaled faces. They are borne
in clusters 1–2 feet (30–60 cm)
above the foliage.

Ideal position Full sun to partial
shade. Protect plants from afternoon
sun when grown in warm zones.
Intolerant of high temperatures.

Ideal soil conditions Average to
humus-rich, well-drained soil.

Cultivation Plants are easy to grow.
Mulch plants to protect them from
winter cold.

Propagation Sow seed in spring or
autumn on a warm (70°F [21°C])
seedbed. Keep the soil moist and
cover with clear plastic wrap to
encourage humidity. Seedlings will
develop in 10–20 days. Divide large
plants in spring or autumn.

Pest and disease prevention No
serious pests or diseases.

Landscape use Plant with spring-
and summer-flowering perennials
for a stunning flower display. Or
plant in partial shade with other
foliage plants.

Iris sibirica

CLIMATE
Zones 3–9.

HEIGHT AND
SPREAD
1–3 feet
(30–90 cm) tall.
1–2 feet
(30–60 cm) wide.

FLOWERING TIME
Early summer;
some cultivars
rebloom.

OTHER COMMON
NAMES
Siberian iris.

IRIS

IRIS'S STRAPLIKE FOLIAGE AND GRACEFUL
FLOWERS COMBINE WELL WITH ROUNDED
PERENNIALS SUCH AS PEONIES.

Description Plants form tight fans of
narrow, swordlike leaves from slow-
creeping rhizomes. Flowers range in
color from pure white, cream and
yellow to all shades of blue, violet
and purple. Some cultivars come
close to true red. The flowers have
three segments, called "falls," which
ring the outside of the flowers. They
are usually reflexed downward and
bear a central white or yellow
blaze. The center has three slender
segments called "standards." They
are often upright but can also be
flat or reflexed.

Ideal position Full sun to partial
shade. Heat- and cold-tolerant.

Ideal soil conditions Evenly moist,
humus-rich soil.

Cultivation Irises are easy-care
perennials. They thrive for many
years without division. If bloom
begins to wane or plants outgrow
their position, divide and replant
into soil that has been enriched
with organic matter.

Propagation Divide plants in late
summer. Seed collected from
cultivars will be variable and often
inferior to the parent plant. Sow
fresh seed of the species outdoors
in summer or autumn.

Siberian iris *Iris sibirica*

Pest and disease prevention
Susceptible to iris borer. Borers also spread bacterial rot, which kills the iris from the ground up. Good culture is the best prevention. Remove dead foliage in spring and autumn. Smash the grubs between your fingers while they are in the leaves. Dig up affected plants and cut off affected parts of rhizome.

Landscape use Plant in formal or informal gardens with perennials, ornamental grasses and ferns. Combine with rounded perennials such as baptisia *Baptisia* spp. and cranesbills *Geranium* spp. beside ponds. Ferns, hostas, primroses and astilbes are good companions.

Cultivars 'Caesar' has blue-purple flowers on 3-foot (90-cm) stems.

'Dewful' has blue flowers on 3½-foot (1.05-m) stems.

'Ego' has rich blue, ruffled flowers on 2½-foot (75-cm) stems.

'My Love' is a soft medium blue with 2½-foot (75-cm) stems.

'Orville Fay' is medium blue with 3-foot (90-cm) stems.

'Sky Wings' is a pale blue bitone with 3-foot (90-cm) stems.

Other species Bearded Hybrids (pictured on page 234) are as popular as Siberian irises. They have showy, fragrant flowers with wide, bearded falls and wide, upright stands. Plants range in size

Japanese iris *Iris ensata*

from less than 1¼ feet (37.5 cm) to over 2⅓ feet (70 cm) tall. They grow in the same conditions as Siberian irises, with good drainage. Hundreds of cultivars are available. Some of the best include 'Beverly Sills', with ruffled, coral-pink flowers, 'Lacy Snowflake', with pure white, fringed blooms and 'Titan's Glory', with purple-blue flowers. Zones 3–8.

I. cristata, crested iris, is an 8-inch (20-cm) spring woodland iris with sky-blue flowers. Prefers semishade. Zones 3–9.

I. ensata, Japanese iris (pictured above), is a wet-soil iris with lovely blue or purple flowers. Many stunning cultivars are available with flattened flowers up to 8 inches

(20 cm) across. Prefers partial shade in hot, sunny climates. Zones 4–9.

I. pseudacorus, yellow flag, is a stout 3–4-foot (90–120-cm) iris with bright yellow flowers. Grows well in full sun to partial shade. Thrives in a water garden. Zones 4–9.

I. tectorum, roof iris, is a short, stout 1–1½-foot (30–45-cm) iris with delicate, flattened, spotted lilac-blue flowers. Prefers sheltered partial shade with protection from hot afternoon sun. Zones 4–9.

I. versicolor, blue flag iris, is a tall 1½–3-foot (45–90-cm) iris with purple-blue flowers. Likes moist soil or shallow water. Zones 2–8.

Kniphofia uvaria

CLIMATE
Zones 5–9.

HEIGHT AND
SPREAD
3–5 feet
(90–150 cm) tall.
2–4 feet
(60–120 cm) wide.

FLOWERING TIME
Late spring and
summer.

OTHER COMMON
NAMES
Common torch lily.

RED-HOT POKER

THE BOLD, VERTICAL FORM OF RED-HOT
POKER ADDS DRAMATIC ACCENTS TO
PERENNIAL BORDERS AND ROCK GARDENS.

Description Red-hot poker is a
commanding perennial with tufts of
narrow, evergreen leaves from a
fleshy, rooted crown. Long, slender
spikes consist of tightly packed,
tubular flowers. The lowest on the
spike are yellow-white and the
upper ones are red.

Ideal position Full sun. Established
plants are quite drought-tolerant.

Ideal soil conditions Average to
humus-rich, well-drained soil.

Cultivation Set out young plants
2–2½ feet (60–75 cm) apart. Leave
established plants undisturbed.
Plants increase to form broad,
floriferous clumps.

Propagation Remove a few crowns
from the edges of clumps in
autumn. Sow seed indoors in winter
after stratification. To stratify, mix
seed with moist peat moss or seed-
starting medium in a plastic bag.
Close the bag with a twist-tie and
place it in the refrigerator for
4–6 weeks. Then sow the mixture
as you would normal seed.

Red-hot poker continued

Kniphofia 'Winter Cheer'

Pest and disease prevention Provide excellent drainage for *Kniphofia* hybrids to avoid crown rot.

Landscape use The bold, vertical form of red-hot pokers adds excitement to perennial borders and rock gardens. Combine with ornamental grasses, wormwoods *Artemisia* spp., sundrops *Oenothera* spp. and other summer perennials.

Hybrids 'Ice Queen' grows to 3½ feet (1.05 m) tall with a spread to 3½ feet (1.05 m). It has lovely, green, budded flowers, which open to pale yellow.

'Little Maid' is a dwarf form that grows to 2 feet (60 cm) with pale green buds opening to cream-colored flowers.

'Percy's Pride' is a taller-growing cultivar, to 3 feet (90 cm), with pale yellow flowers.

'Winter Cheer' (pictured above) grows to 5 feet (1.5 m) with narrow leaves topped by sturdy stalks holding orange tubular flowers, which age to yellow.

Lavandula angustifolia

CLIMATE
Zones 5–8.

HEIGHT AND
SPREAD
2–3 feet
(60–90 cm) tall.
2–3 feet
(60–90 cm) wide.

FLOWERING TIME
Early to late
summer.

ENGLISH LAVENDER

ENGLISH LAVENDER IS A SMALL, ROUNDED, FRAGRANT PLANT BELOVED FOR ITS HERBAL AND ORNAMENTAL QUALITIES.

Description Gray-green leaves clothe soft, hairy stems topped with spikes of purple-blue flowers. The ½-inch (12-mm) purple-blue flowers are carried in tight, narrow clusters.

Ideal position Full sun to light shade. Extremely drought-tolerant.

Ideal soil conditions Average to humus-rich, well-drained soil.

Cultivation Shoots may be partially killed in winter. Prune out dead wood and reshape in spring. Shear plants every few years to encourage growth and promote bloom.

Propagation Layer or take tip cuttings in summer.

Pest and disease prevention No serious pests or diseases.

Landscape use Plant lavender in ornamental and herb gardens. Use as an edging plant or to configure knot gardens. In borders, combine with other plants that need excellent drainage, such as yarrows.

Cultivars 'Dwarf Blue' has dark blue flowers on 1-foot (30-cm) plants.
'Hidcote' grows 1½ feet (45 cm) tall with purple-blue flowers.
'Jean Davis' has pale pink flowers.
'Munstead' has lavender-blue flowers on 1½-foot (45-cm) plants.

Leucanthemum x *superbum*

CLIMATE
Zones 3–10.
Exact zones vary
by cultivar.

HEIGHT AND
SPREAD
1–3 feet
(30–90 cm) tall.
2 feet
(60 cm) wide.

FLOWERING TIME
Throughout
summer.

SHASTA DAISY

SHASTA DAISY IS A SHOWY PLANT. COMBINE WITH OTHER SUMMER-BLOOMING PERENNIALS SUCH AS DAYLILIES AND IRISES.

Description Has dense clusters of shiny, 10-inch (25-cm), deep green, toothed leaves and short, creeping, fibrous-rooted stems. Bright white, 3-inch (7.5-cm) daisies with large, bright yellow centers are carried on stout, leafy stems.

Ideal position Full sun. Extremely cold- and heat-tolerant.

Ideal soil conditions Average to rich, well-drained soil. Tolerates seaside conditions but not waterlogged soil.

Cultivation Shasta daisies are easy-care perennials. Deadhead plants to promote continued bloom. Plants grow quickly, often outgrowing allotted space, especially in warmer zones. Divide and replant clumps in organically enriched soil every 3–4 years to keep them vigorous.

Propagation Remove offsets from the main clump or divide in spring.

Pest and disease prevention No serious pests or diseases.

Landscape use For a delightful seaside garden, plant shasta daisies with blanket flowers *Gaillardia* spp. and coreopsis.

Liatris spicata

CLIMATE
Zones 3–9.

HEIGHT AND
SPREAD
2–3 feet
(60–90 cm) tall.
1–2 feet
(30–60 cm) wide.

FLOWERING TIME
Midsummer.

OTHER COMMON
NAMES
Blazing star.

SPIKE GAYFEATHER

SPIKE GAYFEATHER IS A TALL, LONG-LIVED
PERENNIAL THAT OFFERS AN ABUNDANCE OF
FLOWERS FOR VERY LITTLE EFFORT.

Description The erect stems arise
from basal tufts of grasslike,
medium green foliage. Plants grow
from a fat corm. Rose-purple flowers
are carried on slender flower spikes
in small heads that are crowded
together into dense spikes. The
spikes open from the top down.

Ideal position Full sun. Plants tend
to flop in partial shade.

Ideal soil conditions Average to
humus-rich, moist soil.

Cultivation Clumps increase slowly
and seldom need division.

Propagation Divide plants in spring
or early autumn. Sow seed outdoors
in autumn or indoors in late winter
after stratification.

Pest and disease prevention No
serious pests or diseases.

Landscape use Lovely in perennial
gardens and meadow plantings.
Combine with purple coneflowers
Echinacea purpurea, coreopsis and
with ornamental grasses.

Cultivars 'Kobold' is a popular
cultivar with red-violet flowers on
1½–2½-foot (45–75-cm) stems.

Ligularia dentata

CLIMATE
Zones 3–8.

HEIGHT AND
SPREAD
3–4 feet
(90–120 cm) tall.
3–4 feet
(90–120 cm) wide.

FLOWERING TIME
Late summer.

BIG-LEAVED LIGULARIA

BIG-LEAVED LIGULARIA IS A WONDERFUL,
BOLD ACCENT PLANT FOR MOIST-SOIL
GARDENS. COMBINE IT WITH SPIKY PLANTS.

Description Big-leaved ligularia has 1–2-foot (30–60-cm), round or kidney-shaped leaves on long stalks. Plants grow from stout crowns with fleshy roots. The 5-inch (12.5-cm) bright orange-yellow flowers, carried in open clusters, are like spidery daisies.

Ideal position Light to partial shade.

Ideal soil conditions Consistently moist, humus-rich soil. Plants do not tolerate dry soil.

Cultivation The leaves lose water rapidly. In heat, they can go into collapse but they recover as temperatures cool. The plants form big clumps but don't need frequent division.

Propagation Lift clumps in early spring or autumn and cut crowns apart. Replant into enriched soil.

Pest and disease prevention Slugs may be a problem.

Landscape use Big-leaved ligularias are bold accent plants. Use beside ponds or in gardens with ferns, hostas, irises and grasses.

Cultivars 'Desdemona' has purple spring leaves, which fade to green with purple undersides.

Lobelia cardinalis

CLIMATE
Zones 2–9.

HEIGHT AND SPREAD
2–4 feet
(60–120 cm) tall.
1–2 feet
(30–60 cm) wide.

FLOWERING TIME
Late summer to autumn.

CARDINAL FLOWER

THE BRILLIANT, SCARLET BLOOMS OF CARDINAL FLOWER MAKE AN EYE-CATCHING ADDITION TO ANY GARDEN WITH MOIST SOIL.

Description Has fiery-colored flower spikes on leafy stems and grows from a fibrous-rooted crown. The lance-shaped leaves may be green or red-bronze. Brilliant scarlet tubular flowers have three lower and two upper petals.

Ideal position Full sun to partial shade.

Ideal soil conditions Evenly moist, humus-rich soil.

Cultivation Cardinal flowers are shallow-rooted and subject to frost heaving. Where winters are cold, mulch plants to protect the crowns. In warmer zones, winter mulch may rot the crowns. Replant in spring if frost has lifted them. May be short-lived, but self-sows prolifically.

Propagation Divide in late autumn or spring. Sow seed, uncovered, outdoors in autumn or spring or indoors in late winter.

Pest and disease prevention No serious pests or diseases.

Landscape use Cardinal flowers are used around pools, along streams or in informal plantings. Combine them with irises, hostas and ferns.

Cultivars 'Royal Robe' has stunning, ruby-red flowers.

Lupinus polyphyllus FABACEAE

CLIMATE
Zones 3–7.

HEIGHT AND
SPREAD
3–5 feet
(90–150 cm) tall.
2–3 feet
(60–90 cm) wide.

FLOWERING TIME
Spring and
summer.

WASHINGTON LUPINE

THE SPIKY FLOWERS OF WASHINGTON LUPINE
ARE A CHEERFUL VERTICAL ACCENT IN SPRING
AND EARLY-SUMMER GARDENS.

Description Has conical flower
spikes on stout stems with large,
palmately divided leaves. Plants
grow from thick roots. The ¾-inch
(18-mm), blue-purple or yellow,
pealike flowers are crowded into
1–2-foot (30–60-cm) spikes.

Ideal position Full sun to light
shade. Very sensitive to high
summer temperatures.

Ideal soil conditions Moist but
well-drained, acid, humus-rich soil.

Cultivation Washington lupines are
heavy feeders. Top-dress in spring
with a balanced, organic fertilizer.
Protect plants from hot, dry winds.
They may be short-lived, especially
in warmer zones.

Propagation Remove sideshoots
from around the clump in autumn.
Sow seed outdoors in autumn or
inside in winter. Before sowing
indoors, soak seed overnight and
then stratify by placing in a plastic
bag with moist peat.

Pest and disease prevention No
serious pests or diseases.

Landscape use Plant Washington
lupines with border perennials such
as columbines *Aquilegia* spp. and
cranesbills *Geranium* spp.

Lychnis coronaria

CLIMATE
Zones 4–8.

HEIGHT AND
SPREAD
2–3 feet
(60–90 cm) tall.
1–1½ feet
(30–45 cm) wide.

FLOWERING TIME
Late spring.

ROSE CAMPION

THE SOFT, SILVERY LEAVES AND SHOCKING-
MAGENTA FLOWERS OF ROSE CAMPION ADD
EXCITEMENT TO BEDS AND BORDERS.

Description The deep rose-red,
five-petaled flowers are carried in
open clusters atop woolly stems.

Ideal position Full sun or
light shade.

Ideal soil conditions Average to rich,
moist but well-drained soil.

Cultivation Divide clumps every
2–3 years in spring or autumn to
keep the plants vigorous. Plants
may be short-lived, especially in
rich soil, but self-sown seedlings
are numerous.

Propagation Sow seed outdoors in
autumn or remove small crowns
from the edge of the clump in
spring or autumn.

Pest and disease prevention No
serious pests or diseases.

Landscape use Plant rose campion
in formal and informal beds and
borders or in rock gardens. Use
the strong-colored flowers to spice
up a subdued scheme of blues
and pale yellows. Combine with
catmints *Nepeta* spp., cranesbills
Geranium spp. and blue-leaved
grasses. Plant in color combinations
with yarrows, marguerites
Argyranthemum frutescens and
sundrops *Oenothera* spp.

Macleaya cordata PAPAVERACEAE

CLIMATE
Zones 3–8.

HEIGHT AND
SPREAD
6–10 feet
(1.8–3 m) tall.
4–8 feet
(1.2–2.4 m) wide.

FLOWERING TIME
Summer.

PLUME POPPY

PLANT PLUME POPPY AS AN ACCENT
ALONG STAIRS OR FENCES OR USE IT
LIKE A SHRUB AS A FOCAL POINT.

Description The imposing plume poppy is shrublike in stature with 10-inch (25-cm) lobed leaves clothing erect stems. Plants grow from stout, creeping roots and quickly become invasive. The 1-foot (30-cm) plumes consist of small, cream flowers that give way to showy, flat, rose-colored seedpods.

Ideal position Full sun to partial shade. Stems are not as sturdy on shade-grown plants.

Ideal soil conditions Moist, average to humus-rich soil.

Cultivation Established clumps of plume poppy can double in size each season. Control is inevitably necessary to avert a total takeover. Chop off the creeping roots with a spade as soon as you see new stems emerging.

Propagation Remove new offsets in spring or autumn or take root cuttings in winter.

Pest and disease prevention No serious pests or diseases.

Landscape use Place plume poppies at the rear of borders where there is ample room for them to grow. A mature clump is a lovely sight.

Mertensia pulmonarioides

CLIMATE
Zones 3–9.

HEIGHT AND
SPREAD
1–2 feet
(30–60 cm) tall.
1–2 feet
(30–60 cm) wide.

FLOWERING TIME
Spring.

VIRGINIA BLUEBELL

PLANT ALONG A WOODLAND PATH WITH
SPRING BULBS, SUCH AS DAFFODILS OR
SQUILLS, TOGETHER WITH WILDFLOWERS.

Description Virginia bluebells are
lovely spring wildflowers with
graceful flowers on arching stems
clothed with thin, blue-green leaves.
Plants grow from thick roots and go
dormant after flowering. Nodding,
sky-blue bells open from pink buds.

Ideal position Full sun to shade.

Ideal soil conditions Consistently
moist, well-drained, humus-rich soil.

Cultivation Virginia bluebells
emerge early in spring and go
dormant soon after flowering. Sun
is essential to bloom but plants are
shade-tolerant once dormant. Place
them where you will not dig them
up by accident.

Propagation Divide large clumps
after flowering or in autumn.
Leave at least one bud per division.
Self-sown seedlings are usually
abundant. They will bloom the
second or third year.

Pest and disease prevention No
serious pests or diseases.

Landscape use Interplant clumps of
Virginia bluebells with foliage plants
such as ferns and hostas to fill gaps
left by still-dormant plants.

Miscanthus sinensis

CLIMATE
Zones 5–9.

HEIGHT AND SPREAD
3–5 feet
(90–150 cm) tall.
3 feet
(90 cm) wide or
more.

FLOWERING TIME
Midsummer
through early
autumn.

OTHER COMMON NAMES
Eulalia grass.

JAPANESE SILVER GRASS

JAPANESE SILVER GRASS IS ONE OF THE BEST LARGE ORNAMENTAL GRASSES. IT IS VERY ATTRACTIVE NEAR STREAMS AND PONDS.

Description Large clumps of long, pointed, sharp-edged leaves. Flower plumes above the foliage are in hues from silver to reddish purple.

Ideal position Full sun. Provide shade and extra water in hot climates.

Ideal soil conditions Light, moist, humus-rich soil.

Cultivation Set plants 2–4 feet (60–120 cm) apart in spring. Stake if necessary. Divide in spring when clumps begin to die in the center.

Propagation By seed or division.

Pest and disease prevention No serious pests or diseases.

Landscape use Combine with asters and goldenrods *Solidago* spp. to create a stunning autumn show.

Cultivars 'Cabaret' grows to 6 feet (1.8 m); its leaves have white stripes in the center. The flowers bloom pink in autumn, then become cream colored.

'Morning Light', one of the best cultivars, grows to 4 feet (1.2 m) with narrow, white-edged leaves and reddish bronze autumn flowers that later turn a cream color.

Monarda didyma

CLIMATE
Zones 4–8.

HEIGHT AND
SPREAD
2–4 feet
(60–120 cm) tall.
2–3 feet
(60–90 cm) wide.

FLOWERING TIME
Summer.

OTHER COMMON
NAMES
Bergamot,
oswego tea.

BEE BALM

BEE BALM'S LOVELY FLOWERS ADD COLOR
TO THE SUMMER GARDEN. THE LEAVES GIVE
EARL GREY TEA ITS AROMA AND FLAVOR.

Description Sturdy flower stems
grow from fast-creeping runners.
Tight heads of tubular, red flowers
are surrounded by a whorl of
colored leafy bracts.

Ideal position Full sun to shade.

Ideal soil conditions Evenly moist,
humus-rich soil.

Cultivation Plants spread quickly.
Divide every 2–3 years.

Propagation Divide in spring or
autumn. Sow seed indoors or
outdoors in spring.

Pest and disease prevention
Powdery mildew causes white
blotches on the foliage and may
cover the entire plant. Thin the
stems to allow good air circulation.
Cut affected plants to the ground.

Landscape use Plant in formal or
informal gardens.

Cultivars 'Blue Stocking' has very
pretty violet flowers.
'Cambridge Scarlet' (pictured
above) has brilliant scarlet flowers.
'Mahogany' has ruby-red flowers.
'Marshall's Delight' is a mildew-
resistant pink.
'Prairie Night' is red-violet.
'Snow Queen' is creamy white.

CLIMATE
Zones 3–8.

HEIGHT AND
SPREAD
1½–3 feet
(45–90 cm) tall.
2–3 feet
(60–90 cm) wide.

FLOWERING TIME
Spring through
midsummer.

CATMINT

CATMINT'S SPIKES OF DAINTY, VIOLET-BLUE
FLOWERS ARE PERFECT FOR EDGING WALKS
AND BEDS OR FOR ALONG ROCK WALLS.

Description The wiry stems are
clothed in soft, hairy, gray-green,
oval leaves and grow from fibrous-
rooted crowns. Violet-blue, terminal
flower clusters are carried in whorls
on slender spikes.

Ideal position Full sun to light shade.

Ideal soil conditions Average to
humus-rich, moist but well-drained
soil. Plants tolerate poor, dry soil.

Cultivation Clumps get quite rangy
after bloom. Cut back finished
flower stalks to encourage fresh
growth and repeat bloom.

Propagation Divide in spring or
autumn. Take cuttings in summer.

Pest and disease prevention No
serious pests or diseases.

Landscape use In borders, combine
with bellflowers *Campanula* spp.,
cranesbills *Geranium* spp.,
coreopsis and ornamental grasses.

Cultivars 'Six Hills Giant' has deep
purple-blue flowers.

Other species *N. racemosa*, Persian
nepeta, grows 1–1½ feet (30–45 cm)
tall. Lavender-blue flowers cover the
plants for months. 'Blue Wonder'
has deep blue flowers. 'Snowflake'
has white flowers. Zones 3–8.

Oenothera speciosa

CLIMATE
Zones 3–8.

HEIGHT AND
SPREAD
1½ feet
(45 cm) tall.
2 feet
(60 cm) or more
wide.

FLOWERING TIME
Early summer, only
during the day.

OTHER COMMON
NAMES
White evening
primrose, showy
evening primrose.

SHOWY SUNDROP

SHOWY SUNDROPS LOOK WONDERFUL
MASSED IN LOW-MAINTENANCE AREAS
SUCH AS DRY, SUNNY SLOPES.

Description Showy sundrops spread
quickly by underground runners.
They flower during the day, unlike
the many night-blooming species of
the *Oenothera* genus. White, cup-
shaped flowers, 2 inches (5 cm)
across, fade to soft pink and turn
toward the sun.

Ideal position Full sun to very
light shade.

Ideal soil conditions Well-drained,
average soil.

Cultivation Set plants about 2 feet
(60 cm) apart in spring or autumn.

Can be invasive. Plant where the
spread won't become a problem
or surround the planting with an
edging strip that extends a few
inches below the ground.

Propagation Propagate by division
or seed in spring or autumn.

Pest and disease prevention No
serious pests or diseases.

Landscape use Use this fast-
spreading perennial as a quick
cover for those difficult, full-sun,
dry areas in your garden.

Cultivars 'Rosea' grows to 15 inches
(37.5 cm) and has clear pink, 3-inch
(7.5-cm) blooms.

Paeonia lactiflora Hybrids

CLIMATE
Zones 2–8.

HEIGHT AND
SPREAD
1½–3 feet
(45–90 cm) tall.
3–4 feet
(90–120 cm) wide.

FLOWERING TIME
Spring to summer.

OTHER COMMON
NAMES
Common garden
peony, Chinese
peony, peony.

GARDEN PEONY

COMBINE THE LOVELY GARDEN PEONY WITH
EARLY SPRING BULBS IN BEDS AND BORDERS
OR USE THEM IN MASS PLANTINGS.

Description Shrublike with sturdy
stalks clothed in compound, shiny
green leaves. Plants grow from
thick, fleshy roots and may live
100 years or more. Flowers range
in color from white, cream and
yellow to pink, rose, burgundy
and scarlet and may be single,
semidouble or double.

Ideal position Full sun to
light shade.

Ideal soil conditions Moist,
humus-rich soil. Good drainage
is important to avoid root rot.

Cultivation Plant container-grown
peonies in spring or autumn.
Plant bareroot plants in early and
midspring. Mulch new plants to
protect from frost heaving. An
annual winter mulch is advised
where winter temperatures dip
below 0°F (-18°C). Taller selections
and those with double flowers may
need staking to keep their faces
out of the mud. Plants may grow
undisturbed for years but if roots
become too crowded, flowering will
drop off. Lift plants in autumn,
divide the roots, leaving at least one
eye (bud) per division, and replant
into soil that has been enriched
with organic matter.

Peonies with single and semidouble flowers tend to be more resistant to wind damage.

Propagation Divide in autumn.

Pest and disease prevention Spray or dust foliage with an organically acceptable fungicide such as sulfur or bordeaux mix to discourage the fungal disease botrytis.

Landscape use Spring and early-summer perennials such as irises, foxgloves *Digitalis* spp. and columbines *Aquilegia* spp. are excellent companions.

Cultivars There are many cultivars available in a range of different colors and forms.

'Duchess de Nemours' is an early white double.

'Festiva Maxima' is an early, large, white double, flecked with red that is good for warmer gardens.

'Gay Paree' is a midseason, cerise-and-white anemone.

'Nippon Beauty' is a garnet-red Japanese.

'Sara Bernhardt' is a fragrant, midseason double.

'Sea Shell' is a tall, midseason, pink single.

'White Swan' is a midseason, white single.

Papaver orientale

CLIMATE
Zones 2–7.

HEIGHT AND
SPREAD
2–3 feet
(60–90 cm) tall.
2–3 feet
(60–90 cm) wide.

FLOWERING TIME
Early summer.

ORIENTAL POPPY

ORIENTAL POPPIES ARE PRIZED FOR THEIR
COLORFUL, CRÊPE-PAPER-LIKE FLOWERS.
PLANT THEM WITH BORDER PERENNIALS.

Description Plants produce rosettes
of coarse, hairy, lobed foliage from
a thick taproot. The 3–4-inch
(7.5–10-cm) flowers have crinkled,
scarlet-red petals with black spots
at their base.

Ideal position Full sun to light
shade. Established plants are tough
and long-lived.

Ideal soil conditions Average to rich,
well-drained, humus-rich soil.

Cultivation In warm zones plants
often go dormant after flowering,
leaving a bare spot. In autumn, new
foliage emerges. This is the time
to divide overgrown plants.

Propagation Divide in autumn.
Take root cuttings in late summer,
autumn or winter.

Pest and disease prevention No
serious pests or diseases.

Landscape use Combine with
ornamental grasses and bushy
plants such as catmints *Nepeta* spp.
or asters.

Cultivars 'Bonfire' has red flowers.
'Helen Elizabeth' has pale
salmon-pink flowers without spots.
'Snow Queen' is pure white with
large black spots.
'Watermelon' is rosy pink.

Penstemon barbatus

CLIMATE
Zones 3–8.

HEIGHT AND
SPREAD
1½–3 feet
(45–90 cm) tall.
1–2 feet
(30–60 cm) wide.

FLOWERING TIME
Late spring to early
summer.

COMMON BEARDTONGUE

COMBINE COMMON BEARDTONGUE'S SPIKY FLOWERS WITH ROUNDED PLANTS SUCH AS CRANESBILLS, YARROWS AND CORAL BELLS.

Description Has erect flower spikes clothed in shiny, broadly lance-shaped leaves. Flowering stems and basal foliage rosettes grow from fibrous-rooted crowns. It has 1–1½-inch (2.5–3.5-cm), irregular, tubular pink flowers.

Ideal position Full sun to light shade.

Ideal soil conditions Average to humus-rich, well-drained soil. Good drainage is essential for success.

Cultivation Plants form dense clumps with maturity and benefit from division every 4–6 years. More frequent division is required when plants are growing in rich soil.

Propagation Divide in spring. Sow seed outdoors in autumn or indoors in winter after stratification. Seedlings may bloom the first year.

Pest and disease prevention No serious pests or diseases.

Landscape use Plant beardtongues in formal borders, informal gardens and rock gardens.

Cultivars 'Bashful' has unusually colored, salmon-pink flowers on 12–14-inch (30–35-cm) stems.
　'Elfin Pink' has bright pink flowers on 1-foot (30-cm) stems.

Common beardtongue continued

Foxglove penstemon *Penstemon digitalis* 'Husker's Red'

'Pink Beauty' has pink flowers on 2–2½-foot (60–75-cm) stems.

Other species *P. australis*, Southern penstemon, is a heat-tolerant species with soft, hairy leaves and pale pink flowers. Zones 5–9.

P. digitalis, foxglove penstemon, has 2½–5-foot (75–150-cm) tall stems with clusters of 1-inch (2.5-cm), white flowers and shiny, deep green leaves. Plants thrive in moist soil. 'Husker's Red' (pictured above) has deep ruby-red leaves. Zones 4–8.

P. hirsutus, hairy beardtongue, is a fuzzy penstemon with purple flowers. 'Pygmaeus' is a dwarf selection only 8 inches (20 cm) high. Zones 4–8.

P. pinifolius is a shrubby plant with small, scarlet flowers and stiff, needle-like leaves. Zones 6–8.

P. smallii, Small's beardtongue, has dense clusters of rose-purple flowers. Plants need poor soil and are often short-lived. Zones 6–8.

Hybrids Many hybrids of mixed origin are available.

'Firebird' has scarlet flowers.

'Mesa' has deep violet flowers.

'Prairie Dusk' has pendent purple flowers.

'Prairie Fire' is orange-red.

Perovskia atriplicifolia

CLIMATE
Zones 4–9.

HEIGHT AND
SPREAD
3–5 feet
(90–150 cm) tall.
3–5 feet
(90–150 cm) wide.

FLOWERING TIME
Mid- to late
summer.

RUSSIAN SAGE

THE AIRY, GRAY FLOWER BUDS AND SOFT
BLUE FLOWERS MIX WELL WITH YELLOW,
PINK, DEEP BLUE AND PURPLE FLOWERS.

Description A shrubby, branching
perennial with erect stems clothed
in gray-green, deeply lobed leaves.
Plants grow from fibrous-rooted
crowns. Small, irregularly shaped,
blue flowers are carried in slender
12–15-inch (30–37.5-cm) sprays.

Ideal position Full sun.

Ideal soil conditions Average to rich,
well-drained soil. Good drainage is
essential for success.

Cultivation The stems of Russian
sage become woody with age. After
hard frost, cut them back to 1 foot
(30 cm). In cooler zones, plants die
back to the soil line but resprout
from the roots.

Propagation Take stem cuttings in
early summer.

Pest and disease prevention No
serious pests or diseases.

Landscape use Plant toward
the middle or back of borders.
Combine with yarrow, gayfeather
Liatris spp., balloon flower
Platycodon grandiflorus, sedum,
phlox and ornamental grasses.

Cultivars 'Blue Spire' has violet-blue
flowers on strong, upright stems.
'Longin' has stout stems and
grows 3–4 feet (90–120 cm) tall.

Phlox divaricata

CLIMATE
Zones 3–9.

HEIGHT AND
SPREAD
10–15 inches
(25–37.5 cm) tall.
1–2 feet
(30–60 cm) wide.

FLOWERING TIME
Spring.

WILD BLUE PHLOX

WILD BLUE PHLOX LOOKS GREAT IN SHADE
OR WILD GARDENS WITH SPRING BULBS,
WILDFLOWERS AND FERNS.

Description Wild blue phlox is a
sweet-scented, woodland species
with creeping stems clothed in
evergreen, oval leaves. Plants have
fibrous, white roots. Lavender-blue
to sky-blue flowers are borne in
open clusters, on upright stems.

Ideal position Partial to full shade.
Sun is necessary in spring. Summer
sun protection is critical.

Ideal soil conditions Evenly moist,
humus-rich soil.

Cultivation Divide as necessary to
control spread.

Propagation Divide after flowering.
Take cuttings in late spring or early
summer from non-blooming stems.
Sow seed in autumn or spring.

Pest and disease prevention
Powdery mildew may attack. Spray
with sulfur to contain the disease.

Landscape use Grows well around
flowering shrubs as a groundcover.

Hybrids *P.* 'Chattahoochee' has
clusters of lavender-blue flowers
with violet eyes. Zones 3–9.

Other species *P. stolonifera*,
creeping phlox, forms low mats of
rounded foliage and upright spikes
of blue or pink flowers similar to
P. divaricata. Zones 2–8.

Phlox paniculata

CLIMATE
Zones 3–8. Cold
hardiness varies
with cultivars.

**HEIGHT AND
SPREAD**
3–4 feet
(90–120 cm) tall.
2–4 feet
(60–120 cm) wide.

FLOWERING TIME
Mid- to late
summer.

**OTHER COMMON
NAMES**
Summer phlox.

GARDEN PHLOX

GARDEN PHLOX ARE BEAUTIFUL AND
VERSATILE GARDEN PERENNIALS. COMBINE
WITH SUMMER DAISIES, BEE BALM AND ASTER.

Description Has domed clusters of
fragrant, richly colored flowers atop
stiff, leafy stems. Plants grow from
fibrous-rooted crowns. Flowers are
from magenta to pink and white.

Ideal position Full sun to light shade.

Ideal soil conditions Moist but
well-drained, humus-rich soil.

Cultivation Divide clumps every
3–4 years to keep them vigorous.

Propagation Divide in spring. Take
stem cuttings late spring or early
summer and root cuttings in autumn.

Pest and disease prevention
Powdery mildew is the bane of
phlox growers. It causes white
patches on the leaves or, in bad
cases, turns entire leaves white. To
avoid problems, thin the stems
before plants bloom to increase air
circulation. Select resistant cultivars,
especially hybrids with *P. maculata*.

Landscape use Perfect in informal
situations and on the edges of
lightly shaded woodlands.

Cultivars Dozens of named
selections are available. They vary
in bloom time, mildew resistance,
flower size and cold hardiness.
  'Bright Eyes' is pink with
crimson eyes and is mildew-resistant.

Garden phlox continued

Garden phlox *Phlox paniculata* 'Fujiyama' may rebloom in late summer if deadheaded.

'Caroline van den Berg' has purple flowers.

'David' has large heads of white flowers and is mildew-resistant.

'Dodo Hanbury Forbes' has large, clear pink flowers with rose eyes.

'Fujiyama' (pictured above) is a compact, late-summer white.

'Sandra' is a compact plant with scarlet flowers.

Other species *P. carolina*, thick-leaved phlox, has glossy, oval leaves and elongated clusters of lavender, pink or white flowers in early summer. 'Miss Lingard' has white flowers with yellow eyes. 'Rosalinde' has bright pink flowers. Zones 4–9.

P. maculata, wild sweet William, is similar to *P. carolina* but the foliage is lance-shaped. 'Alpha' has rose-pink flowers with a darker eye. 'Omega' has white flowers with lilac-pink eyes. Zones 3–9.

P. ovata, mountain phlox, is an upright, spreading species with open clusters of pink to magenta flowers. 'Spring Delight' has deep rose-pink flowers in late spring and early summer. Zones 4–8.

Physostegia virginiana

CLIMATE
Zones 3–9.

HEIGHT AND
SPREAD
3–4 feet
(90–120 cm) tall.
2–4 feet
(60–120 cm) wide.

FLOWERING TIME
Late summer.

OTHER COMMON
NAMES
False dragonhead.

OBEDIENT PLANT

USE CULTIVARS IN FORMAL GARDENS WITH
ASTER, GOLDENROD, GARDEN PHLOX,
BOLTONIA AND ORNAMENTAL GRASSES.

Description This perennial is named
for the tendency of its flowers to
remain in any position when shifted
in their four-ranked clusters. Plants
grow from creeping stems. The
tubular, bilobed flowers are
rose-pink to lilac-pink.

Ideal position Full sun to light shade.

Ideal soil conditions Moist to wet,
average to humus-rich soil.

Cultivation Wild tend to flop
in rich soil. Stake as necessary.
Divide every 2–4 years to contain.

Propagation Divide in spring. Take
stem cuttings in early summer.

Pest and disease prevention No
serious pests or diseases.

Landscape use Use in formal beds,
borders and cottage gardens. It is
lovely in any informal planting.

Cultivars 'Pink Bouquet' has
bright pink flowers on 3–4-foot
(90–120-cm) stems.
  'Summer Snow' has white
flowers on 3-foot (90-cm) stems.
  'Variegata' has leaves edged in
cream and pale pink flowers.
  'Vivid' has pretty, vibrant,
rose-pink flowers.

Platycodon grandiflorus

CLIMATE
Zones 3–8.

HEIGHT AND SPREAD
2–3 feet
(60–90 cm) tall.
1–2 feet
(30–60 cm) wide.

FLOWERING TIME
Summer.

BALLOON FLOWER

THE RICH BLUE BLOOMS OF BALLOON FLOWER OPEN FROM CURIOUS, INFLATED BUDS. ENJOY WITH OTHER SUMMER-BLOOMING PERENNIALS.

Description Balloon flowers are showy, summer-blooming plants with saucer-shaped flowers on succulent stems clothed in toothed, triangular leaves. Plants grow from thick, fleshy roots. The rich blue flowers have five-pointed petals.

Ideal position Full sun to light shade.

Ideal soil conditions Well-drained, average to humus-rich soil. Mature plants are drought-tolerant.

Cultivation New shoots are slow to emerge. Take care not to damage them. Remove spent flowers to encourage bloom. Established clumps seldom need division.

Propagation Lift and divide clumps in spring or early autumn. Take basal cuttings of non-flowering shoots in summer. Sow seed outdoors in autumn.

Pest and disease prevention No serious pests or diseases.

Landscape use Plant with summer perennials such as yellow yarrows *Achillea* spp., sages *Salvia* spp. and bee balms *Monarda* spp.

Cultivars 'Apoyama' has blue-violet flowers on 6-inch (15-cm) plants.

'Shell Pink' has pale pink flowers on 2-foot (60-cm) plants.

Polemonium caeruleum

CLIMATE
Zones 3–7.

HEIGHT AND
SPREAD
1½–2½ feet
(45–75 cm) tall.
1–1½ feet
(30–45 cm) wide.

FLOWERING TIME
Throughout
summer.

JACOB'S LADDER

JACOB'S LADDER IS IMPRESSIVE WHEN USED
IN INFORMAL GARDENS WITH ASTILBE, IRISES
AND FERNS UNDER FLOWERING TREES.

Description Jacob's ladder has tall,
leafy stems crowned with loose
clusters of nodding flowers. The
showy leaves are pinnately divided
with many leaflets. Plants grow
from fibrous-rooted crowns, with
saucer-shaped blue or white flowers.

Ideal position Full sun to
partial shade.

Ideal soil conditions Evenly moist,
humus-rich soil.

Cultivation Remove spent flowers
to encourage reblooming. Plants are
care-free and seldom need division.

Propagation Sow seed outdoors in
autumn. Self-sown seedlings may
occasionally appear.

Pest and disease prevention No
serious pests or diseases.

Landscape use Plant in formal
gardens with goat's beard *Aruncus
dioicus*, phlox and ornamental
grasses. Massed plantings are
effective in informal gardens.

Varieties *P. caeruleum* var. *album*
has white flowers.

Other species *P. reptans*, creeping
Jacob's ladder, is a woodland
plant with deep blue flowers on
8–16-inch (20–40-cm) stems. A good
summer groundcover. Zones 2–8.

Polygonatum odoratum

CLIMATE
Zones 3–9.

HEIGHT AND
SPREAD
1½–2½ feet
(45–75 cm) tall.
2–4 feet
(60–120 cm) wide.

FLOWERING TIME
Spring.

OTHER COMMON
NAMES
Japanese Solomon's
seal.

FRAGRANT SOLOMON'S SEAL

FRAGRANT SOLOMON'S SEAL PROVIDES
GRACE AND BEAUTY TO THE SHADE GARDEN.
COMBINE IT WITH HOSTAS AND IRISES.

Description Has graceful, arching
stems with broad, oval, blue-green
leaves, arranged like stairs, up the
stem. Tubular, pale green, fragrant
flowers are carried in clusters at the
nodes. Showy blue-black fruit is
produced in late summer.

Ideal position Partial to full shade.

Ideal soil conditions Moist,
humus-rich soil. Tolerates dry soil.

Cultivation Spreads from thick,
creeping rhizomes to form wide
clumps. Divide to control its spread.

Propagation Divide clumps in
spring or autumn or sow fresh
seed outdoors in autumn.

Pest and disease prevention No
serious pests or diseases.

Landscape use Combine with
hostas, lungworts *Pulmonaria* spp.,
irises, wildflowers and ferns. Use
massed plantings under shrubs.

Cultivars 'Variegatum' (pictured
above) is prized for its broad, oval
leaves with creamy white margins.

Other species *P. biflorum*, Solomon's
seal, grows 1–3 feet (30–90 cm) tall
with narrow, oval leaves and paired
flowers. Zones 3–9.

Primula Polyanthus Group

CLIMATE
Zones 3–8.

HEIGHT AND
SPREAD
8–12 inches
(20–30 cm) tall.
1 foot
(30 cm) wide.

FLOWERING TIME
Spring and early
summer.

POLYANTHUS PRIMROSE

PLANT DRIFTS OF POLYANTHUS PRIMROSE
WITH SPRING BULBS SUCH AS DAFFODILS,
TULIPS AND SPANISH BLUEBELLS.

Description Polyanthus primroses
are hybrids with large, showy
flowers in a rainbow of colors. The
broad, crinkled leaves rise directly
from stout crowns with thick, fibrous
roots. Flat, five-petaled flowers vary
in color from white, cream and
yellow to pink, rose, red and
purple. Many bicolored and eyed
forms are available.

Ideal position Light to partial shade.

Ideal soil conditions Evenly moist,
humus-rich soil. Plants can tolerate
dryness if they go dormant.

Cultivation In cooler zones, mulch
to avoid frost heaving and crown
damage. Divide overgrown clumps
after flowering and replant into soil
that is enriched with organic matter.

Propagation Divide in autumn.
Easy to grow from fresh seed sown
outdoors or indoors in early spring.

Pest and disease prevention No
serious pests or diseases.

Landscape use Combine with
early-blooming perennials such
as hellebores *Helleborus* spp.,
lungworts *Pulmonaria* spp. and
forget-me-nots *Myosotis* spp.
Wildflowers and ferns are
excellent companions.

Polyanthus primrose continued

Drumstick primrose *Primula denticulata*

Hybrids Many hybrids and seed-grown strains are available.

Barnhaven Hybrids are small with large flowers in mixed colors.

Pacific Giant is a seed strain with large, mixed-colored flowers.

Other species *P. auricula*, auricula primrose, is a hardy species with thick, spoon-shaped, evergreen leaves and showy clusters of white, pink, burgundy, rose and bicolored flowers. Zones 2–8.

P. denticulata, drumstick primrose (pictured above), bears round heads of small, pink, lavender or white flowers on tall stalks. Leafy clumps develop as flowers fade. Needs constant moisture. Zones 3–8.

P. elatior, oxslip, has broad, puckered leaves and open clusters of nodding, soft yellow flowers. Zones 3 (with winter protection)–7.

P. japonica, Japanese primrose, has lush, paddle-shaped foliage and pink, rose or white flowers in tiered clusters on tall stems. Zones 5–10.

P. sieboldii, Siebold's primrose, has fuzzy, heart-shaped, toothed leaves and open clusters of pink, rose or white flowers with notched petals. Zones 4–8.

P. veris, cowslip primrose, has fragrant, nodding, yellow flowers and broad leaves. Zones 3–8.

P. vulgaris, English primrose, has wrinkled, tonguelike leaves and flat, pale yellow flowers. Zones 3–8.

Pulmonaria saccharata

CLIMATE
Zones 3–8.

HEIGHT AND SPREAD
9–18 inches (22.5–45 cm) tall.
1–2 feet (30–60 cm) wide.

FLOWERING TIME
Spring.

OTHER COMMON NAMES
Lungwort.

BETHLEHEM SAGE

BETHLEHEM SAGE IS A LOVELY SPRING-BLOOMING FOLIAGE PLANT. IT ADDS A DRAMATIC TOUCH TO SHADY GARDENS.

Description Has wide, hairy leaves variously spotted and blotched with silver. Plants grow from crowns with thick, fibrous roots. The nodding, five-petaled flowers vary in color from pink to blue.

Ideal position Partial to full shade.

Ideal soil conditions Moist, humus-rich soil.

Cultivation Keep soil moist to ensure all-season foliage.

Propagation Divide in spring, after bloom, or in autumn.

Pest and disease prevention No serious pests or diseases.

Landscape use Plant Bethlehem sage with spring bulbs, primroses, foamflowers *Tiarella* spp., wildflowers and ferns.

Cultivars 'Janet Fisk' has densely spotted, white leaves and lavender-pink flowers.

'Mrs Moon' has spotted leaves and pink flowers.

Other species *P. angustifolia*, blue lungwort, has narrow leaves and gentian-blue flowers. Zones 2–8.

P. longifolia, long-leaved lungwort, has spotted leaves and electric-blue flowers. Zones 3–8.

Pulsatilla vulgaris

CLIMATE
Zones 3–8.

HEIGHT AND
SPREAD
6–12 inches
(15–30 cm) tall.
10–12 inches
(25–30 cm) wide.

FLOWERING TIME
Early to midspring.

PASQUE FLOWER

PASQUE FLOWER IS PERFECT FOR PLANTING
IN ROCK GARDENS. IT LOOKS GREAT IN
BORDERS AND IN LARGE CONTAINERS.

Description Pasque flowers are
early-blooming perennials with
cupped flowers over rosettes of
deeply incised, lobed leaves clothed
in soft hairs. Plants grow from deep,
fibrous roots. The purple flowers
have five starry petals surrounding
a central ring of fuzzy, orange-
yellow stamens (male reproductive
structures). Clusters of fuzzy seeds
follow the flowers.

Ideal position Full sun to
light shade.

Ideal soil conditions Average to
humus-rich, well-drained soil.
Does not tolerate soggy soil.

Cultivation Pasque flower begins
blooming in spring and continues
for several weeks. After seed is set,
plant goes dormant unless conditions
are cool. It seldom needs division.

Propagation Divide clumps after
flowering or in autumn. Sow seed
outdoors in autumn or spring.
Self-sown seedlings are plentiful.

Pest and disease prevention No
serious pests or diseases.

Landscape use Great companions
for pasque flowers are bulbs, rock

Pasque flower *Pulsatilla vulgaris* 'Rubra'

cresses *Arabis* spp., basket-of-gold *Aurinia saxatilis*, perennial candytuft *Iberis sempervirens* and columbines *Aquilegia* spp.

Cultivars 'Rubra' (pictured above) has purple- or rust-red flowers.

Other species *P. bungeana* is a tiny species with bell-shaped, violet-blue, upward-facing flowers. This delightful species grows to only 2 inches (5 cm) tall. Zones 4–9.

P. halleri is an unusual species with very hairy, fine, silky foliage. The flowers are white, lavender or purple. *P. hallerie* subsp. *slavica* has hairy, woolly foliage that is less divided than that of *P. halleri*.

It has charming, deep violet flowers. Zones 5–9.

P. montana has very fine, divided leaves. The bell-shaped flowers are deep blue to purple. The flower stems are 6 inches (15 cm) tall but can grow to 1½ feet (45 cm) when in seed. Zones 6–9.

P. patens, prairie pasque flower, has white or pale blue flowers. Plant this species only in sandy, well-drained soil. It goes dormant in hot weather. Zones 3–7.

Rhodanthe anthemoides

CLIMATE
Zones 9–10.

HEIGHT AND
SPREAD
8 inches
(25 cm) tall.
1 foot
(30 cm) wide.

FLOWERING TIME
Virtually
throughout the
entire year.

STRAWFLOWER

THE SMALL, WHITE FLOWERS OF STRAW-
FLOWER ARE ESPECIALLY WELL SUITED TO
MIXED PLANTINGS IN ROCKERIES.

Description Has masses of stiff,
white, papery, daisy-type flowers.
The flowers are 1 inch (2.5 cm)
wide with a yellow center.

Ideal position Full sun.

Ideal soil conditions Well-drained
soil. Will grow in poor soil.

Cultivation Deadhead strawflower
regularly to stimulate more flowers.
Cut back occasionally to maintain
dense growth. It is often treated as
an annual.

Propagation Sow seed in spring.
Propagate cultivars from cuttings
taken in spring.

Pest and disease prevention No
serious pests or diseases.

Landscape use Strawflowers are
a very attractive choice for
rockeries, dry banks and full-sun
meadow plantings.

Cultivars The cultivar 'Paper
Cascade' is good for hanging
baskets or rockeries.

Rodgersia pinnata

CLIMATE
Zones 4–7.

HEIGHT AND
SPREAD
3–4 feet
(90–120 cm) tall.
4 feet
(1.2 m) wide.

FLOWERING TIME
Late spring and
early summer.

OTHER COMMON
NAMES
Roger's flower.

RODGERSIA

RODGERSIA IS A BOLD PERENNIAL IDEALLY SUITED TO BOG AND WATER GARDENS. USE IT WITH OTHER MOISTURE-LOVING PLANTS.

Description Rodgersia has large, pinnately compound leaves. It grows from stout, fibrous-rooted crowns. The small, rose-red flowers are carried in plumelike clusters.

Ideal position Partial to full shade. Protect from hot afternoon sun in warm zones.

Ideal soil conditions Constantly moist, humus-rich soil.

Cultivation Rodgersias form huge clumps from crowns that can remain in place for years. Give each plant at least 3–4 feet (90–120 cm).

Propagation Divide in autumn or spring. Sow seed outdoors in autumn or indoors in spring

Pest and disease prevention No serious pests or diseases.

Landscape use Plant in bog and water gardens or beside streams. Combine with hostas, irises, astilbes, ferns, ligularias *Ligularia* spp. and primroses.

Other species *R. aesculifolia*, finger-leaved rodgersia, has palmately divided leaves and creamy white flowers. Zones 4–7.

R. sambucifolia, elder-leaved rodgersia, is similar to *R. pinnata* but with white flowers. Zones 4–7.

Rudbeckia fulgida

CLIMATE
Zones 3–9.

HEIGHT AND
SPREAD
1½–3 feet
(45–90 cm) tall.
2–4 feet
(60–120 cm) wide.

FLOWERING TIME
Mid- to late
summer.

OTHER COMMON
NAMES
Black-eyed Susan.

ORANGE CONEFLOWER

ORANGE CONEFLOWER IS A VERSATILE
PERENNIAL PERFECT FOR FORMAL BORDERS,
MEADOW GARDENS AND EVEN CONTAINERS.

Description Orange coneflowers are
cheery, summer daisies with oval to
broadly lance-shaped, rough, hairy
foliage on stiff stems. Plants grow
from fibrous-rooted crowns. The
daisy-like flowers have yellow-
orange rays (petal-like structures)
and raised, dark brown centers.

Ideal position Full sun to light
shade. Extremely heat-tolerant.

Ideal soil conditions Average, moist
but well-drained soil. Good
drainage is important.

Cultivation Orange coneflowers are
tough, long-lived perennials. They
spread outward to form large
clumps. The edges of the clumps
are the most vigorous. Divide every
2–4 years and replant into soil that
is enriched with organic matter.

Propagation Divide in autumn
or spring. Sow seed outdoors in
autumn or spring or sow indoors
in late winter.

Pest and disease prevention No
serious pests or diseases.

Landscape use For a wonderful
flower display, plant orange
coneflowers with other

One of the many popular *Rudbeckia* cultivars

daisies, sedums, phlox, bee balms *Monarda* spp., garden mums and ornamental grasses.

Varieties *R. fulgida* var. *sullivantii* is a stout grower with wide leaves. 'Goldstrum' is a popular compact cultivar of this variety. The variety *speciosa* (also known as *R. neumanii*) has narrow leaves and smaller flowers.

Other species There are many species, each with distinctive cultivars. Some are listed below.

R. hirta has the distinctive green-centered cultivar, 'Irish Eyes', as well as golden-orange 'Marmalade'. 'Becky Mixed' is a bushy dwarf cultivar available in a variety of colors ranging from deep orange to light lemon-yellow. Zones 3–10.

R. laciniata is a tall-growing plant with single flowers and is the parent of a number of double forms, including the dwarf-growing 'Goldquelle'. Zones 3–10.

Ruta graveolens

CLIMATE
Zones 4–9.

HEIGHT AND
SPREAD
1–3 feet
(30–90 cm) tall.
2–3 feet
(60–90 cm) wide.

FLOWERING TIME
Summer.

RUE

RUE IS A FAVORITE FOR HERB GARDENS BUT
ITS FOLIAGE LOOKS GREAT IN ORNAMENTAL
PLANTINGS WITH BOLD, COLORFUL FLOWERS.

Description Rue has small, yellow
flowers that are carried in open
clusters above lacy, aromatic,
blue-gray foliage. It is a traditional
herb-garden plant.

Ideal position Full sun or
light shade.

Ideal soil conditions Average to
rich, well-drained soil. Plants
tolerate dry, sandy soil.

Cultivation Rue forms broad, dense
clumps that seldom need division.

Propagation Take stem cuttings in
summer and autumn.

Pest and disease prevention No
serious pests or diseases.

Landscape use Choose rue for herb
and knot gardens or for the front
or middle of beds and borders.
Combine with hyssop *Hyssopus
officinalis*, yarrow, ornamental
onion and ornamental grasses. For
contrast, plant with bold flowers
such as balloon flower *Platycodon
grandiflorus*. Think twice about
planting rue where people will have
to brush by, because it produces an
oil that can irritate the skin.

Salvia elegans

CLIMATE
Zones 6–8.

HEIGHT AND
SPREAD
6 feet
(1.8 m) tall.
3–4 feet
(90–120 cm) wide.

FLOWERING TIME
Summer through
autumn.

PINEAPPLE–SCENTED SAGE

USE PINEAPPLE-SCENTED SAGE IN HERB AND
COTTAGE GARDENS. THE FOLIAGE EXUDES
A WONDERFUL PINEAPPLE SCENT.

Description This perennial has
bright red flowers. In cooler areas it
may not bloom as prolifically as in
warmer areas but the foliage is an
attractive light green. The leaves are
used to flavor summer drinks.

Ideal position Full sun.

Ideal soil conditions Well-drained
soil with adequate summer water.

Cultivation Pineapple-scented sage
tolerates light frosts. Light or partial
shade will produce softer stems
which result in a much more open,
"floppy" plant.

Propagation Take stem or root
cuttings during summer.

Pest and disease prevention No
serious pests or diseases.

Landscape use Use pineapple-
scented sage for structure and
foliage interest in formal beds
and borders. It's a good filler for
the rear of the border or where
its clear, red blooms can be
incorporated into a late-summer
color scheme.

Salvia officinalis

CLIMATE
Zones 4–9.

HEIGHT AND
SPREAD
1–2½ feet
(30–75 cm) tall.
2–3 feet
(60–90 cm) wide.

FLOWERING TIME
Summer.

SAGE

SAGE IS AN AROMATIC HERB THAT BLENDS
EQUALLY WELL INTO FLOWER GARDENS AND
HERB GARDENS. YOU CAN ENJOY IT ALL YEAR.

Description The broad, lance-
shaped, opposite leaves are
sea-green to purple-green with a
crinkled surface. The pink or purple
flowers are less showy than those
of other sages but are an added
bonus to the leaves. Plants grow
from fibrous-rooted crowns.

Ideal position Full sun or
light shade.

Ideal soil conditions Light, sandy
or loamy, well-drained soil.

Cultivation Sage grows to form a
small shrub with persistent woody

growth in warmer zones. Cut plants
back in spring to remove winter-
damaged growth and reshape plants.

Propagation Take stem cuttings
in summer.

Pest and disease prevention No
serious pests or diseases.

Landscape use Use sage in herb
and cottage gardens or for winter
structure and foliage interest in
formal beds and borders.

Cultivars The pretty 'Purpurascens'
(pictured above) has leaves tinged
with purple.
    'Tricolor' has gray-green leaves
tinged with yellow and pink to red.

Salvia pratensis

CLIMATE
Zones 3–9.

HEIGHT AND SPREAD
2 feet
(60 cm) tall.
2–3 feet
(60–90 cm) tall.

FLOWERING TIME
Summer

OTHER COMMON NAMES
Meadow clary.

MEADOW SAGE

MEADOW SAGE IS AN IDEAL PERENNIAL FOR MEADOW PLANTINGS BECAUSE IT DOES NOT REQUIRE SUPPORT OR STAKING.

Description An easy-care herbaceous perennial. The plant forms an attractive mound of basal, gray-green leaves and flowers on stout stems. Flowers vary from pale to dark violet-purple and are sparsely carried on spikes up to 3 feet (90 cm) tall.

Ideal position Full sun.

Ideal soil conditions Well-drained soil with adequate summer water. Tolerates frost.

Cultivation Plant in particularly well-drained soil. Mulch well in early spring.

Propagation By seed or by division or softwood cuttings in spring.

Pest and disease prevention No serious pests or diseases.

Landscape use Well suited to midrow positioning in a border where both the foliage and the taller flower spikes can be fully appreciated.

Cultivars There are numerous cultivars available in colors ranging from white through pink to shades of blue and purple.

Salvia x superba

CLIMATE
Zones 4–7.

HEIGHT AND
SPREAD
1½–3½ feet
(45–105 cm) tall.
2–3 feet
(60–90 cm) wide.

FLOWERING TIME
Early to mid-
summer. Plants
often rebloom.

VIOLET SAGE

THE SPIKY BLOOMS OF VIOLET SAGE
COMBINE WONDERFULLY WITH ROUNDED
PERENNIALS SUCH AS CRANESBILLS.

Description A bushy, well-branched
plant with aromatic, triangular
leaves. It grows from a fibrous-
rooted crown. Violet-blue flowers
are carried on narrow spikes.

Ideal position Full sun to light
shade. Drought-tolerant once the
plant is established.

Ideal soil conditions Average to
humus-rich, moist, well-drained soil.

Cultivation After flowering wanes,
shear back flowering stems to
promote fresh growth and renewed
bloom. Plants seldom need division.

Propagation Divide in spring or
autumn. Take cuttings in late spring
or early summer

Pest and disease prevention No
serious pests or diseases.

Landscape use Plant violet sage
in borders or rock gardens with
early-summer perennials such as
yarrow, lamb's-ears *Stachys
byzantina*, daylilies, coreopsis
and ornamental grasses.

Cultivars 'Blue Queen' has violet-
blue flowers.

'East Friesland' has attractive
purple-blue flowers. It is 1–1½ feet
(30–45 cm) tall.

'May Night' has violet-blue
flowers on bushy plants.

Sanguinaria canadensis

CLIMATE
Zones 3–9.

HEIGHT AND
SPREAD
4–6 inches
(10–15 cm) tall.
6–8 inches
(15–20 cm) wide.

FLOWERING TIME
Early to midspring.

BLOODROOT

BLOODROOT IS A BRIGHT WILDFLOWER,
PERFECT IN WOODLAND GARDENS WITH
SPRING BULBS, HOSTAS AND FERNS.

Description A single, deeply cut,
seven-lobed leaf emerges wrapped
around the single flower bud. Plants
grow from a thick, creeping
rhizome. The snow-white flowers
have eight to 11 narrow petals
surrounding a cluster of yellow-
orange stamens (male reproductive
structures). Flowers last a few days.

Ideal position Light to full shade.
Spring sun is important but summer
shade is necessary. During
prolonged dry spells the plants
go dormant with no ill effect.

Ideal soil conditions Moist,
humus-rich soil.

Cultivation The foliage remains
attractive all summer when ample
moisture is available. Plants form
dense clumps that can be divided.

Propagation Divide in late summer.
Sow fresh seed outdoors in summer.
Self-sown seedlings often appear.

Pest and disease prevention No
serious pests or diseases.

Landscape use Plant bloodroot
under shrubs. Use as a groundcover.

Cultivars 'Flore Pleno' is a stunning,
fully double form with magnificent,
long-lasting flowers.

Sanguisorba canadensis

ROSACEAE

CLIMATE
Zones 3–8.

HEIGHT AND
SPREAD
4–5 feet
(1.2–1.5 m) tall.
4 feet
(1.2 m) wide.

FLOWERING TIME
Late summer and
early autumn.

CANADIAN BURNET

THE TALL BOTTLEBRUSHES OF CANADIAN
BURNET LOOK STUNNING AT THE REAR OF
A BORDER OR GARDEN BED.

Description Plants grow from thick, fleshy roots. Flowers appear in late summer atop stout stems clothed in pinnately divided leaves with oblong leaflets. The fuzzy, white flowers lack petals and are tightly packed into dense spikes.

Ideal position Full sun to partial shade. Intolerant of excessive heat.

Ideal soil conditions Evenly moist, humus-rich soil.

Cultivation Mulch plants to help keep the soil cool and moist. Divide overgrown clumps.

Propagation Divide in spring. Sow seed outdoors in autumn.

Pest and disease prevention No serious pests or diseases.

Landscape use Plant at the rear of the border with phlox, monkshood *Aconitum* spp., asters, boltonia *Boltonia asteroides*, sedum and ornamental grasses.

Other species *S. obtusa*, Japanese burnet, grows to just 3–4 feet (90–120 cm) with drooping, rose-pink flower clusters and blue-green leaves with rounded leaflets. Zones 4–8.

Santolina chamaecyparissus

CLIMATE
Zones 6–8.

HEIGHT AND
SPREAD
1–2 feet
(30–60 cm) tall.
2 feet
(60 cm) wide.

FLOWERING TIME
Summer.

LAVENDER COTTON

PRETTY LAVENDER COTTON IS GREAT TO
EDGE WALKS AND BEDS OR TO CONFIGURE
INTRICATE KNOT GARDEN DESIGNS.

Description Lavender cotton is a
compact, semiwoody plant with
small, white, woolly, pinnately
divided leaves topped with yellow
flowers in summer. Plants grow
from fibrous-rooted crowns. The
button-like yellow flowers are held
above the foliage on thin stalks.

Ideal position Full sun. Plants
tolerate drought, poor soil and salt.

Ideal soil conditions Average,
well-drained soil.

Cultivation Plants need winter
protection in cold areas. Cut back

in early spring to promote strong,
healthy growth.

Propagation Layer in spring. Take
cuttings in summer.

Pest and disease prevention No
serious pests or diseases.

Landscape use Combine with other
perennials that need good drainage,
such as pinks *Dianthus* spp., rock
cresses *Arabis* spp. and sedums.

Other species *S. rosmarinifolia*,
green lavender cotton, is similar but
has deep green foliage.

Saponaria x *lempergii*

CLIMATE
Zones 5–8.

HEIGHT AND
SPREAD
4–6 inches
(10–15 cm) tall.
12–14 inches
(30–35 cm) wide.

FLOWERING TIME
Summer.

SOAPWORT

THE MOUNDS OF PRETTY FLOWERS ON
SOAPWORT LOOK LOVELY AT THE FRONT
OF BORDERS AND IN ROCK GARDENS.

Description Soapwort has mounds
of flowers on sprawling stems with
oval leaves. Plants grow from
fibrous-rooted crowns. The 1-inch
(2.5-cm), deep pink flowers have
five squared petals.

Ideal position Full sun to light shade.

Ideal soil conditions Average,
well-drained soil.

Cultivation Divide to control the
spread. Cut back after flowering.

Propagation Divide in spring or
autumn. Take cuttings early summer.

Pest and disease prevention No
serious pests or diseases.

Landscape use Plant soapworts
along walks, along the edges of
beds, at the front of borders or
in rock gardens.

Other species *S. ocymoides*, rock
soapwort, is a sprawling plant with
clusters of ¼-inch (6-mm), bright
pink flowers. 'Rubra Compacta'
forms tight mounds with deep pink
to crimson flowers. Zones 3–7.

S. officinalis, bouncing Bet, is a
fast-spreading plant with 1–2½-foot
(30–75-cm) stems and rounded
clusters of pale pink flowers.
Zones 2–8.

Saxifraga stolonifera

CLIMATE
Zones 6–9.

HEIGHT AND SPREAD
10–12 inches
(25–30 cm) tall.
1 foot
(30 cm) wide.

FLOWERING TIME
Spring.

STRAWBERRY GERANIUM

IN A SHADY GARDEN, USE THE SILVERY FOLIAGE OF STRAWBERRY GERANIUM WITH HOSTAS, BULBS, WILDFLOWERS AND FERNS.

Description Makes an attractive groundcover with round leaves that resemble bedding geraniums. The evergreen leaves are attractively veined with silver. The small, white flowers have five petals, two of which are longer than the others.

Ideal position Partial to full shade.

Ideal soil conditions Moist, humus-rich soil.

Cultivation Plants spread quickly to form dense, weed-proof mats. Easily pulled if they spread out of bounds.

Propagation Remove and replant rooted offsets in spring or autumn. Sow seed outdoors in autumn.

Pest and disease prevention No serious pests or diseases.

Landscape use Plant as a ground-cover under flowering shrubs and small trees. The plants also perform admirably in pots.

Cultivars 'Tricolor' has pink and cream variegation but is less hardy.

Other species *S.* x *urbium*, London pride, has toothed, spoon-shaped, evergreen leaves and clusters of small pink flowers. Zones 6–8.

Scabiosa caucasica

CLIMATE
Zones 3–7.

HEIGHT AND
SPREAD
1½–2 feet
(45–60 cm) tall.
1–1½ feet
(30–45 cm) wide.

FLOWERING TIME
Summer.

PINCUSHION FLOWER

TO INCREASE THE VISUAL IMPACT OF
PINCUSHION FLOWER, PLANT IT IN GROUPS
WHERE THE FLOWERS SEEM TO DANCE.

Description Pincushion flowers are
old-fashioned perennials that are
regaining the popularity they had in
Victorian gardens. The stems are
loosely clothed in lance-shaped to
three-lobed leaves. The unusual,
soft blue flowers are packed into
flat, 2–3-inch (5–7.5-cm) heads. The
flowers increase in size as they near
the margins of the heads.

Ideal position Full sun to light
shade. Sensitive to high temperatures.

Ideal soil conditions Average to
humus-rich, moist but well-drained
soil. Will not tolerate wet soil.

Cultivation Plants form good-sized
clumps in 1–2 years. Divide if plants
become overcrowded. Deadheading
promotes continued bloom.

Propagation Divide in spring. Sow
fresh seed outdoors in autumn or
indoors in late winter.

Pest and disease prevention No
serious pests or diseases.

Landscape use The airy flowers
look great above low, mounded
plants such as phlox, pinks

Pincushion flower *Scabiosa caucasica* 'Clive Greaves'

Dianthus spp. and yarrows. They combine well with bee balms *Monarda* spp., daylilies and columbines *Aquilegia* spp.

Cultivars 'Alba' has white flowers.

'Butterfly Blue', of uncertain parentage, is long blooming with lilac-blue flowers.

'Clive Greaves' (pictured above) has large, lavender-blue heads.

'Miss Wilmot' is creamy white.

Other species *S. atropurpurea* is a tall, branching, often short-lived plant with wiry stems, which carry deep purple, blue or lavender blooms. Flower season can be extended if flowers are regularly deadheaded. This species has given rise to some elegant double cultivars, including 'Double' and 'Dwarf Double'. Zones 3–7.

S. columbaria 'Pink Mist' has flowers with deep pink petals becoming paler at the center and held over gray-green foliage. Zones 4–8.

S. lucida forms tufted clumps of silvery green foliage with pale lilac summer flowers held erect on thin, wiry stems. Zones 4–8.

S. graminfolia (pictured on page 284) has grasslike foliage topped with blue-violet flowers on slender stalks. Zones 4–8.

Sedum spectabile

CLIMATE
Zones 3–9.

HEIGHT AND
SPREAD
1–2 feet
(30–60 cm) tall.
2 feet
(60 cm) wide.

FLOWERING TIME
Mid- to late
summer.

SHOWY STONECROP

VERSATILE SHOWY STONECROP IS STUNNING
WHEN USED IN ANY FLOWER GARDEN IN
LARGE SWEEPS OR CLUMPS.

Description Late summer perennials
with clusters of pink flowers atop
thick stems clothed in broad, gray-
green leaves. Plants grow from
fibrous-rooted crowns. Small, bright
pink flowers are borne in 4–6-inch
(10–15-cm) domed clusters. The
pale green buds are attractive in
summer and the brown seed heads
hold their shape all winter.

Ideal position Full sun. Extremely
drought- and heat-tolerant.

Ideal soil conditions Average to
humus-rich, well-drained soil.

Cultivation Clumps get quite full
with age and may fall open. Divide
overgrown plants.

Propagation Divide from spring to
midsummer. Take cuttings of non-
flowering shoots in summer. Sow
seed in spring or autumn.

Pest and disease prevention No
serious pests or diseases.

Landscape use Plant in formal
borders, informal gardens and rock
gardens. Combine with yarrow,
purple coneflower *Echinacea
purpurea* and ornamental grasses.

Cultivars 'Brilliant' has pretty
rose-pink flowers.
    'Carmen' is carmine-pink.

Two-row sedum *Sedum spurium* 'Dragon's Blood'

Hybrids Several hybrid cultivars are available. 'Autumn Joy' is similar to *S. spectabile* but more robust and with darker flowers.

'Ruby Glow' has sprawling stems with purple-tinged leaves and ruby-red flowers.

Other species *S. aizoon*, Aizoon stonecrop, is an upright grower with oval, toothed leaves and flat, 3–4-inch (7.5–10-cm) clusters of yellow flowers. Zones 4–9.

S. album, white stonecrop, is a creeping plant with evergreen leaves and 1–2-inch (2.5–5-cm) clusters of white flowers. Zones 3–9.

S. kamtschaticum, Kamschatka stonecrop, is a creeping plant with yellow flowers. Zones 3–8.

S. maximum, stonecrop, is an upright plant with oval leaves and domed clusters of creamy rose flowers. Zones 3–8.

S. spurium, two-row sedum, is a creeper with rounded, evergreen leaves and open clusters of pink flowers. 'Dragon's Blood' (pictured above) has red-tinged foliage and rose-red flowers. 'Tricolor' has leaves variegated with pink, white and green. Zones 3–8.

S. ternatum, whorled stonecrop, is a low, woodland plant with starry white flowers. Zones 4–8.

Silene fimbriata

CLIMATE
Zones 5–9.

HEIGHT AND SPREAD
2 feet
(60 cm) tall.
2 feet
(60 cm) wide.

FLOWERING TIME
Summer.

OTHER COMMON NAMES
Catchfly.

CAMPION

PUT CAMPION IN A ROCKERY OR THE FRONT OF A BORDER WHERE IT WON'T BE OVER-SHADOWED BY MORE AGGRESSIVE PLANTS.

Description Good ground-covering plant with hairy, upright, leafy stems carrying interesting flowers with light green, inflated calyces holding white, fringed petals.

Ideal position Full or partial sun.

Ideal soil conditions Fertile, evenly moist, well-drained soil.

Cultivation Shear flowering stems at end of season to promote growth and next year's blooming.

Propagation Stem cuttings in spring. Sow seed in spring or early autumn.

Pest and disease prevention No serious pests or diseases.

Landscape use Campion makes a wonderful groundcover. It is perfect for rock gardens and sloping beds and borders.

Other species *S. acaulis*, moss campion, is a useful plant for the cooler-climate rock garden. It forms a green mass with pink flowers during summer. Flowering may be sparse if it is not suited to the site. Zones 2–9.

S. uniflora flowers from spring though summer. The double-flowering 'Flore Pleno' is usually seen in cultivation. Zones 3–10.

Smilacina racemosa

CLIMATE
Zones 3–8.

HEIGHT AND
SPREAD
2–4 feet
(60–120 cm) tall.
2–3 feet
(60–90 cm) or
more wide.

FLOWERING TIME
Spring.

OTHER COMMON
NAMES
False Solomon's
seal.

SOLOMON'S PLUME

SOLOMON'S PLUME THRIVES IN SHADE.
YOU'LL ENJOY THE FLOWERS IN SPRING,
FOLIAGE IN SUMMER AND BERRIES IN AUTUMN.

Description Erect, arching stems
bear broad, glossy, green leaves
arranged like ascending stairs.
Plants grow from a thick, creeping
rhizome. Small, starry, creamy white
flowers are borne in terminal,
plumelike clusters. Red berries ripen
in late summer.

Ideal position Light to full shade.
Plants burn in full sun.

Ideal soil conditions Evenly moist,
humus-rich, neutral to acid soil.

Cultivation Divide tangled rhizomes
if plants overgrow their position.

Propagation Divide in spring or
autumn. Sow seed in autumn.

Pest and disease prevention No
serious pests or diseases.

Landscape use Plant Solomon's
plume in woodland gardens with
hostas, bleeding hearts *Dicentra*
spp., columbines *Aquilegia* spp.,
wildflowers and ferns. Use them
as an underplanting for shrubs
and flowering trees.

Other species *S. stellata*, starry
Solomon's plume, has narrow,
blue-green foliage and small
clusters of ¼-inch (6-mm) flowers.
The attractive berries are green with
deep purple stripes. Zones 2–7.

Solidago canadensis

CLIMATE
Zones 3–8.

HEIGHT AND
SPREAD
2–5 feet
(60–150 cm) tall.
3–5 feet
(90–150 cm) wide.

FLOWERING TIME
Late summer into
autumn.

CANADIAN GOLDENROD

PLANT THE VERSATILE CANADIAN GOLDEN-
ROD IN FORMAL OR INFORMAL GARDENS,
MEADOWS AND WILDFLOWER PLANTINGS.

Description A common roadside
wildflower with plumed flower
clusters and toothed, lance-shaped
leaves. Grows from creeping
rhizomes and can become invasive.
The small, bright yellow flowers are
grouped into large, plumed heads.

Ideal position Full sun to
light shade.

Ideal soil conditions Average, moist
to well-drained soil.

Cultivation Spreads rapidly and
needs frequent division.

Propagation Divide in spring or
after flowering has ended. Sow seed
outdoors in autumn. Take cuttings
in early summer.

Pest and disease prevention No
serious pests or diseases.

Landscape use Combine with phlox,
asters, sunflowers *Helianthus* spp.
and gayfeathers *Liatris* spp.
Contrary to popular belief, goldenrods do not cause hayfever. The
culprit is ragweed, which blooms
at the same time.

Hybrids 'Baby Gold' is 2–2½ feet
(60–75 cm) tall. 'Crown of Rays'
has large, flaring flower clusters.

Stachys byzantina

CLIMATE
Zones 4–8.

HEIGHT AND
SPREAD
6–15 inches
(15–37.5 cm) tall.
1–2 feet
(30–60 cm) wide.

FLOWERING TIME
Early summer.

LAMB'S EARS

THE DENSE, PRETTY FOLIAGE OF LAMB'S EARS
MAKES IT AN EXCELLENT EDGING PLANT FOR
GROWING ALONG PATHS AND WALKWAYS.

Description Lamb's ears are eye-catching plants with basal rosettes of elongated, densely white, woolly leaves. The leaves have the same soft feeling as lamb's wool, hence the name. These sun-loving plants grow from slow-creeping stems. Small, two-lipped rose-purple flowers are carried on woolly flower stalks. Many people consider the flowers unattractive and remove them from the plant.

Ideal position Full sun to light shade. Plants are sensitive to hot, humid weather.

Ideal soil conditions Well-drained, sandy or loamy soil. Intolerant of heavy, soggy soil.

Cultivation Lamb's ears form dense, broad clumps of tightly packed foliage. Divide overgrown clumps to control their spread.

Propagation Divide plants in spring or autumn.

Pest and disease prevention In wet, humid weather rot may occur. Cut back affected plants. Proper siting is the best defense.

Landscape use Choose lamb's ears for the front of formal and informal gardens or garden beds. Combine these plantings with irises, coral

Lamb's ears continued

Lamb's ears *Stachys byzantina* 'Cotton Boll'

bells *Heuchera* spp., alliums *Allium* spp., yuccas and sedums.

Cultivars 'Big Ears' grows larger than most lamb's ears and has purple flowers borne on tall spikes.

'Cotton Boll' (pictured above) has larger, less-woolly leaves and flower heads that look like cotton-wool balls. It grows well in the warmer zones.

'Primrose Heron' has soft, primrose-yellow foliage in spring.

'Silver Carpet' is a neat, compact cultivar. It is listed as non-flowering, but it does flower in some gardens.

Other species *S. coccinea*, scarlet hedge nettle, is a long-flowering perennial with red flowers. It grows to 1–3 feet (30–90 cm) tall and 1½ feet (45 cm) wide. It flowers from spring through to autumn. Zones 5–9.

S. macrantha has erect stems that grow to 2 feet (60 cm) tall. It bears purple-pink flowers from summer to autumn. Zones 5–9.

Stokesia laevis

CLIMATE
Zones 5–9.

HEIGHT AND
SPREAD
1–2 feet
(30–60 cm) tall.
2 feet
(60 cm) wide.

FLOWERING TIME
Summer.

STOKES' ASTER

STOKES' ASTER IS ATTRACTIVE IN FOLIAGE
AND FLOWER AND IT LOOKS WONDERFUL
IN FORMAL OR INFORMAL GARDENS.

Description The broad, lance-shaped leaves are deep green with a white midvein. The leaves form a rosette growing from a crown with thick, fibrous roots. The 2–3-inch (5–7.5-cm) daisy-like flowers have ragged blue rays and fuzzy white centers.

Ideal position Full sun to light shade.

Ideal soil conditions Average to humus-rich, moist, but well-drained soil. Established plants tolerate poor, dry soil.

Cultivation Plants grow particularly well when left undisturbed for many years. Divide in spring or autumn as necessary.

Propagation Divide in early spring. Sow seed outdoors in autumn or indoors in winter after stratification.

Pest and disease prevention No serious pests or diseases.

Landscape use Combine with verbenas *Verbena* spp., phlox, goldenrods *Solidago* spp. and ornamental grasses.

Cultivars 'Alba' has white flowers. 'Blue Danube' has very pretty lavender-blue flowers.

Symphytum ibericum

CLIMATE
Zones 3–8.

HEIGHT AND SPREAD
Foliage to 1 foot (30 cm) tall.
2 feet (60 cm) wide.
Flowers to 1½ feet (45 cm) tall.

FLOWERING TIME
Spring.

YELLOW COMFREY

YELLOW COMFREY IS AN EXCELLENT, EASY-CARE GROUNDCOVER FOR DIFFICULT DRY, SHADY SPOTS IN YOUR GARDEN.

Description It produces dense, spreading clumps that tend to crowd out most weeds. Clusters of white to creamy yellow, tubular flowers, ¾ inch (18 mm) long, rise above the foliage.

Ideal position Sun or partial shade.

Ideal soil conditions Light-textured, well-drained soil. Tolerates dry, poor soil once established.

Cultivation Set plants 1½–2 feet (45–60 cm) apart in spring or autumn. Once established, plants need virtually no care.

Propagation Propagate by division in spring or autumn.

Pest and disease prevention No serious pests or diseases.

Landscape use Yellow comfrey is an excellent, easy-care, weed-suppressing groundcover for dry, shaded spots.

Cultivars 'Goldsmith' has pretty green leaves variegated with yellow and cream. Flowers vary in color from pale cream, pink to pale blue.

Thalictrum aquilegiifolium

CLIMATE
Zones 5–8.

HEIGHT AND
SPREAD
2–3 feet
(60–90 cm) tall.
1–2 feet
(30–60 cm) wide.

FLOWERING TIME
Late spring and
early summer.

COLUMBINE MEADOW RUE

COLUMBINE MEADOW RUE PERFORMS WELL
BESIDE PONDS OR ALONG STREAMS WITH
IRISES, HOSTAS, DAYLILIES AND FERNS.

Description Has billowy plumes crowning erect stalks clothed in intricately divided leaves that resemble columbines. Plants grow from fibrous-rooted crowns. The ½-inch (1-cm) lavender or white flowers consist of many fuzzy stamens (male reproductive structures) in dense clusters.

Ideal position Full sun or partial shade.

Ideal soil conditions Evenly moist, humus-rich soil. Plants tolerate wet soil.

Cultivation Clumps spread slowly and seldom need division.

Propagation Divide in spring or autumn. Sow seed outdoors in autumn or indoors in early spring.

Pest and disease prevention No serious pests or diseases.

Landscape use Plant in formal or informal gardens.

Cultivars 'Album' has white flowers. 'Atropurpureum' is violet.

Other species *T. flavum* subsp. *glaucum*, dusty meadow rue, has blue-gray foliage and flattened heads of soft, sulfur-yellow flowers. Zones 4–8.

Thermopsis villosa

CLIMATE
Zones 3–9.

HEIGHT AND
SPREAD
3–5 feet
(90–150 cm) tall.
2–4 feet
(60–120 cm) wide.

FLOWERING TIME
Late spring or early
summer.

OTHER COMMON
NAMES
Carolina
thermopsis and
Southern lupine.

CAROLINA LUPINE

CAROLINA LUPINE IS LOVELY AT THE EDGE
OF AN OPEN WOODLAND OR WITH SHRUBS
IN LIGHTLY SHADED WILD GARDENS.

Description Produces upright flower
spikes atop stout stems clothed in
three-lobed, gray-green leaves.
Plants grow from stout, fibrous-
rooted crowns. Lemon-yellow, pea-
shaped flowers are tightly packed
into 8–12-inch (20–30-cm) clusters.

Ideal position Full sun to light
shade. Heat-tolerant.

Ideal soil conditions Average to
humus-rich, moist, acid soil.

Cultivation Clumps grow to
shrublike proportions but seldom
need division if ample space is

allotted. If foliage declines after
bloom, cut it down to the ground.

Propagation Take cuttings in early
summer from sideshoots. Sow seed
outdoors in autumn. Sow seed
indoors in early spring after soaking
it in hot water for 12–24 hours.

Pest and disease prevention No
serious pests or diseases.

Landscape use Plant toward the rear
of the garden with peonies, willow
blue star *Amsonia tabernae-
montana*, cranesbills *Geranium*
spp. and other rounded or
mounding plants.

Tiarella cordifolia

CLIMATE
Zones 3–8.

HEIGHT AND
SPREAD
6–10 inches
(15–25 cm) tall.
1–2 feet
(30–60 cm) wide.

FLOWERING TIME
Spring.

FOAMFLOWER

AS THE CONSUMMATE GROUNDCOVER,
FOAMFLOWER'S FOLIAGE MATS DISCOURAGE
WEEDS UNDER SHRUBS AND TREES.

Description Woodland wildflowers with fuzzy flowers and rosettes of triangular, three-lobed hairy leaves. Plants grow from fibrous-rooted crowns and creeping stems. The small, starry white flowers are borne in spikelike clusters. They are often tinged with pink.

Ideal position Partial to full shade.

Ideal soil conditions Evenly moist, humus-rich, slightly acid soil.

Cultivation Spreads by creeping stems to form broad mats. Divide plants to control spread.

Propagation Remove runners in summer and treat them as cuttings if they lack roots of their own. Sow seed in spring.

Pest and disease prevention No serious pests or diseases.

Landscape use In woodland gardens combine them with bulbs, ferns and wildflowers such as fringed bleeding heart *Dicentra eximia* and bloodroot *Sanguinaria canadensis*, as well as hostas and irises.

Other species *T. wherryi* is a clump-forming species with many pink-tinged flower spikes rising above deeply lobed leaves in late spring.

Tradescantia Andersoniana Group

COMMELINACEAE

CLIMATE
Zones 3–9.

HEIGHT AND
SPREAD
1–2 feet
(30–60 cm) tall.
2 feet
(60 cm) wide.

FLOWERING TIME
Spring and early
summer.

COMMON SPIDERWORT

EACH COMMON SPIDERWORT FLOWER LASTS
ONLY A DAY, BUT ONE PLANT PRODUCES SO
MANY YOU'LL ENJOY THEM FOR MONTHS.

Description Has satiny flowers
borne in clusters at the tips of the
stems. The 1–1½-inch (2.5–3.5-cm)
flowers have three rounded blue,
purple or white petals. Plants grow
from thick, spidery roots.

Ideal position Full sun to
partial shade.

Ideal soil conditions Moist but well-
drained, average to humus-rich soil.

Cultivation After flowering, plants
tend to look shabby. Cut them to
the ground to encourage new
growth. Plants in dry situations tend
to go dormant in summer.

Propagation Divide in autumn. Self-
sown seedlings often appear.

Pest and disease prevention No
serious pests or diseases.

Landscape use Plant in informal
gardens with bellflowers
Campanula spp., columbines
Aquilegia spp., hostas and ferns. In
formal gardens combine them with
other spring-blooming perennials.

Cultivars 'Blue Stone' has rich
medium blue flowers.
'J.C. Weguelin' is sky-blue and
'Zwanenberg Blue' is purple-blue.
'Pauline' has orchid-pink flowers.

Tricyrtis hirta

CLIMATE
Zones 4–9.

HEIGHT AND
SPREAD
2–3 feet
(60–90 cm) tall.
1–2 feet
(30–60 cm) wide.

FLOWERING TIME
Late summer and
autumn.

COMMON TOAD LILY

COMMON TOAD LILY IS SUBTLE AND IS BEST PLANTED WHERE IT CAN BE FULLY APPRECIATED AT CLOSE RANGE.

Description The tall, arching stems are clothed in two-ranked, broadly lance-shaped leaves that have prominent veins. The purple-spotted white flowers face upward with three petals and three petal-like sepals around a central column. The flowers are carried in the leaf axils on the upper one-third of the stem.

Ideal position Light to partial shade. Full sun will burn the foliage.

Ideal soil conditions Evenly moist, humus-rich soil.

Cultivation Plants spread by creeping stems to form handsome clumps that seldom need division. Plants often bloom in autumn. In cooler zones they may be damaged by frost as they begin blooming.

Propagation Divide clumps in spring. Sow seed outdoors in autumn for best results.

Pest and disease prevention No serious pests or diseases.

Landscape use Large groups of common toad lilies are effective when planted with astilbes, hostas, ferns and other woodland plants.

Tropaeolum speciosum

CLIMATE
Zones 8–10.

HEIGHT AND
SPREAD
9 feet
(2.7 m) tall.
Up to 6 feet
(1.8 m) wide.

FLOWERING TIME
Summer to autumn.

OTHER COMMON
NAMES
Chilean flame
creeper and
Scottish flame
flower.

FLAME CREEPER

A VERY PRETTY PERENNIAL CREEPER, FLAME CREEPER IS PERFECT FOR ADDING COLOR TO THOSE DULL AREAS IN YOUR GARDEN.

Description Flame creeper is a perennial climber. Its delicate shoots are covered with apple-green foliage. This stunning vine has fine, blue-green palmate leaves, and it attracts birds.

Ideal position Sun to partial shade. Ideal for cool, humid areas.

Ideal soil conditions Fertile, moist, well-drained soil.

Cultivation In the colder areas, lift the tubers when plants become dormant and store them in peat in a frost-free garage. Feed monthly and divide tubers in spring. The secret to a healthy flame creeper is good drainage, cool temperatures and just enough moisture.

Propagation Start seed or tubers early indoors and transplant after danger of frost. Be careful when moving them, their roots are very delicate. Take cuttings in late summer.

Pest and disease prevention No serious pests or diseases.

Landscape use Use as a vine or cascading over rocks around a water feature or scrambling over fences. It's perfect in any cool, shady humid part of your garden.

Uvularia grandiflora

CLIMATE
Zones 3–8.

HEIGHT AND
SPREAD
1–1½ feet
(30–45 cm) tall.
1–2 feet
(30–60 cm) wide.

FLOWERING TIME
Spring.

OTHER COMMON
NAMES
Large-flowered
bellwort.

GREAT MERRYBELLS

THE NODDING FLOWERS OF GREAT MERRY-
BELLS LOOK WONDERFUL WITH OTHER SPRING
WILDFLOWERS AND BULBS.

Description Plants grow from
rhizomes with brittle white roots.
The nodding, bell-shaped, lemon-
yellow flowers have three petals
and three petal-like sepals that twist
in the middle and are on slender
stalks clothed in gray-green leaves.

Ideal position Partial to full shade.
Spring sun is important for bloom
but summer shade is mandatory.

Ideal soil conditions Moist, humus-
rich soil.

Cultivation Great merrybells spread
to form tight, attractive clumps.

When flowers fade, the foliage
expands to form an attractive,
summer-long groundcover.

Propagation Divide plants before
flowering in early spring.

Pest and disease prevention No
serious pests or diseases.

Landscape use Plant great merrybells in woodland gardens with
wildflowers such as bloodroot
Sanguinaria canadensis and fringed
bleeding heart *Dicentra eximia*.

Other species *U. sessilifolia*,
strawbell, is a slender, delicate plant
with straw-colored flowers and
narrow leaves. Zones 4–8.

Verbascum chaixii

CLIMATE
Zones 4–8.

HEIGHT AND SPREAD
2–3 feet
(60–90 cm) tall.
1–2 feet
(30–60 cm) wide.

FLOWERING TIME
Summer.

NETTLE–LEAVED MULLEIN

COMBINE NETTLE-LEAVED MULLEIN WITH
FINE-LEAVED PLANTS, SUCH AS CATMINT,
IN INFORMAL GARDENS.

Description Nettle-leaved mullein has thick flower spikes and stout stems with broadly oval, pointed leaves. The small, five-petaled yellow flowers are tightly packed into dense clusters.

Ideal position Full sun to light shade.

Ideal soil conditions Average, well-drained soil.

Cultivation Long-lived plants spread slowly to form clumps and seldom need division.

Propagation Sow seed outdoors in autumn or spring or indoors in spring. Take root cuttings in late winter or early spring.

Pest and disease prevention No serious pests or diseases.

Landscape use Plant in borders with fine-textured perennials, such as thread-leaved coreopsis *Coreopsis verticillata* and cranesbills *Geranium* spp.

Cultivars 'Album' (above) has white flowers with purple eyes.

Other species *V. olympicum*, olympic mullein, has broadly oval, pointed, silver-gray, hairy leaves and yellow flowers. Zones 6–8.

Verbena canadensis

CLIMATE
Zones 4–10.

HEIGHT AND
SPREAD
8–18 inches
(20–45 cm) tall.
1–3 feet
(30–90 cm) wide.

FLOWERING TIME
Late spring through
autumn.

ROSE VERBENA

ROSE VERBENA IS AN EXCELLENT "WEAVER."
USE IT TO TIE MIXED PLANTINGS TOGETHER
AT THE FRONT OF THE BORDER.

Description Rose verbena has deeply lobed leaves and circular flower clusters. Plants grow from fibrous-rooted crowns but also root along the trailing stems. The tubular, lavender to rose-pink flowers have flat, five-petaled faces.

Ideal position Full sun. Plants are heat- and drought-tolerant.

Ideal soil conditions Poor to humus-rich, well-drained soil.

Cultivation Plants spread quickly to form broad clumps. Prune or divide plants that overgrow their position.

Propagation Take stem cuttings during summer.

Pest and disease prevention Powdery mildew may cause white blotches on the foliage. Spray infected plants with wettable sulfur to control the spread of the disease.

Landscape use The stems will cover bare ground between yuccas *Yucca* spp. and mulleins *Verbascum* spp.

Other species *V. bonariensis*, Brazilian vervain, is an upright plant with sparse foliage and clusters of violet flowers. Zones 7–9.

V. x *hybrida*, garden verbena, is a trailing plant with numerous cultivars in many colors. Zones 8–9.

Veronica spicata

CLIMATE
Zones 3–8.

HEIGHT AND SPREAD
1–3 feet
(30–90 cm) tall.
1½–2½ feet
(45–75 cm) wide.

FLOWERING TIME
Summer.

SPIKE SPEEDWELL

SPIKE SPEEDWELL IS A GOOD COMPANION FOR ORNAMENTAL GRASSES AND A WIDE VARIETY OF SUMMER-BLOOMING PERENNIALS.

Description Has pointed flower clusters atop leafy stems. The leaves are oval to oblong and clothed in soft hair. Plants grow from fibrous-rooted crowns. The small, two-lipped pink, blue or white flowers are tightly packed into erect spikes.

Ideal position Full sun to light shade.

Ideal soil conditions Average to humus-rich, moist, but well-drained soil.

Cultivation Plants grow slowly to form neat, attractive clumps. Cut plants back if they get rangy and to encourage fresh growth and continued bloom.

Propagation Divide in spring or autumn. Take stem cuttings in late spring or early summer and remove any flower buds.

Pest and disease prevention No serious pests or diseases.

Landscape use Plant spike speedwells with other summer perennials that need good drainage, such as yarrows *Achillea* spp,. catmints *Nepeta* spp., sundrops *Oenothera* spp. and ornamental grasses. Their spiky forms add interest to plantings.

Viola odorata

CLIMATE
Zones 6–9.

HEIGHT AND
SPREAD
2–8 inches
(5–20 cm) tall.
4–8 inches
(10–20 cm) wide.

FLOWERING TIME
Spring.

SWEET VIOLET

IN INFORMAL GARDENS, PLANT SWEET VIOLET WITH BULBS, WILDFLOWERS, HOSTAS AND EARLY-BLOOMING PERENNIALS.

Description Sweet violets are beloved for their delicate, fragrant, early-season flowers. They produce rosettes of heart-shaped leaves from creeping, fibrous-rooted rhizomes. The deep purple or mauve flowers have five petals. Two point upward and three point outward and down. The two outfacing petals have fuzzy beards.

Ideal position Sun or shade. Sweet violet is widely tolerant of varying soil and moisture conditions.

Ideal soil conditions Moist, humus-rich soil.

Cultivation Violets are prolific spreaders and make themselves at home in any garden. If planting among other plants, don't allow them to run unchecked.

Propagation Divide plants after flowering or in autumn. Plants often self-sow.

Pest and disease prevention No serious pests or diseases.

Landscape use Violets form attractive groundcovers under shrubs and flowering trees.

Sweet violet *Viola*, Perennial Cultivars 'Jackanapes'

Cultivars *V. odorata* has many cultivars. 'Deloris' has lovely, deep purple flowers.

'White Queen' has small, dainty white flowers.

Hybrids Perennial Cultivars are hardy, long-flowering perennials of mixed parentage.

'Huntercombe Purple' has purple flowers wth small cream-colored eyes.

'Jackanapes' (pictured above) has destinctive two-toned (brown and yellow) flowers.

'Maggie Mott' has pretty blue-purple flowers.

'Nellie Britton' has lavender-pink flowers.

'Magic' has deep purple flowers with purple and cream centers.

Other species *V. sororia*, woolly blue-violet, is a stemless perennial with sharply pointed, hairy leaves. 'Freckles' has pale blue flowers flecked with purple.

V. sororia var. *priceana*, the confederate violet, has white flowers with purple-blue centers. Zones 3–9.

Yucca filamentosa

CLIMATE
Zones 3–10.

HEIGHT AND
SPREAD
5–15 feet
(1.5–4.5 m) tall
(5 feet [1.5 m]
is average).
3–6 feet
(90–180 cm) wide.

FLOWERING TIME
Summer.

ADAM'S NEEDLE

THE SPIKY CLUMPS OF ADAM'S NEEDLE ADD
A DRAMATIC ACCENT TO ANY PLANTING.
THE SHOWY FLOWERS ARE A BONUS!

Description It grows from a woody
crown with fleshy roots. Produces
tall, elongated clusters of nodding,
bell-like creamy white flowers and
rosettes of sword-shaped blue-green
leaves. The flowers have three
petals and three petal-like sepals
that form a bell.

Ideal position Full sun to
light shade.

Ideal soil conditions Average to
humus-rich, well-drained soil.

Cultivation Plants thrive for years
with little care. After flowering, the
main crown dies but auxiliary
crowns keep growing.

Propagation Remove young
sideshoots from the clump in
spring or autumn.

Pest and disease prevention No
serious pests or diseases.

Landscape use Plant in dry borders
or rock gardens as accents or in
seaside gardens. Contrast the stiff
foliage with soft or delicate plants
such as lamb's ears *Stachys
byzantina*, sedums and verbenas
Verbena spp.

Cultivars 'Bright Edge' (pictured
above) has tall, striking, yellow-
variegated leaves.

PLANT HARDINESS ZONE MAPS

These maps of the United States, Canada and Europe are divided into ten zones. Each zone is based on a 10°F (5.6°C) difference in average annual minimum temperature. Some areas are considered too high in elevation for plant cultivation and so are not assigned to any zone. There are also island zones that are warmer or cooler than surrounding areas because of differences in elevation; they have been given a zone different from the surrounding areas. Many large urban areas, for example, are in a warmer zone than the surrounding land. Plants grow best within an optimum range of temperatures. The range may be wide for some species and narrow for others. Plants also differ in their ability to survive frost and in their sun or shade requirements.

*PACIFIC
OCEAN*

AVERAGE ANNUAL MINIMUM TEMPERATURE °F (°C)

ZONE 1 Below -50°F (Below -45°C)

ZONE 2 -50° to -40°F (-45° to -40°C)

ZONE 3 -40° to -30°F (-40° to -34°C)

ZONE 4 -30° to -20°F (-34° to -29°C)

ZONE 5 -20° to -10°F (-29° to -23°C)

ZONE 6 -10° to 0°F (-23° to -18°C)

ZONE 7 0° to 10°F (-18° to -12°C)

ZONE 8 10° to 20°F (-12° to -7°C)

ZONE 9 20° to 30°F (-7° to -1°C)

ZONE 10 30° to 40°F (-1° to 4°C)

Canada

United States
of America

*ATLANTIC
OCEAN*

The zone ratings indicate conditions in which designated plants will grow well, and not merely survive. Many plants may survive in zones that are warmer or colder than their recommended zone range. Remember that other factors, including wind, soil type, soil moisture, humidity, snow and winter sunshine, may have a great effect on growth.

Keep in mind that some nursery plants have been grown in greenhouses, so they might not survive in your garden. It's a waste of time and money, and a cause of heartache, to buy plants that aren't suitable for your climate zone.

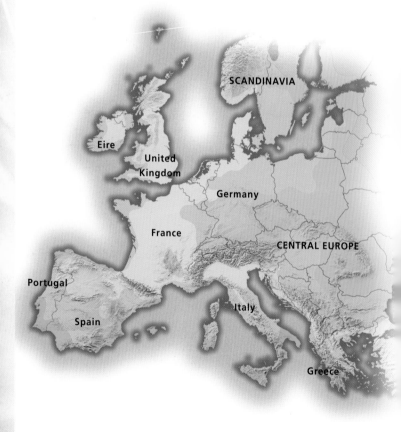

AUSTRALIA AND NEW ZEALAND

These maps divide Australia and New Zealand into seven climate zones which, as near as possible, correspond to the USDA climate zones used in the United States, Britain and Europe and in this book. The zones are based on the minimum temperatures usually, or possibly, experienced within each zone. This book is designed mainly for cool-climate gardens, but the information in it can be adapted for those in hotter climates.

In this book, the ideal zones in which to grow particular plants are indicated and when you read that a plant is suitable for any of the zones 7 through to 10, you will know that it should grow successfully in those zones in Australia and New Zealand. There are other factors that affect plant growth, but temperature is one of the most important. Plants listed as being suitable for zone 10 may also grow in hotter zones, but to be sure, consult a gardening guide specific to your area.

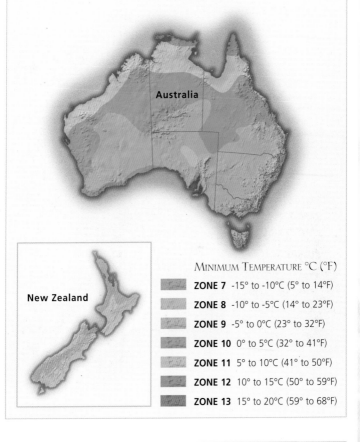

MINIMUM TEMPERATURE °C (°F)

ZONE 7 -15° to -10°C (5° to 14°F)

ZONE 8 -10° to -5°C (14° to 23°F)

ZONE 9 -5° to 0°C (23° to 32°F)

ZONE 10 0° to 5°C (32° to 41°F)

ZONE 11 5° to 10°C (41° to 50°F)

ZONE 12 10° to 15°C (50° to 59°F)

ZONE 13 15° to 20°C (59° to 68°F)

INDEX

Page references in *italics* refer to photos and illustrations.

T

U, V

W, Y

ACKNOWLEDGMENTS

KEY l=left; r=right; c=center; t=top; b=bottom. AA=Allan Armitage; AL=Andrew Lawson; Aus=Auscape; BCL=Bruce Coleman Ltd; CM=Cheryl Maddocks; CN= Clive Nichols; DF=Derek Fell; DW=David Wallace; GB=Gillian Beckett; GPL=Garden Picture Library; HSC=Harry Smith Collection; JC=John Callanan; JP=Jerry Pavia; JY=James Young; LC=Leigh Clapp; PH=Photos Horticultural; SM=Stirling Macoboy; SOM=S. & O. Mathews; TE=Thomas Eltzroth; TR=Tony Rodd; WO=Weldon Owen; WR=Weldon Russell

1t, c LC; b Aus/Rob Walls **2**c WO/JY **5**c TE **6**t TE; c SOM; b AL **7**t SOM; c WO/JY **10**c WO **12**br TE **13**t WO/JY **14**tr, bl WO/JY **15**t PH **17**t WO/JY **18**b PH **19**t WO/JY **20**br PH **21**t SOM; cr PH **22**t WO/JY **23**cl DF; bl WO/JY **25**c WO **26**bl PH **27**tr WO/JY **29**t CN **30**br CN **32**c CN **34**bl PH **35**b CN **36**bl CN **37**tl WO/JY **38**br PH **39**t CN **42**tr WO; br PH **43**t PH **44**tr WO/JY; bl PH **45**tr WO/JY; br PH **46**bl WO/JY; t PH **47**t WO **48**b WO/JY **49**t WO/JY

50b SOM **51**t CN; br WO/JY **52**t JP; b AL **53**t WO/JY **54**t WO/JY **55**tr WO/JY **56**b DF **57**t EWA Photo Library; b SOM **58**t, b WO/JY **59**t WO/JY **60**t WO/JY **61** Aus/Jerry Harpur **62**bl AL **63**t WO/JY **64**b TE **65**t TR; b PH **66**t TE **67** GPL/Roger Hyam **68**t TE **68–69**b WO/JY **69**t WO/JY **70**c BCL/Eric Crichton **72**t, c, b WR **73**t WR **74**t, b CN **76**bl PH; br DW **78**cl CN; bl, br DF **79**t WO/JY; bl, br DF **80**tl, tr WR/CM **81**t GPL **83**c CN **84**tl, tc, tr DW; b AL **85**tr CN **86**c CN **88**bl PH **89**tl DW; br WO/JY **91**tl SOM **93**tr CN **96**br PH **97**tr DW; cl PH **98**b PH **99**tr APL/Corbis/Wolfgang Kaehler **100**bl PH **101** PH **102**c WO; b PH **105**t PH; b Premaphotos Wildlife/K.G. Preston-Mafham **106**b CN **108**cl PH; br GPL/Brigitte Thomas **109**tr, tc, tl DW **110**bl, bc, br DW **111**tr WO/JY **112**c CN **114**t JC **115**t GP.com/Graham Rice **116**t TE **117**t Corbis **118**t WO/JY **119**t TR **120**t PH **121**t GP.com/Judy White **122**t GPL/Mark Bolton **123**t GPL/Brian Carter **124**t WO/JY **125**t TE **126**t JC **127**t WO/JY **128**t GPL/J. Sira **129**t GP.com/Judy White **130**t PH **131**t PH **132**t TE **133**t GPL/John Glover **134**t GPL/John Glover **135**t GPL/John Glover **136**t JC **137**t GPL/Brian Carter **138**t GB **139**t GPL/Gary Rogers **140**t DF **141**t JC **142**t GPL/Neil Holmes **143**t PH **144**t TE **145**t Nancy J. Ondra **146**t TE **147**t TE **148**t TE **149**t PH **150**t PH **151**t HSC **152**t TE **153**t WO **154**t WO/JY **155**t JC **156**t JC **157**t WR **158**t JC **159**t WO/JY **160**t AL **161**t GP.com/Judy White **162**t SM **163**t PH **164**t DF **165**t JP **166**t HSC **167**t PH **168**t HSC **169**t TR **170**t JC **171**t TE **172**t JP **173**t HSC **174**t PH **175**t JC **176**t WR **177**t WO/JY **178**t Anita Sabrese **179**t TE **180**t WO/JY **181**t APL/Corbis/Hal Horowitz **182**t GPL/Mayer/Le Scanff **183**t GP.com/Judy White **184**t GPL/Mark Bolton **185**t GB **186**t WO/JY **187**t JC **188**t GPL/Rajeev Jhanji **189**t WR **190**t WO/JY **191**t JC **192**t GPL/John Glover **193**t GPL/David Askham **194**t WO/JY **195**t GP.com/Judy White **196**t TE **197**t PH **198**t WO **199**t WO/JY **200**t WO **201**t TE **202**t TE **203**t WO/JY **204**t WO **205**t JC **206**t APL/Corbis/Tania Midgley **207**t HSC **208**t GPL **209**t WO/JY **210**t GB **211**t PH **212**t WO/JY **213**t JC **214**t PH **215**t JC **216**t WO/JY **217**t WO/JY **218**t TE **219**t WO/JY **220**t John J. Smith **221**t TE **222**t WO/JY **223**t WO/JY **224**t WO **225**t AA **226**t WO **227**t TE **228**t WO/JY **229**t WO/JY **230**t TE **231**t GPL **232**t GPL/Lamontagne **233**t PH **234**t WO **235**t WO/JY **236**t WO/JY **237**t WO/JY **238**t Aus/Jaime Plaza van Roon **239**t TR **240**t JC **241**t TE **242**t PH **243**t TE **244**t WR **245**t APL/Corbis/Eric Crichton **246**t GPL/Brian Carter **247**t TE **248**t GB **249**t WO/JY **250**t TE **251**t WO **252**t DF **253**t GPL/Marijke Heuff **254**t JC **255**t PH **256**t WO/JY **257**t PH **258**t DF **259**t TE **260**t TE **261**t TE **262**t TE **263**t WO **264**t AA **265**t TE **266**t WO/JY **267**t WO/JY **268**t WO/JY **269**t WO/JY **270**t TE **271**t Michael Dirr **272**t PH **273**t WO/JY **274**t GDR **275**t WR **276**t WO/JY **277**t JY **278**t PH **279**t WO/JY **280**t John J. Smith **281**t TR **282**t TE **283**t TR **284**t GPL **285**t WO/JY **286**t PH **287**t WO/JY **288**t WO **289**t AA **290**t TR **291**t TE **292**t WO/JY **293**t TE **294**t GB **295**t JC **296**t HSC **297**t PH **298**t TE **299**t TR **300**t PH **301**t WO/JY **302**t TE **303**t JC **304**t JC **305**t TE **306**t PH **307**t WO/JY.

Illustrations by Tony Britt-Lewis, Edwina Riddell, Barbara Rodanska, Jan Smith, Kathie Smith.

The publishers would like to thank Puddingburn Publishing Services, for compiling the index, and Bronwyn Sweeney, for proofreading.